ECHOES IN ETERNITY
STREET COP STORIES

JERRY,

THANK YOU!

James Devine

ECHOES IN ETERNITY
STREET COP STORIES

JAMES DISSER

gatekeeper press
Where Authors are Family

Tampla. Florida

Echoes In Eternity: Street Cop Stories

Published by Gatekeeper Press
7853 Gunn Hwy, Suite 209
Tampa, FL 33626
www.GatekeeperPress.com

Library of Congress Control Number: 2023930017

ISBN (paperback): 9781662936647

For The Memory of My Father,
Louis R. Disser,
The Finest Policeman I've Ever Known.

Contents

Forward

All victories result from teamwork. Throughout history, in wartime and peace, success has been a team effort. It's true in military and civilian life, sports, business, relationships, anything you can name; and it certainly applies to law enforcement. All the exciting, significant and worthwhile moments I've experienced in my career happened because of other people who were present for me when I needed them.

The concept of sharing is first taught to us by our parents, and mine certainly impressed that concept upon my sister and me. From childhood to adulthood, I was shown the importance of working toward common goals by teachers, scoutmasters, coaches, mentors and ultimately the leaders I encountered as a young policeman.

As I wrote this book it dawned on me that it's not a journal of my career accomplishments but a testament to the people I worked with and what we accomplished together. For that reason, I decided to celebrate them and describe their contributions and character throughout this narrative.

Perhaps the most significant of those contributions came from my dad, a 33-year police veteran who accomplished so many great things in his career. As a young kid I believed his was the most important job in the whole world, and I still remember asking him, "*Did you catch any bad guys today, Dad?*" when he came home from work. He never said a single word to me about becoming a cop, but all those Tuesday nights together spent watching the TV show 'Adam-12' probably ensured he never had to. It was the only job I ever wanted.

While addressing his cavalry officers just before a battle in the epic film Gladiator, Russell Crowe's Maximus says, "*What we do in life echoes in eternity.*" I believe that. My hope is that these true stories, and the people who lived them, will be remembered.

Introduction

During my law enforcement career in Michigan, I spent 15 years employed by the City of Mount Clemens Police Department and 16 years with the City of Marysville Police Department. I also served a short time with the Grand Rapids Police Department. I had many assignments including road patrol, SWAT, narcotics, and major crimes investigation.

MCPD

The Mount Clemens Police Department (MCPD) was founded in 1892. I was hired following my graduation from Central Michigan University and a short stint working for Manufacturers National Bank of Detroit. I spent 3 months at the Macomb Police Academy before starting at MCPD, which was the first police job offer I received. Back then it was hard to get a job as a cop, with hundreds of applicants for every available spot. As it turned out I needn't have jumped at the first one, but I'm still glad that I did. It's much different today!

Mount Clemens is an old Michigan city that sits alongside the Clinton River. The famous road known as Gratiot Avenue runs right through the middle, on its way from downtown Detroit to Port Huron. Sulfur springs run beneath the city and during the early 20th century there were hotels that tapped the underground springs to offer mineral baths to their guests. Babe Ruth, Jack Dempsey, Clark Gable, Mae West, and William Randolph Hearst were just a few of the famous people to visit Mount Clemens for the world-famous baths.

Mount Clemens was also a destination for criminal gangs that imported booze during Prohibition. Whiskey, rum, and beer would be brought across Lake St. Clair from Canada by men in small, fast boats. They'd shoot up the Clinton River to downtown Mount Clemens, where a system of underground tunnels allowed them to supply hotels and private clubs, and to ship the hooch to destinations like Detroit and Chicago.

Those tunnels still exist and were the scene of a shootout between Mount Clemens police officers and some violent armed robbers. On November 1, 1973, Patrolman Robert Ahrens was sent to a jewelry store on Macomb Street for a holdup alarm. The alarm was a frequent occurrence, so it did not raise much suspicion as Ahrens entered the store. What he didn't know was there were two females in the display area acting as a distraction for two men robbing the establishment in the back.

As Ahrens walked through the door, one of the robbers opened fire. Although Ahrens was able to draw his revolver and return fire, he fell to the floor fatally wounded. When backup arrived, the two women and one of the men surrendered. The other man accessed the underground tunnels from the store's basement and escaped. Three Mount Clemens cops were sent down into the tunnels to find him, armed to the teeth with department weapons which included a Thompson .45 caliber submachine gun. The tunnels are dark and dangerous but when the policemen emerged there was no need for a judge or jury; the suspect met his fate that day.

During my time at Mount Clemens PD, I learned how to be a policeman in a fast-paced urban environment. I made the rank of Sergeant after seven years as a uniformed patrolman, and Lieutenant another seven years after that. Along the way I was a member of the Macomb County SWAT Team and worked undercover for three years while assigned to the County of Macomb Enforcement Team (COMET). In my fifteenth year, the Mount Clemens City Commission made the unfortunate budgetary decision (by a 4-3 vote) to disband the 113-year-old police department and contract the county sheriff to provide all police services. So began the second half of my career.

I'll always look back fondly at the people and places I experienced in Mount Clemens, especially the mentors who taught me so much about police work and leadership.

SWAT

The idea of having a team of police officers trained in Special Weapons and Tactics originated in Los Angeles when LAPD officers were involved in a terrible shootout with a group called the Symbionese Liberation Army, widely considered to be the first domestic terrorist organization in America.

The Macomb County SWAT Team was a collaborative effort between police agencies throughout Macomb County. The team was administered by the Macomb County Sheriff's Office, but at that time included police officers from cities such as Mount Clemens, Sterling Heights, Chesterfield Township, Shelby Township, Fraser, and New Baltimore. The team continues today as a multi-jurisdictional squad, and this concept saves the individual agencies a lot of money while ensuring a qualified response to any potentially violent scenario.

The Macomb County SWAT Team was not a full-time, 40 hour per week assignment like tactical teams in large cities. I retained all my regular duties during my nine year assignment in SWAT. Our team trained locally two to four days per month and annually for a week at a military base in northern Michigan. We were then available 24 hours a day for call outs. Situations that we trained for included barricaded gunmen, active shooter response, hostage rescue, vehicle and bus assaults, and high-risk warrant service.

We often brought in SWAT trainers from outside agencies like the Ontario Provincial Police and Los Angeles County Sheriff Department to teach us current techniques, and frequently had representatives from firearms manufacturers and other companies at our training sessions. That allowed us to test and evaluate the latest products and have the best equipment possible.

Any assignment you can have outside of your normal routine makes you a better police officer. Being assigned as a detective, for example, will make you much better at gathering information from victims and witnesses when you go back to patrolling the streets in uniform. Being part of a SWAT Team is no different. The time spent learning how to properly respond to violent encounters and de-escalate scary situations stays with you for the rest of your career. The ultimate goal of SWAT Teams in any situation is to save lives, and we always strived to do that peacefully.

COMET

As a Detective Sergeant with the Mount Clemens Police Department, I was assigned to a Michigan State Police narcotics task force called the County of Macomb Enforcement Team (COMET) for three years. Like similar MSP teams spread out across the state, COMET was comprised of state troopers and cops from other departments including the Macomb County Sheriff's Office, and police departments from cities such as Mount Clemens, Warren, Clinton Township, and Shelby Township.

At that time there were about 35 detectives assigned to COMET, spread across four teams: Street Narcotics, Conspiracy, Surveillance, and Violent Crimes. Street Narcotics concentrated on developing informants, buying directly from dealers, executing search warrants and many other traditional drug unit activities. The Conspiracy team was smaller, included a dedicated DEA liaison, and assisted us when our investigations needed additional manpower and resources. The Surveillance team often worked long hours tracking robbery suspects and interrupting crimes in progress, while the Violent Crimes team focused primarily on fugitive apprehension. We also had a dedicated MSP property sergeant responsible for the walk-in vault containing the huge quantity of drugs, money, and guns that the teams seized as evidence, and two civilian secretaries.

Each individual team was led by a Detective Lieutenant from the Michigan State Police, with assistant team leaders comprised of Detective Sergeants from outside agencies, like me. The Street Narcotics team, to which I was assigned, was led by Detective Lieutenant Rich Margosian, callsign 'Deak'. He was an intelligent, highly accomplished leader who trusted his hard charging cops and gave them room to operate, while ensuring investigations were completed the right way. Margosian had a great sense of humor, always set an excellent example, and was one of the very best bosses I've ever had.

An undercover assignment to COMET typically lasted three years. The first year is mostly learning how to properly handle informants, conduct surveillance, write search warrants, interview and interrogate suspects, and how to navigate the MSP system of reports and evidence, among other things. The second year you really start to pick up speed as a narcotics investigator, expertly making hand-to-hand drug buys, getting confessions from suspects, and gathering valuable intelligence. By the third year you're rolling along nicely, routinely building cases big enough to require the involvement of outside agencies like the DEA.

Investigations often started with a confidential informant, or 'CI', usually someone who had been arrested for a drug offense and wanted to 'work off' their criminal charges. In exchange for their cooperation, charges were often amended or dismissed. The goal was usually to have the informant introduce a drug dealer to an undercover cop, who would then buy drugs directly from him or her. That person is then arrested and hopefully becomes an informant too, thereby allowing us to climb the ladder of drug networks in our area. Typically, that meant we were conducting operations in the city of Detroit by the second or third bust.

After three years or so, even if you don't want to, you should come out of 'working dope' and move on with your career. Every day that I was assigned as a narcotics investigator, I couldn't wait to get up and go to work. I was on a team comprised of true warriors and it was a different thrill every night, but the environment is stressful and can take a toll on your family. I watched several of my friends get divorced, at least in part because they stayed in narcotics too long.

I learned so much during my time assigned to COMET, acquiring skills and techniques that made me a better policeman and leader. The success I had during that time was, in no small part, due to my wife. Cyndi and I had two kids aged 3 and 1, respectively, when I went to COMET. Her strength and generous support made it easy for me to give 100 percent at work every day. This included operating in dangerous environments and sometimes being gone for days at a time, all the while having a different appearance that made me look more like the people we were trying to arrest. She never complained and wasn't afraid to set me straight when I needed it, which helped me remember that family is much more important than a job assignment.

Marysville PD

When the Mount Clemens Police Department was disbanded, I was offered a job with the Macomb County Sheriff's Department when they took over law enforcement duties in the city. In fact, I could have entered service there as a road patrol sergeant, only dropping one rank from Lieutenant. I respectfully declined the offer, took a deferred retirement from the city of Mount Clemens, and accepted a job with the Marysville Police Department. It meant that I had to start completely over as the bottom man at the lowest rank, and I spent the next decade working the 7pm-7am midnight shift, but there were also advantages.

We had moved to Marysville eight years earlier because of its outstanding public schools and good local government. So, when I started working there, I was home much more than I ever had been before. I was able to see my kids and be present in a way I never was previously. If the kids had a little league baseball or soccer game and I had to work, no problem. I could park my patrol car at the ball field, turn on my portable police radio and watch the game. In fact, the police administration liked having officers walking around at public events to 'fly the colors' and represent the department in a positive way. I even ended up as the freshman baseball and football coach at our local high school for several years. Looking back, I'm very thankful for the way things worked out and all the great experiences I had personally and professionally.

One of those incredible opportunities came to me when I was assigned to the Port Huron Police Major Crimes Unit as a task force detective.

Port Huron Major Crimes Unit

The Port Huron Major Crimes Unit (MCU) was a multi-jurisdictional task force under the direction of the Port Huron Police Department (PHPD). During my five years assigned to MCU, the team consisted of sworn officers from PHPD, Marysville Police Department, St Clair County Sheriff's Office, Michigan State Police, US Customs & Border Protection, and the US Border Patrol. Because of the various agencies that comprised it, MCU had local, state, and federal jurisdiction.

Typical MCU investigations included homicide, robbery, felony assault, human trafficking, home invasion, organized retail crime and fugitive apprehension, among others. MCU was available to assist any police agency with major investigations, including agencies that did not have an officer assigned to the unit. MCU investigators typically had experience as detectives with their respective agencies, or as officers assigned to narcotics task forces, SWAT teams, or other special units, prior to their assignment with MCU.

In today's era it is difficult to recruit, hire, and retain police officers due to the negative perception that is unfairly pushed on the public by certain groups and media institutions. Combined with shrinking budgets and resources, police departments across the nation are largely underfunded and understaffed. Assigning an officer full-time to a task force such as MCU allows smaller departments like Marysville PD to have a fully staffed investigative team available 24 hours per day for the cost of one officer's salary and overtime. MCU could travel wherever needed to track down witnesses, victims, suspects, or to conduct surveillance, gather evidence, or serve search warrants. These activities simply cannot be done by patrol officers with limited jurisdiction, who must respond to never-ending daily calls for service.

Port Huron Police Chief Joe Platzer deserves credit for conceptualizing MCU and breathing life into a team that has done so much good for its community and region. I'm very thankful for the wisdom and leadership of Marysville Police Chief Tom Konik, who allowed me to be part of MCU for so many years.

Euclid Street Scrap

As a rookie cop in my early twenties there was nothing cooler than when COMET came to Mount Clemens to execute a search warrant, conduct undercover operations, or snatch somebody up on a felony warrant. They would often need a uniformed patrolman in a fully marked scout car to make a traffic stop, escort the team to a house being raided, or transport prisoners. Back then I looked up to those detectives as the 'real police'. They got to drive undercover cars and grow their hair long. Their investigations were complex and often dangerous. There was nothing I wanted more than to be assigned to COMET someday. Until that day came, I made it my mission to be the uniformed patrol cop who helped them every time they came to town.

One cold January night during my first year, I was partnered with Officer Jim Grasel. He was a rookie like me, albeit with a few more months on the job. Our similarities didn't end there; we were the same age, his dad was a cop just like mine, we even played quarterback on our respective high school football teams. Grasel was tough. Even though we were both skinny, the guy could punch harder than almost anyone I knew! I don't know if he'd had boxing lessons as a kid or just possessed natural mechanics, but I'd already seen him knock down a couple bad guys who thought they would get the better of us.

"Car 56, 10-19 please," the radio crackled. It was our shift commander, Sergeant Dan Fields, telling us to return to the police station forthwith.

"10-4," Grasel replied over the frequency, as I turned our patrol car in that direction and hit the gas.

The Mount Clemens Police Department occupied the ground floor of City Hall at One Crocker Boulevard. As I turned into the parking lot Grasel pointed at a blue Chevy cargo van positioned near the back, alongside several unmarked sedans.

"Hey, does that look like the COMET raid van?" Grasel asked.

"Sure does!" I replied.

My heart started to beat faster just then; the prospect of assisting COMET with a drug raid was the type of thing I got excited about, and I couldn't park the scout car in one of the reserved spaces fast enough. We walked up the ramp and keyed our way through the employee entrance to the police station.

We turned left into the hallway and then left again into the squad room, where the COMET Street Narcotics team was assembled. The plainclothes cops were about to give a pre-raid briefing and had been waiting for us.

"Well, if it isn't Jimmy and Jimmy here to lend us a hand!" exclaimed Detective Sergeant Steve 'Red Man' Thomas, the team's leader. Employed by the Macomb County Sheriff's Department, Thomas was assigned full-time to COMET for many years.

Thomas was, without a doubt, one of the best cops with whom I ever worked. He was 20 years older than Grasel and me, but possessed a youthful enthusiasm born from his love for the job. He was an even-tempered, approachable leader who wanted his guys to succeed. He got his nickname, or 'call sign', from the tobacco he chewed while playing for the best police softball teams in metropolitan Detroit.

"You guys want to help us out with a search warrant?" Thomas asked with a grin, knowing the answer long before he asked the question. There was nothing we would rather do that night.

The briefing commenced and the target was announced. COMET had secured a search warrant for a house in the 100 block of Euclid Street, just east of Gratiot Avenue on the city's northeast end. The neighborhood was plagued with prostitution and street corner sales of crack cocaine, much of it supplied by occupants of the house on Euclid Street.

It was a square, two-story, bungalow home which sat on the south side of Euclid, before the street ran downhill to the public housing projects two blocks east. Five wide steps led to a covered front porch that spanned the entire width of the structure. The deck, trim, and shingles were shades of green and gray, accenting the structure's white vinyl siding. Alongside the house was an alley which paralleled Gratiot Avenue and ran south to the next block.

Thomas listed each assignment on the whiteboard with a dry erase marker. Grasel and I would park our police car in the alley, then hustle to the rear of the house. I was assigned to watch windows on the east side of the house and Grasel would cover the back door, along with a couple uniformed deputies from the sheriff's department. Thomas's crew would knock on the front door of the home and announce their presence, then knock it down with a battering ram if no one answered. When everyone was clear about their roles, Grasel and I headed outside to our police car. The undercover cops donned their Kevlar raid vests before loading up in the dark blue Chevy van we'd seen earlier.

A lineup of three vehicles drove out of the parking lot in a single file line, Grasel and I leading the way. Behind us was the raid van, followed by a Macomb County Sheriff's unit with two deputies. It was well past sundown and the snow had stopped, but the temperature was dropping in the darkness. A few minutes later we turned onto Euclid Street and all three vehicles killed their headlights.

The accumulated snowfall reflected light from the moon and made it easy for me to see as I turned our car into the alley and accelerated past the house. Grasel had his passenger-side door open before I came to a stop in the dark shadow of a wildly overgrown elm tree. Just as the wheels stopped turning, he was out and gone to cover the backside of the target house. I threw the car into park using the column-mounted shifter, while opening the driver door with my other hand. Before rolling out, I turned to my right and grabbed the black Remington 870 12-gauge shotgun out of its vertical mount between the two front seats. It was a decision I'd later regret.

Once out of the car I closed the driver door quietly, then hustled through the darkness toward the east side of the house. I could see Grasel's silhouette near a detached garage and the two deputies moving south through the alley to help him cover the rear of the residence. As I racked a round into the chamber of the shotgun, I heard Thomas on the front porch.

"Police! Search warrant!" he yelled.

The folks who occupied the house on Euclid Street were notorious criminals, well-known for their violent tendencies and hatred of the police. The COMET crew wasn't going to give them time to arm themselves inside the house; just a beat after Thomas's announcement, the battering ram hit the front door with force enough to break it. The door flung open, and the team moved inside.

From my spot near a tree on the east side, I could hear muffled voices from inside the house; "Police!", "Show me your hands!", and "Get on the floor!". Then I heard a command that was much louder and closer to me.

"Police! Stop!" Grasel shouted.

I've never been one to leave my post, but there wasn't anyone crashing out of the elevated windows I was assigned to cover. I ran around back to help my partner. When I did, I saw Grasel sprinting down the dark alley after a Black man running south. Grasel was a good distance from me, and the two deputies were between us, also chasing the man. Although he was quick, Grasel closed the distance between them and tackled the man as they arrived near the next block.

I ran as fast as I could after them, my pace hindered a bit by the shotgun I carried with both hands. From halfway down the alley, I could see that Grasel was in an absolute donnybrook. They were on the ground throwing punches and elbows, the man fighting to escape as Grasel tried to get him under control. The two deputies arrived just before me and one of them jumped on top of the man. That's when things got scary.

The man had worked his way up to his hands and knees and the deputy was laying on top of him, presumably trying to keep the man down with his body weight. Just as I got close, I saw the man reach straight back with his right hand and yank the deputy's gun from its holster.

As he held the stainless-steel Smith & Wesson .357 Magnum revolver in his right hand, he glanced at Grasel and said, "Look what I got, motherfucker!"

In the split-second it took my brain to process what I was seeing, Grasel snatched the gun out of the man's hand. He even had the presence of mind to cover the gun's rotating cylinder while doing so, to prevent it from firing as he pulled it away. While still kneeling, Grasel turned and handed me the revolver. Now I had two guns in my hands. The man still was struggling to get away, but the gun grab had amped our adrenalin even higher. I tucked the handgun inside my waistband and assisted by using the butt end of my shotgun to help subdue the man, but Grasel was responsible for finally getting him into handcuffs. It's likely that Grasel saved several people from getting shot that night, including the suspect.

As we all exhaled clouds of vapor mist into the cold night air, I saw the deputy standing nearby. He looked shellshocked. I stepped over to him and handed back his gun.

"Thanks," he quietly said.

Everyone knew that deputy as a stand-up guy, and that incident was proof of it. He didn't hesitate to jump in the fray to help a fellow cop, but he was an older man. His recent assignments had primarily consisted of prisoner transports and courtroom security. His physical condition no longer matched his personal courage, and he retired from police work just a few days later.

After a trip to the emergency room at St. Joseph's Hospital, the suspect was lodged at the county jail. He was later convicted of multiple felony crimes for his actions that night, including the load of crack cocaine found by COMET inside the house. It wasn't his first trip to prison, and it probably wasn't his last.

I never again used a shotgun in similar scenarios. It just wasn't practical. The first rule of working outside security during a drug raid is 'Never shoot into the house'. There's never a good reason to risk hitting one of the cops or an innocent person inside. A suspect would have to be hanging outside through a window firing a gun directly at me to justify shooting toward a house during a raid. Having a shotgun also limits your ability to lay hands on anyone. You can't set it down on the ground, nor can you fight with someone and risk them taking it away from you. Perhaps a proper sling would have made a difference. Unfortunately, we were without them back then.

The events that night were intense, but they did nothing to curb my enthusiasm for police work. To the contrary, it was everything I expected and desired, and there was much more to come.

The Salute

I never had much interaction with celebrities during my career, unlike the way I imagined cops in Los Angeles or New York City must, but I did work a bunch of presidential security details. The reason was that the city of Mount Clemens is flanked to the east by Selfridge Air National Guard Base, a 3600-acre US military installation on the shores of Lake St. Clair.

Selfridge ANGB is home to the US Air Force's 107th Fighter Squadron which deploys the A-10 Thunderbolt II, also known as the 'Warthog', to supply close-air support for our troops around the globe. Also housed at Selfridge are the KC-135 Stratotankers of the 127th Air Refueling Squadron, as well as facilities and housing for all other branches of service in the US military and a US Border Patrol intelligence center.

Whenever Air Force One brings the chief executive to the Detroit area, it lands at Selfridge ANGB for security reasons and the base's proximity to Interstate 94. Using a dedicated gate, the presidential motorcade can quickly be on the freeway and enroute to destinations throughout metropolitan Detroit.

This is especially true during presidential election years. My first experience assisting the US Secret Service came on a gray morning in November, just before Election Day. I attended an early briefing and was assigned to a traffic detail with my friend and mentor Officer Lance Folson.

Folson had been my primary Field Training Officer (FTO) from the first day I started on the job, right out of the police academy. I later spent one month each with Officer Mike Santini on the midnight shift and Officer Jeff Benoit on the daytime shift, before returning to Folson until I was cleared for solo patrol. I learned many valuable lessons from Santini and Benoit, things I remember to this day, but it was Folson who built my foundation from the ground up; a framework of skills and philosophies that shaped my career path, especially with regards to investigating narcotics and prostitution.

As a young patrolman I learned to spot hand-to-hand transactions between pedestrians and drivers of cars stopped in the roadway and recognize them as drug deals. Folson taught me that the female walking up Gratiot Avenue, looking over her shoulder and getting picked up by the car I'd seen circling the block, might be a prostitute. He showed me the importance of using the city's Loitering laws to keep the corners clear of pedestrians in high-crime areas, because it was impossible to tell who among them might be dealing the crack cocaine which was destroying the neighborhood. By attacking these problems, we could reduce suffering among all the law-abiding, peaceful residents. Most importantly, Folson taught me to execute these skills safely and professionally. I used to tease Folson by saying he was my big brother "and not because you're tall and Black!" I truly felt that brotherly love for him.

After the assignments were given that day, Folson and I headed out to North River Road to shut down eastbound traffic at the appointed time. This would allow the presidential motorcade to climb the ramp onto the freeway. Just a short while after we arrived, the signal was given, and we parked our patrol cars across both eastbound lanes and activated our emergency lights.

The people who live near Selfridge ANGB are familiar with presidential motorcades, so they're less than sympathetic and completely unimpressed by the official ruckus in their neighborhood. Never is this more apparent than when you prevent them from traveling to and from their homes during an executive visit. On this day a woman started berating me from behind the wheel of her wood-paneled Chrysler Town & Country as soon as we stopped traffic. She was so adamant that she was going to drive past our blockade that I reached inside her minivan and turned off the ignition. I tossed the keys on the passenger seat and told her if she drove past us that she might very well be shot by the Secret Service.

My statement to her was no idle threat, as it had been made clear to us that the roadway between the Interstate and the air base was a "no-go" zone once the motorcade had cleared the gate. I knew that it had because airborne in the distance I could see the helicopter which maintains a constant position over the presidential limousine. It was heading our way, which meant that the motorcade was, too.

I joined Folson as he stood in front of our police cars and watched as the vehicles approached along the curved section of road beneath the overpass. Soon I saw two burly black Cadillac limousines in line behind the lead element, each with a pair of small flags attached above the front bumpers. A sudden motion to my left caused me to turn my head, and I saw that Folson had come to attention and snapped a sharp salute. He knew how to do it properly, having spent four years on active duty in the United States Marine Corps.

Following his lead as usual, I did the same and together we held that position while the line of cars accelerated up the ramp onto Interstate 94. In the second limousine I saw a man in the rear seat lean forward and turn to his left, looking directly at us. It was President George H. W. Bush and, amazingly, he smartly returned our salute as the car passed directly in front of us. Regardless of your political persuasion, that was cool. I was still excited after the motorcade was gone and we began to open the roadway so traffic could flow. I wasn't even mad when the lady in the grocery-getter minivan gave me her most ferocious scowl.

Folson and I recalled that day fondly over the ensuing years, a time when we also played on police softball teams together and helped form the Mount Clemens Police Honor Guard. With his solid guidance I followed in Folson's footsteps to the rank of sergeant and then lieutenant. He even sang at our wedding as a gift to Cyndi and me.

Sadly, Lance Adair Folson left this earth in August 2011 after suffering cardiac failure while waiting for a heart transplant at the young age of 51. I miss laughing with him until my sides hurt, and the way I felt when he would give me an "attaboy" after doing something the right way. I feel his presence often and take encouragement from him even in his absence. His legacy is that he continues to have that same influence on dozens of people whose lives he touched, not just me.

Rookies and Roberta

After a year or so at Mount Clemens PD I had completed probation and generally had it together enough to not screw up everything I touched. I was asked to work some anti-crime assignments along with a couple other new guys. The idea was that criminals wouldn't recognize us as local cops since we were new to the department.

Jim Ochmanski and I had been hired together on the same day a year before. He was a five year veteran of the Detroit Police Department and had worked the mean streets of the 10th Precinct, along with a three year assignment to their Narcotics Section. Jim Grasel was a rookie and second-generation cop, like me, with street smarts and a great sense of humor.

Late on a sunny summer day we were tasked with working prostitution enforcement. This was long before I knew anything about human trafficking, and the women who walked the streets of the city back then were generally drug addicts who operated on their own to feed their habits. Looking back, I realize that period of my career was a perfect training ground for future assignments investigating narcotics and human trafficking.

The supervisor coordinating these anti-crime details was Sergeant Dan Fields. He was a Vietnam veteran who had served with a Search and Rescue helicopter crew in the US Air Force. As a police officer he was a natural at investigating narcotics while assigned to COMET, due to his amazing ability to talk to people. Over the years I saw him arrest countless criminals and not lay a single hand on any of them. He could usually talk them into a set of handcuffs and right into the back seat of a police car. I never mastered that trick, but Fields was a huge influence on my career and one of my most trusted mentors.

Our job during the sting on this day was to pick up a prostitute along Gratiot Avenue, then drive to a predetermined location at a parking lot alongside the Clinton River where Fields would be waiting. The challenge, of course, was getting the prostitute to say what she was willing to do and how much it was going to cost. She had to be the one to say those things to establish probable cause for arrest and avoid a valid defense of police entrapment. A daunting task for a rookie cop, trust me.

Before we left, Fields had an important tip for us to remember.

"At some point, she's going to ask if you're a cop." Fields said. "When she asks, pull the car to the curb and stop. Reach over and open her door, then tell her to get the fuck out".

I was a bit confused by this tactic. "Sarge, won't that kind of ruin the whole thing?"

He told me to trust him and just do as he said. What I didn't understand then was the concept of flipping the script, which makes her believe that you think SHE is an undercover police officer.

It didn't take long for me to spot a woman walking on a sidewalk north of downtown. She had long dark curly hair and was wearing a dirty white tank top untucked from her faded jeans shorts. On my first pass she looked over her shoulder at me, and when I came around again, she waved me over. I had no sooner stopped the blue GMC Jimmy than she opened the door and hopped in the front passenger seat.

"Hey, baby!' she said.

I didn't know it at the time, but this was a woman called Roberta who had been arrested many times and was referred to by some older cops as 'Filthy McNasty', due to her personal grooming habits.

She told me to drive. I pulled away from the curb while trying to act cool, although the butterflies in my stomach were working overtime. She asked me what I was looking for, so I told her "A date" and asked if she was working. She told me that she was indeed and said it would cost me 20 bucks for a blow job. So far, so good! Then, just as Fields had predicted, came the magic words.

"You're not a cop, are you honey?" Roberta asked.

I steered over to the curb on South Gratiot Avenue and stopped, with the car still in gear and my foot on the brake. I reached across her lap and opened the passenger door.

"Get the fuck out," I told her. "I haven't done anything wrong, and I don't want any trouble."

Roberta looked me dead in the eye for about five seconds while the gears turned inside her head.

Then she said "Oh! No, darlin'. I promise I'm not a cop. Look!"

With both hands, Roberta pulled her shirt almost over her head and showed me her boobs which, to be honest, were something I never wanted to see again. The hard life Roberta had lived to that point was not kind to her body, and the lifting of the shirt revealed a powerful odor associated with poor personal hygiene.

But the sage advice from Fields had worked perfectly, and I drove to the meet spot while chatting her up. When I pulled into the parking lot and stopped, he opened Roberta's door and placed her under arrest.

Recognizing him immediately she said, "Goddammit, Fields! Stop sending these young guys after me!"

I used that same 'flip the script' technique many times in different situations while investigating narcotics and human trafficking. It was almost always successful.

First Homicide

I was excited to start my shift one spring Saturday afternoon during my second year on the job. The weather was warm, so I knew we'd have a busy night, but there was a bonus; my father was in town visiting and was going to ride along with me. I was still a rookie but gaining experience quickly in the diverse urban environment of Mount Clemens, and I was anxious to show my dad what I'd learned.

I introduced him around the police station, and he joined us during our daily briefing. The shift commander, Sergeant Dan Fields, told us about some recent citizen complaints of drug dealing on the north end of town and encouraged us to back each other up on traffic stops. After Fields dismissed us from the briefing we headed outside to the row of black-and-white Chevrolet Caprice patrol cars parked neatly alongside the city building. Car 56 was my usual ride, so I unlocked the trunk and stowed my patrol bag inside.

I slid behind the wheel as my dad climbed into the front passenger seat and clicked the seat belt. When we left the parking lot I made a pair of right turns and headed for the Dunkin Donuts shop at the intersection of Cass Avenue and Groesbeck Highway. Unfortunately, the coffee had to wait because I was almost immediately dispatched to an unarmed robbery complaint outside the Cass Party Store.

A man in the parking lot there had a gold chain snatched from his neck by a perpetrator who ran north up a nearby side street. We checked the area, but the suspect was nowhere to be found. I saw a girl named Tammy walking alone on Cass Avenue a short time later. I knew Tammy was a prostitute and that she always walked in that area with her 'boyfriend' named Draymond. The fact she was alone was highly unusual and I suspected Draymond was probably the necklace thief. I included his name in my police report so that detectives could follow up with him and then went back on patrol.

We stayed busy for an hour or two, making some traffic stops and answering a few more calls. Just before we planned to have a meal the radio came to life yet again.

"Station 50 to Car 56, copy information on a stabbing that just occurred" the dispatcher said, her voice clear but just a bit elevated in pitch and volume.

I wrote the address on the back of a log sheet attached to my clipboard as the dispatcher gave the details over the police radio frequency. A man had stabbed his son inside a home on Mulligan Drive, a residential neighborhood on the city's south end. An ambulance was already in route and the man with the knife was still on the scene.

From downtown it took only a couple minutes to arrive at the house, a two-story 1950's brick colonial in a neighborhood of similar structures near Shadyside Park. The residents in the area were almost exclusively Black and though there were a few trouble spots nearby, most people clocked 40-hour work weeks at nearby automotive factories and maintained their homes with pride.

I parked my patrol car left wheel to curb just west of the address on the same side of the street, and saw that Officers Jim Ochmanski and Jim Grasel were exiting their car just to the east of it. (We actually had a fourth 'Jim' on our shift, Officer James Walker, but he was off duty that day)

As I exited the car and walked up the cement sidewalk towards the house, a middle-aged man wearing a short-sleeved button-down collared shirt pushed the screen door open from inside. He stood in the doorway holding the screen door open with his left hand. In his right hand he gripped a huge kitchen knife, the type used for slicing a Christmas ham or Thanksgiving turkey. His right arm was soaked in blood up to the elbow.

I used a nearby tree in the yard for cover and drew my 9 millimeter Glock Model 17 from the Bianchi leather holster on my gun belt.

"Drop the knife!" I shouted at the man as Ochmanski and Grasel maneuvered toward the porch from the east, their movements hidden from the man by a large, attached garage.

The man appeared to be a bit shocked at the whole situation but, after a brief pause, he complied. As he tossed the knife onto the cement porch below his feet, Ochmanski and Grasel rounded the corner and pulled him the rest of the way outside. The man didn't resist as they handcuffed him, patted him down for any other weapons, and seated him on the molded concrete porch steps.

Ochmanski stayed outside with the man as Grasel and I went into the home. Stepping through the front door and the foyer behind it, we found ourselves in a living room ringed with an English sofa and two recliner chairs. A younger adult man laid face up on the living room carpet gasping for air. A woman sobbed uncontrollably in the kitchen, just out of our sight.

I heard the ambulance come to a stop in the street outside, so I asked Ochmanski to send the paramedics in while Grasel attended to the woman in the kitchen. The man on the floor had a vacant look in his eyes that I would see many more times in my career, the gaze of a person near death. I saw blood on his clothing which also stained the dark blue shag carpet beneath him. When the man's shirt was cut away by the paramedics, the true extent of the damage became immediately apparent.

Pink fluid and small bubbles surrounded each of the seven stab wounds in the man's chest. As he struggled to breathe I heard a slight hissing sound from the terrible cuts known as 'sucking chest wounds'. The two paramedics worked frantically, removing clear plastic seals from paper packaging and applying them to the punctures spanning the man's upper body. As soon as they were able, the paramedics loaded him onto a gurney and wheeled him outside to the waiting ambulance. As the emergency medical unit pulled away from the curb, its engine roared and the siren began to wail. They covered the short distance to Mount Clemens General Hospital quickly, but their efforts were in vain. The man was pronounced dead upon his arrival in the emergency room.

We secured the handcuffed man in a police car and I radioed the dispatcher to request a detective to the scene, which had been properly cordoned off using crime scene tape kept in the trunk of every patrol car. My dad, who was an expert homicide investigator, had not engaged in the investigation at all, since he was out of his own jurisdiction and we seemed to have the situation under control. Dad had remained outside, watching our backs while we did the job.

He did have one nugget of wisdom for me that day, though; when I grabbed a plastic evidence bag to collect the murder weapon, he reminded me that a cardboard box, or even a paper bag, were better options. A blood soaked knife inside a plastic bag would be very messy and not conducive to examination by crime laboratory scientists.

Two hours later we had dropped the arrested man off at the police station and I'd completed my portion of the homicide report, adding the boxed knife as an item of evidence and describing my actions in the narrative section of the computerized form. We headed back out on the street and managed to have a couple burgers and cokes at a local diner, discussing the day's action and aftermath as we ate.

Nearing the end of the shift, just before midnight, I drove back to the police station. I noticed the booking room and holding cell were empty, so I assumed the arrested man was still being interviewed in the detective bureau. When I found Sergeant Fields in the squad room, I offered to transport the man to the county jail; surely that was his final destination that day.

"That won't be necessary," Fields replied, shaking his head with resigned frustration.

The man told detectives that his son, who had a history of mental problems and domestic violence, had threatened to hit him with a cast iron skillet. As he picked up the heavy pan from the kitchen stovetop, his father stabbed him with the knife we'd recovered. The man's statement was corroborated by his wife, who had witnessed the entire altercation. When the detectives contacted the prosecuting attorney's office to discuss the appropriate criminal charges, the on-call prosecutor declared that the man had acted in self-defense and ordered him released.

I was stunned. Seven stab wounds seemed like a lot. More than a defensive action, it struck me as a violent expression of rage and anger. At the very least I believed it was a matter for a judge or jury to determine at trial, instead of an attorney whose job was to prosecute criminals, not to defend or excuse them. Then again, I was a young fired-up cop and hadn't been present during the interview. Perhaps there was more to the situation than I understood.

My first homicide investigation had provided a good lesson: do your job well and don't get too wrapped up in the actions and decisions of lawyers and judges. The man's release was frustrating, but it wasn't something I could control, so worrying about it was pointless. Plus, I got to spend a great day with my dad and show him that I was learning and growing as a professional police officer.

Wall of Flames

"Station 50 to Car 52," the dispatcher said over the radio. "Go ahead," I replied from the passenger seat of our patrol car, a white Chevrolet Caprice with blue stripes and city shields emblazoned on the front doors.

"Assist the fire department in the 200 block of Cass Avenue," she said. "Report of a house fire with smoke showing."

I turned and said to my partner, Officer Jim Grasel, "Dude we're a block from there!"

I needn't have said anything, he knew. With a nod, Grasel made a right turn onto Moross Road from Church Street and gunned it. A few seconds later I keyed the microphone of the Motorola radio and replied again to the dispatcher.

"Car 52 on location."

As Grasel made another right turn onto Cass Avenue, the main artery connecting Gratiot Avenue and Groesbeck Highway, we saw the house. It was one of dozens along that stretch of road constructed many decades prior for the city's elite. When Mount Clemens was a destination for the rich and famous to utilize bathhouses which tapped natural underground mineral springs, the population expanded. Doctors, lawyers, and successful businessmen built the homes along Cass Avenue; some had stood for a century.

This house had smoke seeping from windows on the upper floors. Like almost every one of the grand structures nearby, it had long ago been converted from a single-family residence into apartments. A house this size could easily contain 10 separate flats, each one a former room inside the mansion. They usually housed people who were down on their luck, their rent paid each month with 'Section 8' funds from the federal government.

Being so close when the call was dispatched was great, except that the firemen would need at least a few minutes to spin up their engines and gear, then travel from their stationhouse a mile away. It was still daylight on that April afternoon and as people started to gather, they naturally expected us to do something.

Grasel powered our police car over the cement curb and came to a stop on the sidewalk in front of a neighboring house, thereby keeping the front yard clear for the fire department. He killed the motor and we hopped out, then sprinted toward the steps of the massive front porch. The huge house was three stories of architectural mishmash. The porch's red painted awning was attached to white wooden siding of the home's second floor, below a triangular dormer featuring windows on the third story.

Two screen doors marked separate apartments accessed from the front porch. Grasel took the door on the right. As I pounded on the other, it was answered by a sleepy-looking, shirtless white guy with a cigarette dangling from his mouth as he spoke.

As he pulled back the door with his right hand, he scratched the back of his head with the left and asked, "What's all the fuss?"

"Sir," I said. "The building is on fire. Get out now."

"Oh, come on man," he replied. "This is bullshit! Ain't no fire in my apartment."

Normally I would pause to ponder stupidity that profound, but on this day, I just didn't have the time.

"Hey!" I said, more forcefully. "Grab your shit and get your ass out of there now!"

Sometimes you must speak language that a person will understand.

Behind Grasel's door were residents who had the good sense to listen and immediately exit their apartment. We moved quickly off the porch, boots barely touching stairs on the way down. Barreling around the corner of the house we raced across the faded grass to the rear. There we found two more apartments, near the corner of the building on the ground floor. Pounding on the locked doors, we received no response from inside. We had to move on. Both were later determined to be vacant.

A wooden outdoor staircase led from the grass in the backyard to a rickety landing in front of an outer door on the third floor. We hustled up the old staircase, careful not to slip on the faded treads. It needed fresh paint and had wobbly handrails that were missing quite a few spindles.

Arriving atop the landing, Grasel ripped back the thin metal storm screen and shouldered open the main entry door. We pushed through and entered a narrow, dark hallway. I couldn't see far enough to determine what was at the other end because the small space was clogged with black smoke. It dawned on me just then that we were officially inside a burning building.

Two doors on each side of the corridor marked four additional apartments. Instinctively we moved toward them, knowing there may be residents inside. Abruptly, we both stopped. Neither of us could breathe. The smoke was unlike anything I'd encountered before or since. It wasn't like the smoke that gets in your face around a campfire, or the type that fills up your kitchen when something burns inside the oven. This smoke was choking us. We quickly turned around and went right back out the door.

Outside on the landing we each took a deep breath and held it. Back inside we went, moving quickly to each door. The old interior doors were thin and easily breached. We kicked the doors open and found three of the flats to be empty. One man must have awakened about the time we showed up and realized what was happening. He hustled out of the fourth apartment and down the stairs. When I reached the end of the corridor, I witnessed a sight that will never leave me.

A wide and ornate interior stairwell led upward from the ground floor, turning 90 degrees at each landing until it terminated where I stood. But for the smoke, I could have seen all the way down to the foyer where the main entrance existed many years ago. Across the open space from me a wall, once wood-paneled but now covered in layers of paint and wallpaper, was being consumed by flames.

The fire wasn't raging, it was creeping. A horizontal line of flame extended 10 feet from left to right, advancing slowly upward. Below the line, low flames of yellow and orange rolled over the black remains of the wall's burned coatings, similar in appearance to plasma or lava. Above the line, a century's worth of craftsmanship waited to be devoured. Standing at the top of that banister holding my breath, I was mesmerized. But just for a moment.

"Let's go!" Grasel shouted.

I turned and ran down the short hallway, through the open door and into the late afternoon sunshine. Inhaling the fresh air, we scrambled carefully down the outer steps and onto the grass. We could hear the engines and air brakes of arriving fire engines, and by the time we rounded the corner into the front yard, the firemen were charging hoses and donning air tanks over their turnout gear.

I never learned the cause of the fire, just that it had started on the second floor. That explained why residents on the ground floor had been initially unaware of it, including the rocket scientist I had encountered. Nobody was killed.

Another set of uniforms went in the trash; it's tough to wash away the powerful smell of black smoke from blue polyester. But the City paid for replacements. Cops like to say that firemen spend their time eating until they're tired, then sleeping until they're hungry; but I'll give them credit when its due. After that small adventure, I don't want to be in a burning building ever again.

Pub Lessons

On the west side of Mount Clemens stood a pub called Mangan's Irish Hut, named for its owner Bill Mangan. Mangan was born and raised in the Bronx, New York City, not long after his parents immigrated from Ireland. While serving in the U.S. Air Force, Mangan was stationed at nearby Selfridge Air Force Base. When his service was up, Mangan planned to return home. He didn't like the Detroit area and longed for the Bronx, where his family still lived. But then Mangan met the love of his life, June. They were soon married and Mangan made Mount Clemens his home, tending bar at a tough saloon called Bill Murray's to earn a living. After years of hard work and saving, Mangan opened his own place, and a legendary cop bar was born.

The 'Hut', as it was widely known, opened at 0700 hours each morning to serve the many late shift workers at local factories, but for many rookie cops like me it was a place to unwind after our tour ended at midnight. The bar had an excellent juke box that played everything from Van Halen to Hank Williams and, of course, traditional Irish music. Occasionally, when we were lucky, Mangan treated everyone to a traditional ballad like 'Danny Boy'. His powerful tenor voice filled the barroom and always ended with a huge cheer from the patrons.

We'd play darts, watch a late ballgame on TV, or talk to girls who were hanging out, but I enjoyed hearing the stories. Cops from neighboring agencies sat with us at square tables drinking bottles of beer and eating salty popcorn or a famously delicious Hut burger, served with peppers and raw onions. Everyone recounted the crazy calls they'd had that evening: car crashes, drug busts, domestic brawls; it ran the gamut. Sometimes it helped emotionally to tell the story over a couple beers, if it was a tough scene like a homicide or suicide.

The stories I enjoyed most were from the veteran cops who'd experienced events stranger than fiction. Their tales were often accompanied by a lesson. Mistakes they'd made or injuries escaped due to pure luck were shared, so that we could learn by example rather than experience. Humility and self-deprecating humor made their lessons resonate with me, though there were other reasons.

Since we usually didn't arrive until half an hour after the shift ended at midnight, nobody had time to get too inebriated before closing time. A couple friendly admonishments from Mary, the nighttime bartender, would have us filing out through the big wooden doors shortly after 0200 hours. On just such an evening, one of those veteran cops, a sergeant whose every word I hung on, tapped me with his elbow when we reached the parking lot.

"Hey," he said. "You got your gun with you?"

He knew me better than I knew myself. Young, dumb, and cocky are a few words that described me accurately in that moment. There wasn't a doubt in his mind that I had a gun tucked into my waistband and that I'd be more than happy to show it to him.

"Hell yeah, I do!" I replied.

"Let me see it," he said.

Just before Jim Ochmanski and I were hired together, the entire police department had gone through transitional firearms training. Trading in their old revolvers, each officer went through a week of instruction and practice before being issued a brand new 9-millimeter Glock Model 17. Since the department hadn't yet scheduled another week of the training, Ochmanski and I still carried our revolvers six months later.

For Ochmanski, that meant a big blue-steel wheel gun with checkered wooden grips, chambered in .45 Long Colt, which he brought with him following his service with the Detroit Police Department. Mine was purchased prior to entering the Macomb Police Academy; a Smith & Wesson Model 686, chambered in .357 Magnum with black stainless-steel finish and Hogue rubber grips. It was a beast.

Thumbing my shirt up a few inches, I removed the gun from behind my right hip and handed it over.

"Wow," he said. "That's a nice gun."

"Thanks!" I said, beaming with rookie pride.

BOOM!

BOOM!

BOOM!

BOOM!

BOOM!

BOOM!

Flashes of orange flame, caused by high-powered Winchester Silvertip ammunition, briefly illuminated the asphalt around us each time the gun was fired into an elevated old sign, perched atop the abandoned K-Mart building next door.

Slack-jawed, ears ringing, and pride demolished, I accepted the now-empty gun which was handed back to me.

"Never surrender your gun to anyone," he said, smiling. "Ever".

"Ok," I replied, nodding my head. "Thanks. Good to know."

It was a different time. Though not an advisable action in any era, we've laughed about it for years. And, to date, I've never again handed over a gun to anyone. Lesson learned.

He never knew

As a young patrolman I was expected to work traffic enforcement whenever the volume of regular police calls would allow. Whether that meant stopping cars for disobeying traffic signals, speeding, or other violations, we were each expected to write 50 tickets per month. If we didn't reach that goal, we might have a surprise guest in our patrol car for the next few nights; the shift commander, Lieutenant Dave Chisholm.

Chisholm was a US Navy veteran of the Vietnam War, and I was scared to death of him when I started on the job. He had reddish-brown hair with a matching mustache and reminded me of Yosemite Sam from the Bugs Bunny cartoons I'd watched as a kid. He had Sam's temper, too, and he wasn't a big fan of college boys like me.

In the summer of my first year, I failed to reach the designated 50 ticket monthly quota and found myself as Chisholm's chauffeur for an afternoon shift. He told the dispatcher not to assign us any calls for service; we would be working traffic enforcement for the entire evening. In that single eight hour period we wrote 33 tickets. And we didn't issue any driver more than one violation (that was frowned upon back then); we made 33 traffic stops.

The directive had been delivered loud and clear. On Chisholm's shift you were expected to work hard. And his secondary message, which I didn't understand until later, was that by making all those traffic stops you'd find yourself discovering drugs and guns and fugitives. It wasn't just about writing tickets. Chisholm was a hard character who'd experienced a lot of tragedy in his life, and he shaped my career in many ways. I look back fondly at the time I spent with him, and earning his respect was one of my proudest accomplishments.

Chisholm's wisdom was exemplified on a hot summer day not long after our ride along. I was positioned alongside Gratiot Avenue just south of the Dairy Queen near Joy Road, using my radar instrument to clock northbound traffic. The speed limit in that area was 35 MPH. I normally wouldn't stop anyone until they reached at least 50 MPH and then, if everything else was in order, I would issue the driver a ticket for just 5 MPH over the limit (40/35). The message to slow down in that area was thus delivered, but the driver was spared some of the costs and avoided excess points on their driver's license.

My radar instrument suddenly emitted a high-pitched whine, so I looked up and observed an old blue Chevrolet Malibu northbound at a rate of speed that was clearly over the limit. I glanced at the radar's digital readout and saw that it recorded a speed of 65 MPH for that Chevy sedan. I dropped my patrol car into gear and pulled out behind the car, which was now well past me and approaching Joy Road.

I had to step hard on the accelerator of my Chevy Caprice to catch up to the vehicle, which had turned right and was now eastbound on Joy Road. I hit the overhead lights on the police car and the Chevy Malibu pulled over immediately, stopping near Colchester Street. I walked up to the car and saw that the driver was the only person inside. He was a white man about 30 years old and he had a death grip on the steering wheel.

His window was already down when I arrived at his door, so I greeted the man and asked for his driver's license. He exhaled a deep breath and reached into his back pocket for a big leather wallet, attached to his belt by a chrome link chain. He just nodded silently as I told him that he'd been stopped for driving 65 MPH in a 35 MPH zone.

I returned to my police car and used the police radio to run the man's name through the Law Enforcement Information Network. The dispatcher told me that the man didn't have any warrants for his arrest, but his driver's license was suspended. It's not customary now to physically arrest someone for the offense called Driving While License Suspended, but it was then (on Chisholm's shift, anyway). Rather than issuing a misdemeanor ticket and releasing the driver, we were required to impound their car and transport them to the police station where they'd be required to post $100 to get out of jail.

I again walked up to the car, informed the man that his license was suspended, and asked him to step out of his vehicle. The man's facial expression told me he was still really upset about something, but he remained silent and did everything I asked him without a word. I handcuffed the man behind his back, patted him down for weapons (he didn't have any), then walked him back to the police car and placed him in the back seat.

As I walked back to the car to search it, I used the portable police radio on my gun belt to request a tow truck. I had no obvious reason to suspect drugs or weapons inside the car, but

I'd learned my lesson well from Chisholm. I didn't find any contraband inside the man's vehicle, but I did find a sleeveless denim jacket on the front passenger seat.

When I picked it up and looked at the back panel, I saw a white rocker patch across the top with the words 'Devils Diciples' in blue letters. The misspelling was an intentional signature of the notorious outlaw biker gang, along with crossed red tridents over a 12-spoked wheel. The rocker across the bottom which said 'Michigan' identified the man as a member of their local chapter in Mount Clemens, which also served as the club's national headquarters.

I returned to my patrol car and stopped in front of it. I placed the sleeveless jacket, known as a 'cut', on the hood of my car and folded it carefully. I then placed it gently on my front passenger seat, all within plain view of the man watching me from the back seat. I had no love for his club. They were known for running illegal drugs and guns across the United States, and their reputation for violence was well-earned.

But sometimes a little bit of respect goes a long way. The man had given me no trouble during his arrest, and I was curious about his intentions and destination that day. When we arrived at the police station I fingerprinted the man, took his photo for the criminal file, and issued him a ticket. As most outlaw bikers do, he had a crisp $100 bill folded inside his wallet to post his own bail. I gave the man a receipt for his money, along with his cut, and as I walked him toward the door he finally spoke.

"Officer, I just want to thank you for saving my life" he said.

His statement caught me off guard. I didn't understand so I asked him what he meant.

"I just came from the hospital. My little girl lives with my ex-old lady at the trailer park up on Joy Road. Her new boyfriend has a pit bull that attacked my baby today, and she's in surgery now. I was on my way to the house to kill him".

I just nodded as my mouth hung open. I asked him if he still intended on going there. He shook his head.

"No. I was so angry I couldn't think straight. I just wanted to kill that dude, but then I would've gone to prison for the rest of my life. I'm fine, just want to get back to the hospital. Thanks, man."

I sent the outlaw biker on his way, and he kept his word. He returned to Mount Clemens General Hospital and never did go after the owner of the pit bull. That man in the trailer park never knew it, but the philosophy of aggressive traffic enforcement passed down to me by Lieutenant Dave Chisholm probably saved his life that day.

Cass Avenue Crash

There exists in law enforcement a concept called 'Criminal Patrol'. At least, I think it still exists. It's what every hard-charging uniformed cop on patrol longs for; time during a shift when the police radio is quiet, and dispatchers are not sending him (or her) on a steady barrage of bullshit calls for service. The domestic family disputes and traffic crashes slow down for a while. The guy who wants to report that someone he's never met threatened him over Facebook has gone to bed, and the lady who reported her car broken into twice this month actually remembered to lock the vehicle this time.

It's a moment when cops can focus on catching criminals. Driving slowly down a dark alley with the headlights extinguished might reveal someone kicking in the back door of a business, or a couple sketchy dudes doing a hand-to-hand drug transaction beside a dumpster. Tucking the scout car behind a fence could allow you to see a prostitute getting picked up on the boulevard by her john, who you can then stop for any number of traffic violations. If he gives you consent to search his car, you might find drugs or a gun, or both. And its almost certain that some of these folks will have fugitive warrants for their arrest. In other words, criminal patrol is what cops are supposed to be doing when they're not taking reports. Police work.

I'm not saying every officer I worked with embraced this philosophy, but the ones I most admired always did. There were countless tips and techniques I learned as a young cop to detect crimes in progress and, ultimately, to help protect our community. Some of them became routine things that I did almost unconsciously. An example is the practice of looking through the big glass window of a liquor store or grocery when driving past it, to see the cashier inside behind the counter. You certainly hope that person is not being robbed at gunpoint, but you'll never know if you don't look. It's a small action, but one that could save a life and put a serious felon behind bars. It also falls under the category of knowing your patrol area or 'beat' and understanding the movements of people within it, something every police officer should view as a professional responsibility.

I did exactly that one evening while traveling westbound on Cass Avenue in Mount Clemens. I was approaching the Dairy Mart, an establishment comparable to 7-11 and Circle K in other parts of the country. In Michigan, they're known as 'party stores' and this one was on the south side of the street, so I looked to my left. It was just a brief glance that revealed nothing out of the ordinary. As my eyes returned to the road in front of me, they beheld a sight that made time stop for a moment.

My right foot reached for the brake pedal, but never made it. In the travel lane before me was a dark blue 4-door Ford sedan that had just pulled out of a parking lot on the north side of the street. My police car struck it at full speed, impacting just below the center post which separated that car's front and back doors. It was the type of crash known by street cops as a 'T-bone'. Instantly, the front air bags of my black-and-white Chevy Caprice deployed, striking me full in the face and shattering my windshield on the passenger side.

After both cars slid to a stop, completely blocking traffic in both directions, I learned that airbags are filled with a chemical called sodium azide. When it receives an electrical charge, it explodes and is converted to nitrogen gas which fills the airbag. In fact, I learned that later, but the dusty residue of the explosion filled my lungs when I tried to speak over the police radio. I could barely utter my location to the dispatcher before I had to exit and inhale some fresh air.

I made my way to the other car and found a young white female with blonde hair behind the wheel. She was wearing a burgundy blouse over blue jeans and was conscious but stunned. Two white males were also in the car, one each in the front passenger seat and rear compartment. As I leaned into the driver window to speak with them, I could smell the alcohol. Everyone seemed to be OK, though the young man in back was moaning from the impact. Regaining my voice somewhat, I used my handheld radio to call for paramedics to check them out.

Learning that a police officer has been involved in any kind of critical incident will cause other officers to respond in a hurry. This dynamic is enhanced when the officer is heard over the radio barely able to speak. I was swiftly surrounded by the other officers on my shift and medics from the fire department, as well as some deputies from the Macomb County Sheriff's Office.

It was those deputies who were ultimately tasked with investigating the crash. That is the standard operating procedure in such situations, to avoid any appearance of impropriety that having a police agency investigate its own officer's crash might confer. The deputies' investigation quickly focused on the young female driver's level of intoxication. Just 19 years old, her blood alcohol content (BAC) was recorded at .23. Sadly, it was to be her second drunk driving arrest at that young age. In her heavily intoxicated state, she had failed to yield the right of way to oncoming traffic (me) when she entered the roadway from the parking lot.

"*Well, if you hadn't been distracted while looking at the party store clerk, you could have avoided the crash*," I can hear some of you saying. A fair point, though that conclusion is doubtful. If the young woman hadn't violated traffic laws while driving with a BAC almost three times the legal limit, the crash certainly would never have happened.

As for criminal patrol, it's a dying concept. I fear it might already be dead. Proactive police work in America is now met with derision by many in our society who've been conditioned to abdicate personal responsibility for their actions, and to shriek and wail against law enforcement at every turn. Physical assaults against officers, criminal indictments for merely doing the job, and the absence of courageous police leadership at the executive level cause many young people who would've pursued our honorable profession to look elsewhere. Who can blame them? Meanwhile, as calls to defund the police cause politicians to shrink budgets nationwide, there are fewer cops on the street to handle the ever-increasing calls for service.

We've created a vicious cycle, and I hope that we reverse course before it's too late.

Crazy Sam

Like every place in Mount Clemens, the building at 101 North Main Street has a lot of history. Today it's a beautiful custom built wood-paneled Irish pub that serves craft beer and premium whiskey, a great place for date night or watching a ball game with buddies. One hundred years ago during Prohibition it was a speakeasy, just a block from the Clinton River; a waterway used by mobsters to run illegal booze that had crossed Lake St. Clair from Canada.

But during the last decade of the twentieth century the bar at 101 North Main Street was known as Chrissy's Lounge and it wasn't a place people traveled great distances to visit. It was a neighborhood joint in a downtown that was yet to be revitalized, with plenty of vacant storefronts and empty parking spaces on the block. If craft beer had been a thing back then, it wouldn't have been served at Chrissy's. There was a juke box near the door and a pool table in back, but you'd better order a shot and a beer if you didn't want to attract attention.

One weekend night a man named Sam walked into Chrissy's Lounge and it wasn't long before the bartender called the police. Sam had long since been banned from the establishment for fighting and busting up the place, and the bartender wasn't going to give him a chance have a go with anyone.

Sam was an older Black man with unkempt gray curly hair and a noticeable limp. He was one of those guys who never lifted weights in his life and had the diet of a billy goat but was built like a pro athlete. Combined with a mind warped by drugs and alcohol over the years, Sam was an absolute handful when he was feeling unbalanced or agitated. The limp was from being shot in the leg by a man with a 30-06 hunting rifle after the man had come home from work and found Sam in bed with his wife.

I'd had a couple run-ins with Sam, and they couldn't have been more different. The first time was during my initial training period as a brand new police officer. I was dispatched to St Joseph's Hospital with my Field Training Officer Mike Santini for a disorderly man in the emergency room. When we arrived a shirtless Sam was in the lobby acting like a complete animal, knocking over chairs and screaming threats at anyone he saw.

Santini was a strong guy who stood about 6 foot 3 and worked construction during his off duty time. He could definitely handle his business in a fight, but he always taught me the importance of working smarter rather than harder. I once watched Santini talk a man having a psychotic episode down from the top of a tree he'd climbed. Santini knew that the man smoked, so he fished a Marlboro Light out of his uniform shirt pocket and held the cigarette up for the man to see. When the man climbed down, Santini even lit the smoke for him before placing handcuffs on his wrists and transporting him to a local hospital.

When we walked up the long ramp from the ambulance parking area into the ER, I immediately noticed that all the employees were locked in the nurses' station and they looked scared to death. While looking away from where my attention should have been focused, Sam attempted a roundhouse kick directly at my head. Santini, who was accustomed to protecting unsuspecting rookie cops like me, pushed me back a few inches; just enough to avoid being struck by Sam's steel toed boot.

I had put on my black leather gloves when I exited the patrol car because I figured we might be in for a fight. Santini noticed Sam's eyes locked on my gloves and told me quietly to take them off. I was a clueless rookie back then, but I knew enough to listen to my FTO without questioning him in a situation like that. I calmly took the gloves off and put them in my back pocket. Sam calmed down then but the look on his face said that he didn't trust me. He would only listen to Santini and that was just fine with me. I stood by while Santini talked Sam peacefully down the hallway into the area where psychiatric evaluations were administered.

The second time I met Sam was when I stopped a car which had been speeding down Gratiot Avenue. When the car pulled over I walked up to it, only to see old Sam behind the wheel. Everyone knew Sam didn't have a driver's license, including Sam. I couldn't let him drive away just because I was afraid of dealing with him, so I asked him to step out of the car. He knew exactly why I asked him that question (he was going to jail), but he did as I requested.

Standing outside of the car he pointed at a box of Newport's on the front seat and said, "Hey officer, can I have one of them smokes?"

In my mind I thought '*You're goddamn right you can*', but I just said "Sure, Sam. Let me light it up for you".

I then placed the handcuffs on his wrists but kept them in the front so he could have his cigarette. On the way to the police station Sam started to sing an old Dean Martin song at the top of his lungs.

"Volare! Oh, oh!" Sam belted out. "Cantare! Oh, oh, oh, oh!"

I don't know if he was back on his meds or just having a good day, but I was happy to let him have a good sing and a smoke before we arrived at the jail.

When I walked into Chrissy's Lounge on that Saturday evening with my partner Jim Ochmanski, the patrons were unusually quiet. They looked up as we entered and then collectively looked toward the pool table where Sam had just knocked a striped ball off the top rail cushion into a corner pocket.

We walked slowly toward the back of the smoke-filled tavern and Sam looked up at us when we cast a couple shadows over the green table. I said hello and tried to gauge how Sam was feeling that day. He seemed OK so I told him that it wasn't anything personal, just business, but he was not allowed in Chrissy's anymore and had to leave.

"Come on, Disser," Sam said. "I got three bucks in this game".

I looked over at the bartender who nodded, confirming that Sam had put three dollars in the machine.

Just then Ochmanski reached in his pants pocket and pulled out two single bills. He looked at me and said, "You got a dollar?"

I pulled out my wallet and handed over the cash.

Ochmanski placed the three dollars on the table and said, "There you go, Sam. Whaddaya say?"

It was brilliant.

We avoided a potential brawl with a dude that no one in their right mind wanted to fight, and it only cost us three bucks. Sam was happy, we were happy, the bartender was happy. Sometimes it pays to work smarter, not harder.

Bred to Kill

During my time at Mount Clemens PD there was a nationwide explosion in the popularity of pit bull dogs. Regardless of the genesis of the trend, it became fashionable to have them. Just as cellular phones, gangsta rap, and sagging pants were all the rage, pit bulls were suddenly everywhere.

Don't get me wrong. I had to have a cellular phone as soon as they became available, too. I also happen to dig Snoop Dogg, and I was cool with dudes who belted their pants below their boxer shorts because they couldn't run very fast; it made foot chases a lot easier.

Unfortunately, there was a barbaric undercurrent to the trend, the atrocious blood sport of dogfighting. A few houses in Mount Clemens, and dozens more in Detroit, were dedicated to hosting dog fights. We would encounter them occasionally when I was working undercover in COMET, since they often doubled as dope houses, and uniformed patrol officers would also see the signs.

Just like drug dealers, dog fighters employed lookouts throughout a neighborhood when a fight was planned. If you drove onto a block in a marked police car and suddenly heard a series of whistles, those were lookouts signaling to one another that the cops were nearby. Whether the whistles were intended to alert the dope man or the dog fighter was sometimes difficult to tell, but there were other clues.

A rubber tire hanging by a rope from a tree branch conjures an image of children playfully swinging from it; but what if the tire seems oddly higher than a child could reach and there doesn't seem to be any kids in the area? It's a good bet the tire is being used to build bite strength in a pit bull. If a police officer is dispatched to a house for an unrelated incident but finds a large wooden frame on the basement floor that is stained with blood, there's a good chance they're fighting dogs in that house.

Disturbing as it sounds, numerous police reports of stolen or missing dogs in a particular neighborhood can be an ominous red flag. Dog fighters will sometimes steal regular non-aggressive dogs and put them in the pit with their fighting dog, so that it can acquire a 'taste for blood' and become accustomed to killing. The mindset of a human being who could watch an innocent dog, someone's beloved pet, suffer such a merciless and violent death was something that gave me pause during my career. I can't say that I've ever developed a sound theory as to why or how they can be so cruel. The only remedy that gave me any satisfaction was locking them up at every available opportunity. Neither did I shed a tear when such a person met their demise in some violent way, as happened occasionally in that subculture.

It's easy to also blame the dog, and for a long time I did. A pit bull's appearance lends itself to the image of fighting due to its broad skull, powerful jaw, and heavily muscled frame. Over the years I saw some pit bulls that were absolute demons, trained to fight other dogs or defend drug houses, and I was always apprehensive when executing a search warrant at a drug house that was known to have pit bulls inside.

On a Sunday morning in Mount Clemens, one of our patrol officers encountered a dog which had escaped from a house that belonged to a dog fighting suspect. The dog was roaming the neighborhood and posed a significant threat to the residents, especially children living in that area near Gratiot Avenue and Robertson Street. When the black pit bull snarled and charged at the officer, he was forced to shoot it. That dog took nine shots from a .40 caliber handgun before it finally fell to the ground and died. It had deep scars on its face and was missing pieces of its ears, all injuries suffered from fighting, and the dog's toughness and resilience was displayed that day.

One of the most heinous 'training' methods I ever encountered occurred at Shadyside Park in Mount Clemens, a city-owned 40-acre recreation area on the banks of the Clinton River. At the extreme eastern end of the park, far from the playground and parking lot, was a small dock along the water's edge. The dock hadn't been cared for during the decades since its installation, evidenced by the peeling paint and missing planks.

I was away from daily operations at the police station, assigned full-time to COMET, the day one of our police officers was dispatched to an animal cruelty complaint at the dock. A man walking his dog through the park had witnessed something he almost couldn't believe. Two pit bulls were tethered by chains to the far end of the dock, where the river's current was strongest. Someone had thrown them into the river, which forced the dogs to swim against the current or drown.

When Officer Susan Sherwood arrived, she saw one of the pit bulls was struggling mightily to paddle while keeping his head above water. The other dog's body, sadly, hung limp under the surface of the flowing water at the taut end of its chain. Sherwood loved animals and had a special affinity for dogs, so she had to set her emotions aside in that moment as she pulled in the dogs, first the trembling survivor and then the remains of the other.

The detectives at Mount Clemens PD tracked down and arrested the dog fighter who had placed them in the river, believing it would improve their endurance and survival instincts. The better the dogs fought, the more money he could make fighting them. That man was convicted of animal cruelty and, amazingly, received a harsh prison sentence due to his long previous criminal record.

My border collie, Jake, loved to herd things even though he didn't understand why. I never trained him to do that. It was likely from his ancestors being trained to do so for many generations, going back to Scotland. For the same reason, I'm still wary around pit bulls because of their fighting heritage. But I've become much better at reading their demeanor and I've found that if the dog is wagging its tail when it approaches, it's probably not trying to attack me.

The vicious dogs I've encountered during my career were certainly made so by their owners, and I understand that a properly trained and cared for pit bull is probably no more dangerous than any other breed.

Ice Cream Monster

I don't understand pedophiles. I never much wanted to, except as it pertained to identifying, apprehending, and prosecuting them. I didn't enjoy interviewing or interrogating them because my interview style, developed over many years, relied on empathy (both feigned and genuine). I tried to relate to people as much as possible during an interview, to make them feel comfortable telling me things. It didn't always work, but it worked best for me.

This approach was often much appreciated by victims and witnesses who, after our conversations, felt glad they'd contributed to justice being served. Perhaps it also humanized the police in their eyes. Sometimes even criminal suspects felt some degree of relief after confessing to me because they believed that I understood them or, at least, had tried to do so. Other times, when they realized that their factual statements to me had done nothing but ensure their prolonged incarceration, some accused persons felt quite differently. I make no apologies to them. My efforts always had one goal; to elicit the truth.

It's tough to relate to a pedophile. I don't understand the etiology of that horrific disorder, but I understand that suffering sexual abuse as a child can often contribute to it. In one of my all-time favorite movies, *Manhunter,* the lead character Will Graham describes his sentiment about a serial killer when he considers the man may have been abused as a child, after his boss incredulously asks if Graham has empathy for him.

"Absolutely... My heart bleeds for him, as a child. Someone took a kid and manufactured a monster. At the same time, as an adult, he's irredeemable. He butchers whole families to pursue trivial fantasies... As an adult, someone should blow the sick fuck out of his socks!"

Obviously, the film portrayed a fictional story (although it was based on Special Agents from the FBI Behavioral Science Unit, an actual entity). But that movie line, delivered so expertly by actor William Petersen, accurately summarizes my thoughts on rapists who prey on children. Alas, ending their lives was not my duty; I merely had to build solid cases against them and assist in their prosecution.

A characteristic shared by many pedophiles, in my experience, is that they are opportunistic. They seek places and arrangements which offer access to children, obviously. But also desirable are positions of trust and authority. That combination of factors affords them the ultimate opportunity to determine the most vulnerable kids in their midst and to prey on them.

The notorious serial child molester Jerry Sandusky, a former football coach for Penn State University, founded a charitable sports program for troubled youth called the Second Mile Foundation. People thought him a hero for it. He also adopted six children with his wife and fostered many more in their home. Under the guise of these apparent good works, Sandusky had unfettered access to dozens, perhaps hundreds, of at-risk kids. Sandusky secretly terrorized those children for years and was never suspected, until he was caught in the act of raping a teenage boy in the Penn State football locker room by a fellow coach.

The Roman Catholic Church has mandated since the Middle Ages that their priests be celibate. A popular belief is that because Jesus was unmarried and without children, priests should emulate that behavior. The actual decree by Pope Gregory VII in the year 1075 had more to do with the Church enriching itself with a priest's money and property after his death, but the effect is the same pertaining to pedophiles. Celibate priests don't morph into child molesters. Pedophiles are attracted to that position because of the trust and blind faith of churchgoers. A family atmosphere in the parish rectory would discourage their presence, if not totally eliminate it, as would the ordination of female priests. As someone born and raised in the Church, I'm ashamed of its leaders for their refusal to see this obvious reality and change that tradition.

Whether it's a coach, priest, scout troop leader, childcare worker, school bus driver, or any other position; where there is authority, power and trust, there exists the opportunity for abuse.

As a young cop in uniform, I had one of my first encounters with a child predator on a warm spring day in Mount Clemens. As I steered my patrol car slowly through the public housing projects near Clemens Street and Court Street, I heard the familiar tinny sound of '*Turkey in The Straw*' coming from a cheap loudspeaker one block to the east. It was a bit unusual. The ice cream man didn't normally come down in the 'hood. In fact, it was the first time I ever saw an ice cream truck there.

I turned left past the clustered examples of 1960's urban design; boxy brown brick townhouses, two stories high with rooflines that seemed to fold over the walls. The matching asphalt shingles came halfway down the brick siding. The rectangular structures held two to four residences each, and in the middle of each building cluster was a courtyard with a playset for kids: dark blue climbing ladders and platforms, bright yellow slides and handrails. The fresh sod installed by the city was long ago destroyed by small feet of kids in the daytime, plus the crackheads and dealers who traversed it after dark.

The nearer I got to North Broadway Street, the louder the crappy music became. Another left turn and I saw it; the boxy old, converted Chevy step van was traveling slowly north. Painted a drab olive color years ago, it had a few brightly colored advertisements for different treats and ice cream. But the signs did not command my attention that day.

The truck was covered in kids. Four sat on the rear bumper while two more stood on either end of it, holding awning brackets for balance. Several children were running back and forth inside the truck, visible through the opening in the side panel where the ice cream was ordered and received.

I shot quickly north and activated the overhead red and blue LED lightbar on my police car. A short blast of the siren caused the driver to lean left in his seat and see me in the big side view mirror. He was only traveling about 5 miles per hour, so it didn't take him long to curb the truck and come to a stop. When he did so, each kid on the back bumper took off running in a different direction. I used the police radio to tell the dispatcher that I was stopping a vehicle on North Broadway near Clara Street.

As I climbed out of my driver seat under the clear blue sky, I could see him still watching me in the mirror. I crossed in front of my car behind the ice cream truck and approached on the passenger side where the sliding metal door was already retracted, revealing the steps that led upward into the vehicle's interior. Seated on those steps? More kids. Most of them were holding ice cream sandwiches or bomb pops.

They sat on the step momentarily frozen with eyes wide until I waved them out and told them to go home. I grabbed the short aluminum handrail with my left hand while planting a black Hi-Tec Magnum boot onto the second step. I stepped in and peered around the corner to where the ice cream and popsicles were stored in stainless steel cabinet freezers. I waved out the kids I'd seen through the window, satisfied the step van was now empty except for the driver and me.

I stared lasers through the driver's eyes. This was weird. An otherwise normal-looking white man about 40 years old and of average height and build, something was definitely strange about this guy.

"Did those kids buy that ice cream from you?" I asked.

"Well, yeah," he replied, eyes rolling as if it was the dumbest question he'd ever heard.

"Driver's license, please," I said. "Also, your commercial vehicle insurance and registration. While you're at it, I'm gonna need your official city vendor license and county health department inspection certificate."

I was bluffing that last bit. I suspected he didn't have a vendor license and, frankly, was merely guessing that an ice cream truck needed a health department inspection. Turns out I was right on both counts. Unfortunately for him, he possessed only a driver's license.

"Ah come on, officer," he whined, handing me the license. "I'm just a vet trying make a living. Why ya' gotta harass me?"

"Oh, you're a veteran?" I asked. "What was your MOS?".

MOS is an acronym for Military Occupational Specialty. It's the occupational role that each member of the armed services is assigned after boot camp, and every single veteran in America can recite theirs. In fact, if someone doesn't answer that question immediately with *"11 Bravo, sir"* (indicating they served in the US Army Infantry), or some similar response, its likely they're lying about having served in any branch of our military.

This guy just scoffed, shook his head, and stared out straight ahead through the windshield.

"Step out of the vehicle," I said. "Keep your hands where I can see them."

My intangible sense for people and situations, or 'cop radar', was not yet fully developed at that point in my career, but I felt strongly the man was wrong on some level. Who drives around an ice cream truck without a proper license and lets little kids ride along? I walked him back to my police car, placed him firmly against the side of it, and handcuffed him.

"You're under arrest for operating a commercial vehicle without proof of insurance and selling goods in the city without a vendor's permit," I told him.

If his driver's license was valid and he had no arrest warrants, I could still release him with a ticket later if I wanted to do so. But at this point there was enough probable cause to believe that he'd violated the law, so into the back seat he went. It was one of many solid tactical operating procedures taught to me by my primary Field Training Officer, Lance Folson. You can always take the handcuffs off.

While walking around the back of my car toward the driver door, I noticed one of the kids who'd previously been sitting on the truck step. She was 20 yards away near one of the project houses on North Broadway standing on the sidewalk next to a woman, presumably her mother. Still holding an ice cream in one hand, the girl was pointing at me while her mother scowled.

I opened the door and sat back down in my seat. I rotated the Mobile Data Terminal on its mount toward me and retrieved the man's license from my uniform shirt pocket. It was only then I noticed it was issued by the state of Ohio. Metropolitan Detroit isn't too far from the Ohio border, but it was another oddity. Why would someone from Ohio be selling ice cream in Mount Clemens?

Beneath the small display monitor of the MDT was a keyboard. I used it to enter the man's name and check his driving status in Ohio and Michigan. The query would also run his name through Michigan's Law Enforcement Information Network and the National Crime Information Center, to check for criminal arrest warrants in Michigan and nationwide. It took less time for the computer to return my information than it took for me to read it, though the messages jumped off the screen:

Missouri Query: *Felony Warrant*
           566.062 – Statutory Sodomy in the
           First Degree
           Deviate Sexual Intercourse with a
           Child less than 14 Years Old

Kansas Query: *Felony Warrant*
21-5503(3) – Rape
Sexual Intercourse with a Child less
than 14 Years Old

As I mentally processed that data and thought about all the kids this creep had just enticed into his ice cream truck, my face turned red as I looked at him in my rear view mirror. Our eyes met briefly before he turned and looked away. Lips pursed almost into a sneer, he wore a look that was equal parts defiance and resignation.

From a metal clip on the dashboard, I grabbed the microphone attached by black spiral cord to the Motorola digital radio below. Before depressing the microphone's transmit key with my thumb to call for a commercial tow truck, I noticed a half dozen adults standing to my left, where the girl and her mother had been. They looked pissed. I rolled down my window.

"Everything ok, folks?" I asked.

"What … you gotta arrest the ice cream man for coming to our neighborhood?" asked a heavyset woman, head swaying and finger pointing at the van. "Our kids can't have no ice cream?"

I was stunned.

"No ma'am," I said, shaking my head. "It's not like that."

"Mm hmm," she replied, nodding. "It surely does look like that."

Pressing the transmit key, I said, "Radio from Car 56. Send me a tow truck to this location." Looking at the growing crowd, I added, "And send me another unit, please."

Hearing my request for a tow truck, the jerk in my back seat began to wail.

"Oh, come on, man!" he cried. "You can't tow my rig! All the ice cream's gonna melt!"

"Tough shit, asshole," is what I thought but didn't say. As far as I was concerned, that was his problem. Don't want to lose your inventory? Don't cruise the project playgrounds looking for little kids to molest while illegally selling ice cream in a truck with no insurance.

The man continued to protest loudly while the group of angry people on the sidewalk started to chatter and woof veiled threats in my direction. Between this rock and hard place of evil and ignorance, I contemplated my options.

One alternative was to exit my police car and have a little conference with the angry folks from the neighborhood. I could tell them all about how this man was wanted in multiple states for brutally raping children, but that those states might be too far away for the police to extradite him on the warrants. And so, I'd explain to them, he would just be released here on the scene. It would relieve the erroneous belief that the police department was denying their children the God-given right to enjoy cool treats on a hot day, and it would deliver to this man the punishment he richly deserved for his sins here on earth. He wouldn't make it one block before they descended on him like pirhanas chasing a goldfish.

That's not what happened, of course. Air brakes suddenly hissed as the big blue flatbed truck from Nick's Towing Company angled in front of the ice cream truck and came to a stop. Simultaneously, another black and white patrol car glided in behind me. I conferred briefly with the two cops who'd arrived so quickly to back me up, thanking them and telling them what I'd discovered. They told me they would stand by while the ice cream truck was impounded, so I headed straight for the county jail.

Our dispatcher had called the police departments in Missouri and Kansas, and the arrest warrants had been confirmed. If we would lodge the man in jail, they said, extradition would be forthcoming. I was more than happy to oblige.

It wasn't my last encounter with a pedophile, nor was it the most heinous. But in retrospect, it was a good example of the way child predators manipulate people and create situations which give them access to kids. Not many institutions are less threatening than the friendly ice cream man, and on a hot day kids will run to the sound of his call.

To this day, I can't stand ice cream trucks. When one drives down my street, I point to the next block and tell the driver to keep moving. When they were little, the only time my kids got ice cream from a truck is when I wasn't home, and their mother gave them the money. Poor kids, they were lucky to have her.

Prom Night

When I was 15 years old, my parents got divorced. It was the worst age for me to be, since I was old enough to understand what was happening but too young to process my own emotions rationally. The result was some pretty awful behavior on my part, but kids are resilient, and I bounced back. Later in my life the experiences also informed the way I interacted with teenagers as a police officer.

One Saturday summer night my friend Rick and I were out cruising in the red 1970 Chevy Chevelle SS he bought with money from after-school jobs. Rick was restoring the old beast one piece at a time and his first order of business had been the engine; that car was fast. We screamed down the country roads outside of town, then cruised Main Street blasting Judas Priest and Motorhead tunes from the cassette player Rick had installed. After a few hours we found ourselves in the parking lot of the big Meijer grocery store on the north end of the city. It was late and the lot was empty, so Rick hit the gas.

As we raced through the parking lot approaching 60 miles per hour, we failed to notice a police car parked in the shadow of a gas station at the intersection. Just as we fishtailed from the parking lot into the roadway, rubber burning and heavy metal music blasting, red and blue flashing lights filled the Chevelle's rear view mirrors. Rick pulled over immediately, stopping along the curb as the police car's spotlight illuminated us.

The youthful feeling of being angry at the world disappears quickly when the shadow of a policeman approaches your car. As he bent forward to look through the driver door window, I saw recognition in the cop's eyes. He knew who we were and was well-acquainted with our fathers. He ordered us both out of the car.

We stood on the grass in the bright lights next to Rick's Chevelle as people drove past, stealing looks at the two cocky kids who were in a lot of trouble. After removing a half case of empty beer bottles and a half case of full ones, the policeman placed them on the car's rooftop alongside a shoebox full of firecrackers and bottle rockets we had been firing from the moving vehicle. It seemed like an eternity standing there. But a short time later we found ourselves at the police station, waiting for our fathers to arrive. Rick left with his stepdad, Ray, and so I spent some lonely moments in the lobby waiting for Lou to show up. When he did, a cold stare and a slight lift of his head told me to follow him outside.

Not a word was spoken as we climbed into his silver Oldsmobile 98, parked in a metered space across the street. As we drove the three miles home, to a place where he no longer lived, the silence grew deafening. My dad pulled into the garage and stopped, then used the remote control clipped to the visor to close the garage door. Still, not a word. After a few minutes there in the dark, my dad finally spoke.

"I'm very disappointed in you" he calmly said.

He remained there for another quiet moment, then got out of the car and walked into the house, presumably to tell my mom what had happened before leaving again. I sat in the dark for a while longer, the weight of his words hanging on my heart. At that moment I wished he'd have just hit me; it would have hurt less. It must have been embarrassing for my dad to have to pick up his son from the police station where he'd spent years working, not to mention the concern and worry he surely had about a kid who clearly wasn't reacting well to the marital discord. I ended up grounded for a couple weeks and received a 'juvenile diversion' deferment for the charge of being a minor in possession of alcohol, but the worst punishment was knowing how I'd let my father down.

Plenty more delinquent behavior unfortunately followed. Most of it went undiscovered but there was another rendezvous at the police station. Following that incident my friend Kevin and I had to repair the lawn at an apartment complex with rakes and shovels, destroyed when we'd done a huge burnout in Kevin's Ford LTD. The reckless stunt had spilled from the parking lot asphalt onto the newly seeded turf, and the police stopped us a few miles away after angry residents called 911. Lou and Kevin's dad, Chet, shook their heads grimly as they supervised our landscaping work. As they smoked and chatted quietly that day, they probably wondered how they'd managed to raise such complete knuckleheads.

Somehow I managed to avoid a criminal record and being disowned by my parents. I played sports and graduated high school with grades decent enough to gain admission at Central Michigan University. Around the time I turned 18, I had decided to stop feeling miserable and sorry for myself because of my parents' divorce. Once I realized that it wasn't my fault and nothing I could do would change the situation, I simply stopped thinking about it. In retrospect, it was the strong positive influence of coaches, teachers, and others in our community, in addition to family, that kept me from straying too far from the right path. No one ever gave up on me; to the contrary, they always held me to a high standard. Their lessons stayed with me, and I appreciate those generous people even more as the years go by.

As I've encountered kids in situations similar to my own growing up, my decisions as a police officer have always been guided by my experiences. I never liked writing tickets for 'Minor in Possession'. Because that misdemeanor violation attaches to your driving record, it's a conviction that stays with you for a long time. I've known law enforcement professionals who encountered difficulty obtaining a promotion or security clearance in their late twenties because they received an 'M.I.P.' ticket when they were 19 years old.

I always asked kids in that situation to tell me about themselves, to get a read on what type of person they're becoming or want to be someday. Were they involved with sports, marching band, or choir? Did they enjoy acting in the school play or making an argument on the debate team? Every kid has something going for them even if it's not immediately obvious, and they deserve a second chance when they screw up. Not that there shouldn't be consequences; bad behavior needs to be clearly defined, so that educated choices are made in the future.

As a young patrolman in Mount Clemens, I had a sweet spot for catching speeders with the radar gun. It wasn't a speed trap; the limit on Gratiot Avenue was 35 MPH all the way through town. But as the four-lane southbound section of the divided highway crossed the Clinton River, a rise in the middle of the bridge obstructed the view of drivers as they came upon Wellington Crescent Road, just south of the river. A traffic light has since been installed there, but back then it was a very dangerous intersection.

One spring Saturday I started my shift at 1600 hours and, after grabbing a large cup of black coffee at the nearby Tim Horton's, settled into my favorite radar spot alongside Gratiot Avenue south of the Clinton River. I hadn't even peeled back the coffee cup's plastic lid when I heard the radar instrument whine. I actually heard the red Ford Mustang GT convertible before I saw it cross over the bridge, becoming ever so slightly airborne on the downhill side as it zoomed through the intersection at Wellington Crescent Road. The bright red digits on the radar showed 70 MPH.

The Mustang raced south almost to 16 Mile Road before I could catch up and activate the patrol car's overhead lights. The driver slowed and steered two lanes to his right, coming to a stop along the curb in front of a huge car dealership known then as Jim Causley Pontiac GMC. I walked up to the driver's door and saw a kid wearing a black tuxedo with a hot pink bowtie and cummerbund. It was senior prom night at Mount Clemens High School.

The young man handed over his driver's license which showed he was 17 years old. The muscle car belonged to Enterprise Leasing, having been rented exclusively for the evening's festivities, and the kid was in route to pick up his girlfriend. They planned to have dinner at a restaurant with friends before the big dance.

On the front passenger seat of the car was a clear plastic case containing a wrist corsage with pink flowers; no doubt purchased to match his girlfriend's prom dress. Next to the corsage box was a six pack of Budweiser beer, the condensation on the bottles indicating they were still cold. The kid was stone cold sober, and the beer wasn't open, but he swallowed hard and told me the truth; he had asked a friend of age to purchase it for him so they could party that night.

I returned to my police car and thought about my options. The kid had a clean driving record, did well in school, and he'd told me the truth. Blasting over a bridge and through an intersection at double the posted speed limit could be considered Reckless Driving, a misdemeanor for which he could have been arrested and the car impounded. Taking that course of action would certainly have ruined prom night, but it wouldn't have been unjustified. I decided to write the young man a speeding ticket for 40 MPH in a 35 MPH zone. In addition to costing him $100 the speeding ticket would impact his insurance rates, but that was too bad; consider it another lesson learned. The 30 mile per hour difference between the cited and actual speeds would save him $150 and a couple points on his license, which would have resulted in revocation for a teenager.

Returning to the Mustang, I told the kid to grab the six-pack and step out of the vehicle. After we walked up onto the grass shoulder, I directed him to crack open the bottles of beer and pour each of them out onto the ground. When he'd finished, I had him put the bottles back in the cardboard container and stow it in the trunk of the car. I handed him the ticket and reminded him that by allowing him to drive their little girl to prom, his date's parents trusted him with her life. Her safety and her future depended on his ability to make good decisions. The kid demonstrated his maturity by thanking me and looking me dead in the eye as he shook my hand. I knew then that I'd made the right decision.

That traffic stop was just one of hundreds, maybe thousands, of contacts I had with children and young adults throughout 30 years of police work and coaching sports; they weren't all so easy, nor did they always end well. Some were tragic. Many resulted in incarceration. But even in those difficult scenarios, especially then, it's important for cops to look beyond the surface and try to keep a kid on the right path.

Contact with a police officer can be a critical moment in any young person's life, and it's an opportunity for every police officer to make a huge impact. I'm thankful there were people available to help me through my struggles as a teenager, and glad that I positively affected some kids in return.

A Wee Go-Round

There was a fantastic pub in Mount Clemens called The Last Drop. Named after a similar establishment in Edinburgh, Scotland, it was owned by a man called Jim Morris.

The two-story pub stood on Macomb Place, a paved brick avenue which ran through the heart of downtown and attracted lots of pedestrian traffic. Situated across the street from a covered stage and adjacent to several good restaurants, the pub even had an old red phone booth like the kind seen commonly in the U.K., on the sidewalk outside its main entrance.

Inside, the design was old school British and featured intricately carved hardwood pieces throughout the space. Flags and memorabilia of Glasgow Rangers Football Club added splashes of royal blue, white and red to the wood-paneled walls, along with framed photos of famous golfers and plaques imparting Gaelic wisdom. Along the back wall was a long dark bar with colorful tap handles and bottles of single malt whisky lining the shelves. I loved the place. It made me want to crush a pint of Belhaven or Carling each time I visited.

I never enjoyed working the midnight shift, but I got stuck on it for a year due to seniority (or a lack thereof). Young cops were usually stranded on the afternoon shift when bids were taken every six months, but that suited me fine. It was the busiest time to work (1600 to 2400 hours) and there was no place I'd have rather been. But because someone who usually worked the late show wanted a different spot, I found myself there for two consecutive bids of six months each.

Like most police departments, Mount Clemens PD was perpetually understaffed. Each patrol shift had a minimum number of officers and supervisors necessary to provide proper coverage of the streets. When multiple officers utilized earned time off or called in sick on the same day, it often caused a shift to fall below the minimum level of staffing. That resulted in overtime; an off-duty officer would be called in to work at 1.5 times the normal rate of pay (double time if it was a holiday). It was a good way to boost a pension if you were nearing retirement, or supplement income if you were a cop with a young family; almost like having a second job. It's not a great way to run a police department, however. Too many people get burned out, production suffers, and it's unsafe to be in dangerous situations when you're tired.

On a chilly night during my year of forced overnight patrols, I had an opportunity to work with a supervisor I greatly admired. Lieutenant Smith was the dayshift commander and almost never worked nights. But he was approaching retirement and recently divorced, so perhaps he wanted to give his paycheck a shot in the arm. Smith was an experienced and decorated cop who was respected as a leader in the police department. Whenever I had the chance to work overtime on his shift during the daytime, I always seemed to learn something. Smith was interested in the younger officers and solicited their input when it was appropriate. On more than one occasion I told him about some experience or bright idea I had. He'd listen earnestly and then ask me a couple questions which inevitably made it clear that I had more thinking to do. I appreciated his wisdom and common sense, especially years later.

During the shift that night I was dispatched to a commercial burglary alarm at The Last Drop. It was the small hours of the morning, after the bars had closed but long before sunrise, when I turned onto Macomb Place from North Walnut Street. I extinguished my headlights and parked in the shadows, half a block from the front door.

The entire block east of The Last Drop was a succession of businesses and buildings which abutted each other, with no breaks in between. I moved quickly along the sidewalk, careful to stay close to the storefronts and out of sight as much as possible. Reaching the end of the frontage, I hustled across an open space under a streetlight into the shadow of the red British phone booth.

Once there I was able to see Smith standing against the wall near the entrance. I moved to the wall on the other side and listened quietly. The dispatcher had informed us the alarm was activated by motion detectors inside the main barroom. There was a faint light behind glass block windows lining the entrance, and I could hear the distant hum of an electric motor. With a nod to Smith, I pulled on the twisted iron handle and found the heavy oak door to be unlocked.

We moved quickly through the opening and silently in opposite directions as we crossed through the foyer and into the main room. This movement gets officers out of an area called the 'fatal funnel' when entering a space. The term describes the view of someone inside lying in wait to ambush anyone coming through the door. The tactic also creates an L-shaped field of fire should we encounter an armed suspect.

We did encounter someone inside. She was a middle-aged Latina woman clad in sweatshirt and jeans, running a vacuum between high-top tables and stacked barstools.

Slowly, we moved through the darkened space toward her. Surely this cleaning lady had accidentally or unknowingly activated the alarm. I flashed a few bright bursts from the rechargeable Maglite in my left hand, so that we didn't startle her. Without even shutting off the vacuum, she turned to us and pointed at the stairwell. She looked unimpressed.

I looked to the top of the stairwell just as a teenaged boy started to round the corner from an upstairs hallway. He took one look at us, turned on his heel, then went straight back the way he'd come and out of my sight. I heard an upstairs interior door slam.

Smith and I climbed the wide staircase, which was to the left of the long bar and led to the business office and storage areas on the second floor. Once in the upstairs hallway, Smith knocked on the first door we encountered and then turned the knob. We both stayed in the hallway as Smith pushed the unlocked door inward. Inside, the business office contained three drunken teenagers, each of them about 19 years old. One of them was a son of Jim Morris.

The boys had clearly been tapping the old man's inventory after hours without his knowledge. In addition to being underage, the act was a violation of Michigan Liquor Control laws; one that could lead to revocation of the bar's liquor license. It also happened that Smith oversaw all liquor license applications, inspections and compliance for the police department.

"All right, boys," Smith announced. "Come on out of there. Down the stairs you go."

They dutifully complied, though I gave them each the stink eye on their way out just to let them know we weren't screwing around. When we arrived on the ground floor, the cleaning lady had vanished. Smith directed the boys to remove three stools from a stack, place them in front of the bar, and take a seat. All of them except young Morris.

"Ok, son," Smith said, motioning to a landline phone behind the bar. "Get your father down here. Right now." The kid looked mortified. His head sank and his shoulders slumped, but he trudged around the bar to make the call.

By all accounts, Jim Morris was a good man. From Scotland he'd emigrated first to Canada, then to the USA where he opened his dream pub in Mount Clemens, Michigan. I'd been told he was a policeman in Glasgow or Toronto before his arrival here, perhaps it was both. My few contacts with him had been positive, and the consensus around town was that he was a friendly, hard-working business owner and family guy. It took him an amazingly short amount of time to arrive.

Morris blasted through the front door. Stepping quickly, fists clenched and jaw protruding, the fire in his eyes gave me a fair shot of adrenaline. I wasn't sure what was in store. Morris stopped near me, placing Smith and me between him and the boys.

"Morning, Jim," Smith said. "Thanks for coming straightaway. It looks like the boys got into the booze after you closed up."

"Aye," Morris said quietly, his accent pure Glasgow. "That it does, mate."

"As you know," Smith continued, "that could have serious consequences. You might even lose your license to sell alcohol, at least for a time."

Morris nodded, his eyes burning a hole through his son, who wouldn't meet his gaze. Pointing at the boy he snarled, "Coom he-are, lahd."

The kid took a single step toward his father, then stopped. He was six feet in front of me, his dad to my right.

"Naw, son," Morris continued, pointing at a spot on the floor before him. "R-r-right fookin' he-are!"

The younger Morris took another step. Before his foot landed on the floorboard, his father's fist landed in his solar plexus. To the young man's enormous credit, he didn't go down. But as he stumbled backward, his father advanced.

Instinctively, I moved to stop him. Smith shot his right arm out to the side, palm against my uniform shirt, and stopped me. I stood by as Morris landed a few more blows, full force without consideration for age or inexperience. Fortunately for the son, they were body shots. Morris probably didn't want to ruin the kid's dental work he'd already paid for. As they neared the far wall, I made eye contact with Smith. He gave me a nod.

I reached Morris in three strides and wrapped him in a bear hug from behind. Lifting him a few inches off the ground I spun, then walked him behind the long bar. I pressed him up against the rail and didn't let go until I was sure he was done. The kid was a little worse for wear but uninjured. He was tough as nails, too; without a doubt he possessed his dad's grit.

"Well, Jim," Smith declared. "It looks like you have things under control here. I don't think we need to take any further action. So long as it never happens again, we'll just consider this a warning."

Breathing heavily, Morris nodded. "Cheers, mate," he said. "Ull no let ya doon."

And he didn't let us down. I don't recall any liquor laws being broken at The Last Drop after that night. And a kid with a wild streak was made immediately aware of his transgression, swiftly punished, and kept out of the criminal justice system. Surely some would disapprove of such old school tactics, and many cops didn't possess Smith's wisdom or balls to make that decision in such a moment, but I thought it was bold and effective.

As we exited into the cool darkness, I inhaled a deep breath and let it go.

"Thanks for the backup, Lieutenant!" I said.

"Anytime, Diss," Smith replied with a chuckle. "Anytime."

Full Moon

There's an unwritten rule among cops, nurses, and a few other professions that when there is a full moon, chaos often ensues. I don't have any scientific proof that it's true, but I believe it. There have been countless nights when I've silently asked myself '*What the hell is going on out here?*', only to look up in the sky and see that bright round heavenly body staring back down. One such night I saw two full moons.

I'd spent most of an afternoon patrol shift driving from call to call; domestic disputes, loud music complaints, a car crash. We didn't even squeeze in a meal break that night. Just before we were scheduled to go off duty at midnight, the dispatcher hailed me on the police radio.

"Station 50 to Car 56."

"Go ahead" I replied, after a pause that probably told her I wasn't thrilled.

"Respond to the area of St Joseph's Hospital," she said. "Security reports a man trying to escape from the ER. He was scheduled for an EPE and was waiting to go upstairs."

"10-4," I said. "On the way."

The third and fourth floors of that hospital, commonly referred to as St. Joe East, were designated for psychiatric patients. In fact, the facility was the intake point for all patients throughout Macomb County into the state mental health care program. Before being accepted upstairs for an Emergency

Psychiatric Evaluation, patients were required to be medically cleared in the Emergency Room. This sometimes resulted in a patient who didn't want help, or understand the need for it, taking off on foot into the neighborhood.

The possibility of an escapee was one of the reasons they had security guards on duty at the hospital 24 hours each day. Unfortunately, the security guards were good at not laying hands on anyone until they were officially off the hospital's property. Then they would say they couldn't touch anyone who was not on the property, for fear of being sued. It was a convenient way to avoid physical confrontations. The result was that Mount Clemens PD often had to do their job, in addition to our own.

From downtown I drove up North Avenue, the main divider of residential areas between the city's main thoroughfares, Gratiot Avenue and Groesbeck Highway. I approached Parkview Street, which formed the southern border of the hospital's footprint. On the corner I saw two of the hospital's finest. They wore matching black trousers and black sweaters with the SJE logo on the chest. They both excitedly pointed west, presumably the direction of the fleeing would-be psych patient.

"Thanks, fellas," I thought out loud.

I turned left onto Parkview Street and saw, staggering down the center of the roadway, the escapee-in-question. In his right hand he clutched the tall metal post of an intravenous bag hangar, its four wheels allowing it to roll down the street beside him. The bag itself was still attached to the man's right arm via the IV line which had been inserted by a skilled nurse. But the most obvious thing illuminated by my patrol car's headlights was the man's big bare ass, exposed by the untied hospital gown he was wearing. He was a large guy; well over six feet tall and 250 pounds.

As my car drew closer to the man, he looked over his shoulder at me but kept on moving. His unkempt beard and the hair flowing behind him as he ran made him look a bit like Grizzly Adams. I considered hitting my lights and siren, just for fun, but I knew that would probably frighten him. I used the microphone on my car's Motorola police radio to tell the dispatcher that I had the man in sight.

My friend and fellow SWAT operator Patrick Carson, a former Detroit police officer, keyed up on the radio next.

"Hey Jim," Carson asked. "What's the physical description of this guy?"

"Don't worry, brother," was my reply. "You can't miss him."

Carson arrived in his patrol car just as the man reached the corner of Parkview and Madison Street, coincidentally the southwest border of the hospital's property. When he saw there were now two cops, the man stopped running. This poor guy didn't want any trouble, he'd just made a bad choice during a stressful time. We placed handcuffs on his wrists just as the two security guards approached the intersection on foot, careful to stay out of the street and on the hospital property, of course.

They huffed and chuffed a few words about having us follow them back to the ER. Instead, I walked Grizzly Adams out of the street and up onto the sidewalk. I handed him over to the two gentlemen, who were both starting to lose color and breathe a bit heavily. I asked them to walk the man back inside and leave my handcuffs at the nurses' station; I could pick them up the next night.

Carson and I didn't make it back to the police station before midnight, but we did have laughs over beers about the incident later that evening at the 'Hut'.

Bottles and Sockets

Five years into my career I felt like I was exactly where I belonged. My wonderful wife, Cyndi, and I were approaching our second anniversary on Labor Day of that year, and every day at Mount Clemens PD seemed like an adventure. It was a fast-paced environment and I'd gained much valuable experience in a short time. Late that holiday evening I would experience something unlike anything I'd ever seen previously.

I'd spent a busy but largely uneventful 8-hour shift on patrol and ended my day at midnight, or so I thought. At that time Cyndi and I were renting a house just 15 minutes away from the police station, and when I walked in the door following my short drive home the house phone was already ringing.

The midnight shift commander, Lieutenant Harry Reynolds, had just come on duty when he received an urgent message from the Sterling Heights Police Department. A labor strike by the unions representing workers at the Detroit News and Detroit Free Press had been raging for several weeks, but on this night, it reached a new level. The factory in Sterling Heights where the daily papers were printed was under siege by protestors and the situation had turned violent. The police department there was requesting immediate help from any available agency.

"Hey, Jim. It's Harry. Thanks for picking up." Reynolds said when I answered the phone. He continued, "I know you just got home but, you want to go to Sterling Heights?"

"Sure, L-T. Right now?" I asked the lieutenant.

"Yep. Sounds like it's off the chain over there. They're asking for any help they can get. You'll need to get back here quick, grab some gear, and load up with a few other guys who volunteered. They're almost ready to leave."

I hung up the phone and turned to Cyndi, who had been waiting for me in the kitchen with an ice-cold beer. I gave her the short version of events and a kiss on the lips, and then turned for the door.

"Be careful!" she said, a phrase she would repeat countless times throughout the next few decades.

Some traffic laws may have been broken on my return to the police department, but I arrived safely just after 0030 hours. Walking through the back entrance of the building, I was met by Reynolds in the armory room.

Standing along one wall of that room were some old gray metal lockers which I'd never really noticed and certainly had never opened. From one of those lockers Reynolds removed a blue riot helmet featuring a clear plastic face protector, a gas mask and filter, one handheld shield with "POLICE" emblazoned across the middle, and a wooden baton three feet in length with knurled grips and a looped leather strap attached to one end.

Reynolds handed the items over to me quickly and I placed the helmet on my head to check for a good fit. It seemed to be fine but when I removed the helmet, I felt some material trickling down the back of my neck. I brushed the stuff from my shoulders and looked inside the helmet. It was dry rot. I later was told the equipment had last been used in 1967, when officers from Mount Clemens had been sent to assist the Detroit Police Department with the infamous riots that took place that summer. To his credit, Chief Mike Lubeckyj placed an order the very next day to replace the 30-year-old gear.

I loaded up into a spare patrol car with three other cops who'd also ended their regular tour of duty at midnight: two in the front seat, two of us in the back. It was a quick shot south on Gratiot Avenue to 16 Mile Road, then 8 miles at high-speed due west to Mound Road. As our car turned onto southbound Mound Road, the scene before us resembled a war zone.

"Holy shit," I whispered.

Mound Road is a major north/south thoroughfare crossing multiple jurisdictions in metropolitan Detroit. In Sterling Heights, it features four lanes in each direction, separated by a grassy median about 20 feet wide. As far south as my eye could see there were police cars parked on that median with smashed windows, their shattered glass littering the ground all around them. We didn't have time to be scared as we were waved up onto the median by a helmetless weary-looking cop directing traffic in his sweat-stained blue uniform.

The newspaper plant occupied about 12 acres on the southeast corner of Mound Road and 16 Mile Road. The plant's main gate was accessed on the northbound side of Mound Road, and it was there a battle was being waged between the picketers and the Sterling Heights Police Department.

The protesters carried picket signs that were often stapled to 2" x 2" pieces of hard lumber, an effective weapon with which to club cops over the head along the skirmish line. The Sterling Heights police officers were in full head-to-toe riot gear and were deploying oleoresin capsicum (OC) pepper spray, fired at the picketers from large canisters.

On the southbound side of Mound Road, across four lanes from the median, was a long grassy berm which formed a natural barrier between the heavily trafficked roadway and the Meadowview Village condominium complex. On that lengthy stretch of lawn stood about 2000 people. Many of them were United Auto Workers, Teamsters, or members of other unions across the Midwest and southern United States who had come to support the strikers. Some of the people were residents who desired a front row seat to the action, and a few of them were just drunken yahoos acting like jackasses.

At strategic intervals in the median there were crossovers. These curved concrete lanes allow cars to flip from northbound travel to southbound, or vice versa. Directly across the northbound lanes of Mound Road from the factory's main gate was a crossover. If the Sterling Heights police could clear the picketers from blocking the main gate, the Detroit News trucks were scheduled to roll out across the northbound lanes of Mound Road, through the crossover, and south to deliver their papers to destinations throughout southeast Michigan.

With about a dozen other cops from various police agencies, I was assigned to keep that crossover clear and open. We marched the 100 yards from a makeshift command post to the crossover in a tight group, heads on swivels, the picket line battle raging to our left as we moved. We spread out inside the curbed crossover in a line from north to south.

I tried to find a semi-comfortable position in which to stand while holding the shield and baton, but it wasn't easy. There was plenty of action taking place to hold my attention, however. Directly across southbound Mound Road from us, perhaps 40 feet, were the thousands of people stretched along the embankment. As we stood our post while the main gate battle raged behind us, the people across the street hurled profanities and threats our way. They cursed our families and called us every name in the book, even a few I'd never heard before. I didn't care about the words they screamed at us; you must ignore that stuff and I actually thought some of it was funny. Not so amusing were the objects that started to be launched through the air at us from cowardly souls hiding amidst the huge mass of humanity.

One memory which will never leave me is seeing a glass bottle taking off like a missile from somewhere in the middle of the crowd. It tumbled through the air seemingly in slow motion. As it descended toward my face shield, I was able to read the 'Welch's Grape Juice' label on the front. I sidestepped it and heard it shatter on the concrete behind me. It was frustrating not to be able to wade into the crowd with batons and find the person who threw the bottle, but maintaining discipline was much more important. Our job was to stay together and keep the crossover clear. That became more difficult just a short while later.

My good friend Brian Kozlowski from the Macomb County Sheriff's department, with whom I would later serve in COMET and SWAT, was on the far end of our line, about

20 feet to my right. Amidst the cacophony of loud noise all around us, I heard a thump and whooshing sound, followed by a rising cheer from the crowd across the street. The sound had come from my right. I turned to see Kozlowski fall.

My instinct was to run toward Kozlowski, but several other cops near him were already present, assessing his injury. I thought he had been shot. Remembering my assignment and the importance of holding the line, I kept my position. I was seriously pissed off then and I scanned the crowd, hoping in vain to identify the person who'd hurt my brother. The word was passed down the line that Kozlowski had been hit in the throat with a large wrench socket, the type you'd use to remove lug nuts from a truck wheel.

Thirty minutes later a U-Haul truck ambled north on Mound Road, turning left into our crossover when the driver found himself blocked by the picket line skirmish near the main gate. We knew that there was a police blockade of traffic northbound on Mound Road at 15 Mile; this truck clearly had no business in the area. We stopped the truck and identified the driver by his Tennessee operator's license and Teamsters union card. The man obviously didn't possess any knowledge of the assault on Kozlowski, because he consented to a search of his vehicle. When the U-Haul's roll-up door was lifted, I saw the storage area was empty but for one item. A large, heavy wooden box sat alone on the floor, near the rear bumper. Inside the box were a couple dozen large wrench sockets.

Rounding the rear corner of the truck on the driver side, I quickly realized I was too late to ask the driver any questions about his cargo. He was being yanked through the driver door window by more cops than I could count. We drove the U-Haul truck up onto the median and out of the crossover. I never saw that man again and I have no idea what became of his truck, although the box of sockets was taken as evidence.

Sometime around 0300 hours, the order went out for everyone to don their gas masks. It wasn't hard to conclude what was about to happen. I removed my helmet briefly, pulled the ancient rubber mask over my face, and tightened the straps around the back of my head. It didn't fit well, wasn't comfortable, and had a leaky seal around the filter, but it was better than nothing.

Just then I heard a sound: 'Tunk'. Then a whole bunch of them, one after another for the next few minutes. 'Tunk, tunk, tunk ...'. It was the sound of tear gas being fired from 40-millimeter grenade launchers. I saw the canisters shoot across the roadway in front of us, a cloud of bluish-gray gas slowly rising in front of the crowd. Just then, each one of the in-ground sprinklers spread throughout the grassy embankment sputtered to life. It was amazing. I don't know if the sprinklers were turned on purposefully or were operating on a timer, but the result was immediate.

A combination of nasty CS tear gas and an unexpected cold shower drove the crowd away rapidly. Fifteen minutes later I looked about and saw the streets empty except for exhausted cops and gear strewn everywhere. The picketers on the skirmish line were also gone, and we were soon dismissed for the night. As we trekked north along the median, back to our trashed police cars, I heard engines roar and turned to see the Detroit News trucks rolling through the main gate.

The Detroit Newspaper Strike occurred after the newspaper ownership attempted to break up the unions inside their shops. Despite union claims of unfair labor practices being denied in federal court, the cost to ownership was heavy; an estimated $40,000,000 was spent on private security and reimbursement of police overtime, and much of the papers' circulation was forever lost. The unions paid dearly, too. The Teamsters were said to have spent in excess of $30,000,000 in legal fees and strike benefits for their membership.

I was in police unions my entire career, first the Fraternal Order of Police Labor Council and later the Police Officers Association of Michigan. If it wasn't for police unions, we'd all be making peanuts and pensions would have been a pipe dream. Some of the striking newspaper workers and protesters accused us of being pawns for the newspaper ownership. Their claims were bolstered when an idiotic, high-ranking member of the Sterling Heights Police Department was famously photographed kicking a striking worker while on the ground, but that was an anomaly.

Speaking for myself and my guys, nothing was further from the truth. We did our job when the strike became violent. To have done anything less would have been a betrayal of our oath to serve and protect all citizens. On a personal level, I may have even sided with some of the grievances raised by the unions; but that was completely irrelevant. The trust placed in us by the communities we served transcended labor issues, so we did our duty; nothing more, nothing less.

I Hate Bombs

As the sergeant on an afternoon patrol shift, my leave days never coincided with those of the lieutenant, ensuring that one of us was always on duty to supervise our team of police officers. At the conclusion of our daily briefing one overcast Sunday, I asked Patrolman Mark Bratton to work in the office and supervise the dispatch, so I could work road patrol.

I didn't like being in the office. I much preferred leading troops out on the street to hearing complaints at the front desk or reviewing reports, though I knew that was also part of my job when the lieutenant was gone. Bratton was the senior officer on the shift but, even if he hadn't been, he was the best choice to hold down the fort in my absence. I knew he would call me right away, if necessary.

After grabbing a large black coffee from the Tim Horton's on Gratiot Avenue near 16 Mile Road, I assisted one of our units on a traffic stop and then headed for the 'hood'; an area encompassing the northeast section of our city where the supply of drugs and prostitutes was exceeded only by the demand. Amidst the federally subsidized housing projects were homes owned by hard-working people who deserved and demanded police presence; it was my favorite area of the city to work.

As I was cruising south on Orchard Street toward the basketball courts, my cell phone chirped, and I saw that

Bratton was the caller. I tapped the green button and answered the call.

"Hey, brother," Bratton said. "You better get in here right away."

He sounded alarmed, which was highly unusual for the squared-away Bratton.

"Ok. Why, what's up?" I replied.

"Some asshole brought a bomb into the lobby," he said. "And the dispatcher accepted it through the package portal. It's sitting on the front desk."

Bratton's tone clearly conveyed his concern about the bomb, along with his disbelief and displeasure with the dispatcher's decision to accept the device behind the bullet-resistant glass. In his defense, the dispatcher was a 19 year old kid who thought he was doing the right thing while Bratton was out of the room for a moment. What he should have done was stay in the dispatch center and let Bratton handle the front desk when he returned, and I later made sure he understood that fact.

I made a hard left on Jones Street and got back to the police station in about two minutes. When I pulled my black-and-white Chevy Caprice into a parking spot near the back door, Bratton was waiting. Together we entered the building through the door usually reserved for officers bringing prisoners into the lockup area.

We advanced up the hallway past the dispatch center to an open room containing rows of metal cabinets filled with criminal files. I peered over the cabinets to the far side of the room, which looked out through the protective glass into the hallway of the city building. On the wide wooden counter beneath the glass sat a large, nasty-looking pipe bomb.

The 12-inch cylinder was made of heavy-gauge steel and featured a pair of thick metal caps threaded onto either end. A black and green safety fuse extended about four inches from a hole which had been drilled in the top endcap. Taped to the outside of the device were about a dozen flat-head roofing nails.

In the police academy there had been a day dedicated to instructing recruits about explosive devices. A bomb technician from the Detroit Police Department taught us the dangers of various bomb types; most of them fairly obvious, others not so much. Regarding fuses and detonators, our instructor had a display board to which he'd affixed different systems for igniting explosives.

I hadn't enjoyed the class that day. Even though all the objects on display had been inert, they still made me nervous. But thanks to the basic instruction, I recognized that the device we were dealing with probably wouldn't explode without putting a flame to its fuse. Still, it was possible, if not likely, that a mercury switch or remote detonator could cause the pipe bomb to go off. For all these reasons, we left it right where it was and slowly walked back down the hallway.

I directed our young dispatcher to disconnect one of the multi-line phones at his workstation and reconnect it in the squad room at the back of the building. Along with a hand-held portable police radio, he could now handle phone calls and radio traffic from a safe distance. While Bratton used crime scene tape to ensure that no one could enter the building through the main door, I stepped outside to call the chief of police.

Chief Mike Lubeckyj was a United States Marine Corps veteran of the Vietnam War and an expert in firearms and marksmanship, having been the agency's primary instructor for most of his 25 year career before being appointed to the top post. His calm demeanor and great sense of humor had inspired me since I was a rookie assigned to his shift years before. Lubeckyj was at home on that Sunday afternoon and answered my call on the third ring.

"How ya doing, Jimmy?" he asked.

"Not bad, Mike," I said. "Except, well … there's a bomb inside the police station."

"You don't say!" he replied. "How the hell did that happen?"

I brought him up to speed and assured him there had been no injuries, but he decided to drive in from home and assess the situation for himself. As someone accustomed to leading from the front, that move was not out of character for Lubeckyj. He gave me clearance to call the Michigan State Police Bomb Squad, which I did as soon as we disconnected.

The MSP technicians didn't arrive until four hours later, so I used some of that time to interview the man who had walked into our building with the pipe bomb. He told me that he woke up that day and walked outside to the silver Honda Accord parked in the driveway of his house on South Avenue. As he opened the driver-side door and started to enter, he saw a metal object partially protruding from under the rocker panel of his car. On his hands and knees, he got a close look at the object and recognized it. Wanting to keep his neighbors safe and avoid a disturbance, he had tossed the bomb onto the passenger seat and drove to the police station to drop it off. The guy's heart was in the right place, but his judgement was extraordinarily poor.

As for why there had been a large explosive device underneath his car, the man described an ongoing dispute with his ex-girlfriend. He reckoned that her new boyfriend might have placed the bomb there. But he had no evidence of that and didn't seem very disturbed by the whole episode. Before he left for home I told him our detectives would follow up on Monday and to stay far away from his ex and her new man. Years later I learned that the man had been a confidential informant for a commercial auto theft task force in Detroit, but that never came to light during our investigation.

Two Explosive Ordnance Disposal technicians finally arrived in a dark blue GMC box truck emblazoned with the famous MSP shield and lightning bolt on both sides. After giving them each a detailed briefing about our situation, we stood by while they donned their bomb suits; the same as worn by explosive ordinance disposal units around the world.

They disappeared into the building through the same door Bratton and I had used, and when they emerged I was even more concerned. In their padded suits and helmets the two men looked like a pair of astronauts having an intense conversation on the moon. They wobbled past without a word to us and retrieved a device from their truck that was unlike anything I'd ever seen.

It was a tracked vehicle constructed of shiny aluminum, about three feet long and two feet wide. At the top of a post extending up from the center of a flat metal frame perched a cylindrical cannon called a Projected Water Disruptor. Alongside it, a movable arm with claw grip and a remote on-board video camera completed the loadout. A handheld controller allowed the technicians to move the robot with precision and see through the camera's eye via a small high-definition monitor.

The slow-moving parade passed by again and the technicians entered the vacant police department like surgeons into an operating room. Minutes seemed like hours as they deployed the robot, and I waited patiently outside with Bratton and Lubeckyj. Suddenly we heard a muffled 'boom' that didn't quite sound like an exploding pipe bomb but was startling, nonetheless.

One of the bomb techs came outside just then and gave us a 'thumbs up'. He walked over to us while removing his protective helmet, and then explained that the noise we'd heard was the water cannon being fired at the pipe bomb. The water charge was precisely aimed and delivered, striking the device with such force that it separated one of the threaded end caps from the main cylinder. After checking with his partner over a radio contained within the bomb suit, he invited us inside to have a look at their handiwork.

We retraced our steps up the corridor and past the dispatch center, then around the file cabinets to the front desk. The bomb techs had used the claw arm to place the pipe bomb on the floor prior to deploying the water cannon. The end cap was several feet away from the rest of the remains, which were surrounded by a large amount of black powder fanned out across the tan Berber carpet. The bomb techs explained that if the device had detonated, it would have destroyed the entire front desk area and much of the dispatch center.

I truly appreciated the expertise of the bomb technicians, but under no circumstances was I envious of their assignment. The apprehension I felt that day in the police academy was confirmed. It's tough for me to articulate why bombs bother me so much, but the incident disturbed me for a long time afterward, more so than other scary scenes like shootings and stabbings. Fortunately, there are men and women in law enforcement dedicated to handling them, so I don't have to.

Momma's Boy and a Blood Bath

It's common for people to use the word "psycho" when describing those acting in a violent or destructive manner, and the word conjures images associated with Halloween or scary books and movies. But it's likely that they're not actually witnessing psychotic behavior when using that word to describe another person's actions.

Psychosis is an extreme symptom of mental illness like schizophrenia, but it can also be genetic or caused by other conditions such as chronic drug abuse or severe trauma. It causes people to lose touch with reality, seeing and hearing hallucinations they believe are real. A doctor once told me that a person in psychosis doesn't know if they are experiencing reality or a dream.

In over 30 years on the job, I witnessed what I believed to be true psychosis just a handful of times. It's a scary moment when it dawns on you, and you realize that the person you're speaking with is completely disconnected from reality. A couple of those moments still resonate in my mind.

As a uniformed patrol sergeant working afternoon shift in Mount Clemens, I once heard a call go out over the police radio to check an address for a man who hadn't been seen in several days. His mother reported that the man had suffered from mental illness most of his life and she wanted a police officer to check his residence. The officer sent to the scene, Kevin Gloude, was a rookie fresh from completing his field training program. Since it was a busy day with many calls for service, no other units were immediately available. I left the police station and drove out to back up Gloude.

We arrived simultaneously at the small bungalow on Cass Avenue. We both parked on a side street to the east, and I examined the house carefully as we walked around to the front. A car was parked in the driveway and curtains in the home's windows were pulled open. The grass needed a cut but otherwise everything appeared normal.

I arrived at the front door and climbed four steps to the small concrete porch, while Gloude kept watch on the windows from his position in the yard. I spent several minutes alternately knocking on the door and ringing the doorbell with no response from inside. I leaned over the wrought-iron railing to my right so that I could peer inside the living room window. Just then, I heard rustling and mumbling sounds directly below me.

Seated in the dirt, leaning against the brick siding below the big glass window was a short, stocky man; his arms were clutching his knees to his chest. He had been hidden from our view by a large green landscaping bush. I saw that his dark long hair was matted, and he clearly hadn't shaved in a couple weeks. He was rocking very slightly forward and back, talking softly to someone only he could see.

"Sir, are you OK? It's the police," I said, waving Gloude to a position on the man's left, near the front corner of the house.

He looked up and to his right without moving his head, eyeing me as if he wasn't sure I was really there. I listened as he continued to quietly speak words that made absolutely no sense. The verbs, nouns, and adjectives he used just didn't go together grammatically as he described the people and places he was seeing. It was then I realized that his mental state was dangerously unbalanced, and he desperately needed treatment at St. Joseph Hospital East, a facility with a psychiatric ward, which was luckily just a short distance away.

Calling for an ambulance to transport the man would also bring a fire engine, an annoying protocol in Mount Clemens that I never understood. The prospect of three firemen in full turnout gear and helmets dismounting a big red machine with air brakes and flashing red lights didn't appeal to me at all; it might cause the man to have a bad reaction.

A plan to lay hands on the man, handcuff him, and force him into the back of a police car was an alternative, but not a very good one. That scenario could get ugly fast. People with severe mental problems, in my experience, often displayed incredible strength; more than you'd expect given their physical stature. Fighting with the man could also lead to his injury and perhaps necessitate an escalation of force if he reached for one of our guns. I thought it was best to keep that option in our pocket as a last resort.

As the man continued to mumble, I asked him if he'd like to see his mom.

"Yeah," said the man as he stood up behind the bush.

"Ok, bud. We'll take you to see your mom," I said quietly. Pointing to Gloude, I continued, "Just follow my partner."

The man turned to his left and slowly walked out from behind the landscaping. As Gloude led him toward the closest patrol car parked on the side street, the man stopped several times as if unsure whether he should continue. He shrunk from us when we got close, a clear indication he didn't want to be touched. We kept talking to him in low tones and promising that he could see his mom. As we did so I closely eyed the man's waistband and clothing, looking for any suspicious bulges that might conceal a weapon. I didn't see any.

When we arrived at the police car it took a moment to coax him into the back seat, but we stayed on message. When he was finally seated inside and the car door was closed, the man wasn't handcuffed, and he hadn't been properly searched. That was a blatant breach of our rules and regulations, one that was entirely my responsibility as the sergeant and more experienced police officer.

The eight block trip due north to the hospital took just a few minutes and we left the man in the back seat upon our arrival. I walked up the ramp leading to the Emergency Room and asked for two attendants to bring a wheelchair down to the police car. I let them do what they do best, removing and securing the man and then wheeling him inside the facility.

Before we left I explained to Gloude my reasons for handling and transporting the man without properly searching and handcuffing him. I made him promise not to mistake my decision that day for any type of standard operating procedure going forward, and to always be conscious of safety first. The situation worked out for the best and the man received proper care and treatment after our peaceful resolution to his crisis.

A psychotic episode which proved to be much scarier and more violent involved a man who lived just a few blocks away from the first. With Cass Avenue as its northern border and Robertson Street to the south, three tree-lined roads comprised an area populated with beautiful older homes reminiscent of more affluent communities such as nearby Grosse Pointe and Birmingham. The middle of the three thoroughfares was Moross Street. Not to be confused with Moross Road in Detroit, its old-growth oaks shaded the meticulously manicured lawns of brick ranches and large colonial homes.

One dark, moonless night a young woman dialed 911 from a single-story older home on Moross Street, pleading for police and an ambulance to come and help her husband. She reported that her husband was trying to kill himself and was locked in the bathroom. My partner that night was Officer Don Sepke, and as we pulled into the driveway I noticed two other patrol cars already on the scene.

Sepke and I got out of our patrol car and walked through the open garage. When we got to the entryway leading into the home, I looked through the screen door and saw a woman crying while holding a small baby in her left arm, across an area dissecting the kitchen and living room. Her right hand rested on the head of a little boy hiding behind her leg. Perhaps it was because of the age of the houses on the block, but I hadn't expected this one to be occupied by a young family.

As I pulled back the screen door and entered, she looked up and saw me. I waved her over as I heard loud voices down a hallway to my right. She walked toward me, the toddler in tow behind her. I asked her to take the kids into the garage and wait there until an officer came for them. She nodded and walked outside. As she passed, I saw that her face was wet with tears.

"He has a knife," she said.

Sepke and I made our way down the hallway to find Officer Maurice Carter with his gun pointed at the bathroom's closed door. He was directing the man to open the door, without success.

"Sir! Have you been drinking?" Carter shouted at the door.

I looked at Carter curiously and silently wondered why he would ask such a dumb question. I tried the doorknob and found it to be locked. I looked at my partner, who was shaking his head.

Channeling Moe Howard from the Three Stooges, Sepke said "Spread out."

I moved aside quickly because I knew what was coming.

Sepke was a big Polish kid who was built like a brick shithouse. He'd been an offensive lineman for the Eastern Michigan University football team, and that bathroom door was about to get flattened. Sepke didn't even have to kick the door, he just shouldered it, and the door flew inward on its hinges. Behind the door was a scene unlike anything I'd ever witnessed.

From a kneeling position in the hallway, I peeked around the doorframe from the right side; Sepke was on the left. The small bathroom featured a standard sink, cabinet and mirror on the right side. On the left was a closet for towels and supplies. Directly in front of us, against the back wall, was the bathtub. For a quick moment, I thought it was filled with blood.

The 33-year-old husband of the woman I'd just encountered sat with his back pressed against the tub wall to my right. His feet were pressed against the other tub wall, where drops of water dripped from the chrome faucet. In his right hand he gripped a large Buck knife, the folding type often carried by hunters and sportsmen. He was using that knife to saw off his left hand.

The man had started behind his thumb and progressed down through the small carpal bones in his wrist. His left hand was just hanging there by some skin, cartilage, and tendons near the ulna bone. The man was bleeding profusely, so much so that it had turned the bath water to an opaque red. When the door flew open the man turned his head and looked at me. I'm not sure that he actually saw us with his thousand yard stare; if he did, did he believe we were real? He was silent and completely void of any visible emotion. He gave no sign that he was in any physical pain. No one moved as the surreal scene made a quiet moment seem much longer.

The stillness was broken just then as Carter leaned in between Sepke and me, firing a full can of OC pepper spray into the bathroom directly at the man. I was flabbergasted by his stupidity, but I couldn't say I was surprised that Carter had done it. He had a history of making poor decisions when the use of physical force was imminent.

"Dude! What the fuck was that?" I shouted, as Sepke used his big paw to push Carter back into the hallway and away from us.

Carter probably didn't even mind; I knew that he wanted no part of fighting this lunatic. Unfortunately, that meant that Sepke and I now had to find a way to secure the man and get him to the hospital, all while holding our breath to avoid being overcome by pepper spray. Carter had made a dangerous situation much worse.

The moment Carter had depressed the plunger on his can of OC pepper spray, the man submerged himself in the tub. I couldn't see him through the impenetrable bloody bathwater; it was like he'd vanished! We knew we couldn't be that lucky and just then the man emerged from the muck and leaped to his feet. Still in the tub the man faced us; completely naked, knife still in hand. He was so completely covered in blood that had we not known he was white, it would've been tough to determine his race.

The battle that ensued over the next few minutes started with Sepke knocking the knife out of the man's grasp onto the bathroom floor. We then tried to tackle the man to the floor so we could handcuff him. We hadn't yet thought through the detail of his partially detached hand; we were too busy slipping and sliding with him back and forth like wrestlers in a bloody cage match. Every time we thought we had him pinned, the man would slip away like a greased pig.

Finally, Sepke got a handcuff on the man's right wrist. We struggled to bring his hands together behind his back, but it seemed that we never would. While the man's severely damaged left hand was flying around, I felt a warm liquid spray cross my face from left to right. The man's blood had spurted directly into my eyes.

I couldn't believe the man's strength and determination, given his blood loss and severe self-inflicted injury. During the brawl he tried to reach for the gun in my holster, but I twisted my hip away from him, putting it just out of reach.

Because the circumstances were so dire and getting worse from exhaustion, I decided to render the man unconscious if I could. With Sepke holding the cuffed wrist and leaning his full body weight down on the man to limit his movement, I disengaged from him. I moved back, still on my knees, and wound up, then spun my hips and struck the man with my fist as hard as I possibly could, directly on the hinge point of his right jaw. Still, the man fought. I stepped back and hit him again with every ounce of strength I had remaining, right on the same spot.

Mercifully, the man started to fade. It was probably from his massive loss of blood more than my punches, and he wasn't completely out yet, but we were able to get the other handcuff onto his left wrist. Unfortunately, the cuff immediately sank deeply into his grotesque wound. I didn't know what else to do and didn't much care at that point. We radioed for the EMTs to enter and then assisted them in securing the man tightly to the gurney with straps and buckles.

As the medics wheeled the man outside to the ambulance, Sepke and I looked at each other. Our uniforms were wrecked. My eyes were crusting over as the blood dried, so I needed to get to the hospital. When I arrived at Mount Clemens General, the nurses ran a stream of saline water over my eyes for half an hour to clean away the blood. The man was transported to Detroit Receiving Hospital for emergency surgery to reattach his left hand, and I later heard that the operation was successful. While at DRH he was tested for HIV and other communicable diseases, thankfully with negative results.

We learned the man had a history of severe mental illness and had stopped taking his medication. His bizarre behavior began suddenly and had terrified his wife and children. I wish the incident could have been a more peaceful resolution, but we didn't have many options that night.

The Ricochet Adventure

The Macomb County SWAT Team usually trained locally two days per month, in addition to one week each year at a military base in Northern Michigan and whatever additional instruction we could persuade the sheriff to fund for us. The monthly training was held at various gun ranges, industrial complexes, or high rise buildings; anywhere we could practice skills and techniques to stay sharp and competent for every real-life scenario we might face.

One of the cool places we were able to use was a huge commercial sand and gravel pit near Romeo, Michigan, owned by a businessman who supported our mission. The pit was about one square mile in total area, sunk below ground level with huge piles of dirt, sand, and rock spread across the property. We were easily able to set up live-fire scenarios for our sniper team and two entry teams, and often combined all three elements in unique and useful drills.

Our team was frequently provided rifles, handguns, shotguns, and other equipment from manufacturers who wanted us to test and evaluate their products. Glock, Heckler & Koch, Benelli, Fabrique Nationale (FN), Benchmade, and Nike are just a few of the companies who sent representatives to our training dates over the years, and the Romeo gravel pit was an ideal location for putting any new tactical product through its paces. One of those training days at the pit became quite memorable for me.

The training schedule that day called for our two entry elements to work on pistol and submachine gun drills at a 25 yard range in the morning, while our snipers put their bolt-action .308 caliber rifles through paces at much longer distances. After lunch, the whole team would assemble and combine for coordinated drills. Prior to getting underway, however, we had a new rifle to assess. The gun was a precursor to the FN15 Tactical II CA chambered in 5.56 x 45mm (.223 Rem).

Our portable bench rest had been deployed 25 yards away from a steel-framed target holder. The frame had been fabricated using thin angle iron by one of our teammates and held a standard 2' x 3' cardboard backer and target steady even under heavy use. On top of the bench rest were stacked several bags of sand, each of them made of canvas and weighing about 12 pounds each. These were used to form a comfortable and solid base from which to fire the rifle while holding a steady sight picture. Our assistant team commander would do the honors that day using only the rifle's stock iron sights to aim, since it did not come equipped with optics.

The rest of the team assembled in a semi-circle behind him as he prepared to fire several three-round groups. This practice allows one to see where each group strikes the target and then adjust the gun's sights until it hits the bullseye every time, otherwise known as being 'zeroed'. There was no horseplay. Nobody was cracking wise or acting foolish. We were all relaxed but focused, each man hoping he'd get a chance to fire the weapon once it was dialed in. I was positioned near the middle, just to the left of the bench rest. Unfortunately, this product evaluation consisted of exactly one shot.

After our man eased in behind the rifle, lined up the iron sights, and then took a breath and exhaled, he began to smoothly press the trigger. The muzzle flashed and the report was loud, even as we all wore proper ear protection. Simultaneously, I got a punch in the face that felt like Kirk Gibson swinging a ballpeen hammer.

Before I realized what had happened, I was spun around 180 degrees. My palms were flat against my knees, and I was bent over at the waist when I opened my eyes and saw blood pouring from my face like a faucet. It puddled in the brown dirt below me. It was only a few seconds, but seemed longer, before I saw a big balled-up wad of gauze bandage coming up from underneath me. A teammate pressed it hard against the wound to my left cheekbone, his other hand against the back of my head.

It was later determined that the rifle's sights had come from the factory so out of whack that even when it was aimed dead-center at the target, the round struck the steel frame and ricocheted backward and slightly to the left. Lucky me.

Things started to move quickly. Someone said they would call for an ambulance.

"Screw that!" I said loudly. Then, more calmly, "I'm not waiting out here for 45 minutes until two minimum-wage EMT's show up and try to do surgery on me. Let's just get in the truck and go." (Side note: I have nothing against EMTs. At the time, the ambulance service in that area was way below par. I worked with many paramedics after this incident, particularly in Marysville, and watched them save lives on numerous occasions.)

I was able to press and hold the gauze bandage wad against my face while one of my teammates opened the passenger-side door of the unmarked black Ford F-250 pickup truck assigned to the SWAT team. We normally used it to haul an 8.5' x 20' enclosed trailer that contained everything from portable target systems to vests and tools, anything that needed to be transported. I climbed inside as he slammed the door shut, hustled around the front of the truck and clambered in behind the wheel.

As the ignition key was turned and the big 10-cylinder engine roared to life, our team commander, Lieutenant Craig Sparks, leaned in through the driver door window and said, "Get him to Providence Hospital in Rochester; it's the closest. I'll meet you there."

"No way, Sparky," I said. "Let's go to General. My bosses from MCPD are gonna want to be there and it's not that much farther away. I'll be fine." My face and mouth felt strange as I spoke. Maybe I wasn't going to be fine? Turns out the bullet clipped a nerve in my face that affected the muscles. As a result, I wasn't able to smile for about six months without my upper and lower lips going in opposite directions. But the nerve grew back, and that little side effect faded away.

"Fine," replied Sparks. "Get moving. Now!"

I don't remember much about the 20 mile trip to Mount Clemens General Hospital, except that we flew down Van Dyke Avenue to 16 Mile Road, then east to Groesbeck Highway and north one mile to the hospital at Harrington Road. As soon as I climbed down out of the truck under the overhang at the Emergency Room entrance, a nurse in royal blue scrubs pointed at the gurney she'd brought outside and told me to lay down. Her demeanor was friendly but quite serious. I did as I was told.

Still pressing the gauze to my face as I was wheeled into the ER, I recall seeing Lieutenant Mike Convery from Mount Clemens PD standing over me briefly and giving me some words of encouragement. I don't remember exactly what was said but definitely recall feeling grateful for his presence. Convery was the patrol shift commander that day and he was there to make sure one of his guys was looked after properly. I appreciated that very much.

After an initial examination, X-rays, and a change into a surgical gown, I only had to wait a short while before being wheeled into an operating area on the ground floor near the ER. Once there, I received shots to the face of a different sort. They came from a long needle and contained local anesthetic. A physician administered them strategically around and inside the wound and told me that I would be awake for the surgery. Though initially nervous about that prospect, I actually didn't feel a thing except some pulls and tugs over the following couple of hours. I listened to the doctors speak to each other about their progress and next steps and I learned that there are a lot of muscles in your face that complicate matters such as the removal of high-velocity projectiles.

Removed from the cheekbone below my left eye was a jagged piece of .223 caliber metal jacket approximately 1 inch in length, with a small piece of the bullet core inside. I'm very thankful that most of the lead bullet must have ricocheted in a different direction. Ammunition of that caliber designed for target practice travels around 2,800 feet per second, depending on bullet weight and barrel length. The jagged bullet jacket with just a fraction of the lead core slowed down significantly after striking the target frame. I'm also grateful for where the bullet hit me; through the mouth would've certainly knocked out some teeth or worse, and my shooting glasses may not have stopped me from losing an eyeball.

Before closing the surgical procedure, the doctors told me that there would be swelling and some fluid buildup inside the wound for a few days. They gave me two options. They could sew the wound closed and avoid a visible scar down the road, but the fluid might cause an infection requiring more treatment. Or they could insert a drainage tube which would allow me to lean over the sink every hour to let any fluid run out. That option would avoid infection but probably leave a scar. I chose the second option because having an infection in my face sounded worse than the original injury. The tube was a clear plastic straw about three inches long and a quarter inch in diameter. It looked amazingly similar to the straws used when drunk drivers are required to blow into a breath test instrument.

I was a little groggy when I found myself being wheeled into a hospital room, but not so much that I didn't see my lovely bride, Cyndi, there waiting for me. She'd received a phone call from a teammate, telling her that I was OK but at Mount Clemens General and unable to come to the phone because I was in surgery. Not exactly a reassuring combination of facts, to say the least. But it wasn't the first time she received such a message and wouldn't be the last. She left Cameron Medical Center for Animals, where she was employed as the surgical veterinary technician, and drove quickly but safely to be with me.

I didn't expect to be required to stay the night and told the doctor as much when he visited the room a short while later. He insisted. The staff wanted to make sure there were no complications or clots overnight but said I could leave first thing in the morning if I had a good night's sleep. After a few hours, Cyndi had to head home to relieve our babysitter. She knew I was going to be fine and that I could watch the Red Wings playoff game that evening in the hospital as easily as I could in our basement. Some SWAT teammates and Mount Clemens cops had already stopped by to visit and would continue to do so throughout the remainder of the day. A couple guys even brought me a can of Skoal and a pint of Jim Beam. That's true friendship.

The next morning, I was given a ride home by the SWAT team assistant commander, who felt so bad that I thought he was going to be sick. Poor guy. I assured him that the incident was not, in any way, his fault and that although I would tease him about it for the rest of time and use it to secure free beer from him frequently, I wasn't mad. A few days later I returned to the hospital and had the drainage tube removed. It only took a minute and a thin, two-inch square, flesh-colored band aid was installed in its place.

I attended a KISS/Ted Nugent concert over the weekend with the band aid on my face, then returned to work the following Monday. After putting on my uniform and gear in the locker room, I crossed the hallway at 1600 hours and entered the squad room to give the afternoon patrol shift briefing. All the cops were present and accounted for, some sitting in roller chairs and others leaning on desks, each of them with a clear plastic breath test tube taped to their face. Those assholes. It was dead silent for a beat, until we all cracked up laughing. I miss them.

Canfield Street

One cloudy spring Sunday, officers from the Mount Clemens Police Department were called to a house on Canfield Street because neighbors reported some loud noises coming from a residence in the middle of the block. The neighborhood was a pleasant working-class area of small but well-kept ranches and bungalows.

When they arrived, the three policemen saw a large man lying face down in the front yard. They picked up their pace as they approached, because they could see the man was bleeding and unconscious. When they reached him they saw that the man had been shot multiple times. Rather than wait for an ambulance, these cops lifted and carried the man toward a police car so that he could quickly be transported to St Joseph's Hospital, just a few blocks away. While they were doing this, they heard gunshots coming from inside the house.

The supervisor on duty that day, Lieutenant Mike Convery, was one of the officers first on scene and had helped carry the man out of the line of fire. Convery was a veteran cop, born and raised in Mount Clemens, and he immediately recognized the dire and exigent circumstances. He didn't hesitate to call out the Macomb County SWAT Team while ensuring that responding officers established a perimeter around the house, to protect the lives of neighbors and prevent traffic from passing through the area.

After the initial callout we had a command post established nearby in less than an hour, and gradually started to replace patrol officers on the perimeter with operators from the SWAT Team. These operators, including myself, were members of our two designated entry elements. We also had Team members qualified and assigned as snipers and they deployed around the house, though it was very tight quarters in that neighborhood with small properties grouped closely together.

While the deployment of the Team was unfolding, we learned that the courageous actions of the first responding officers had been in vain; the man found in the front yard had died at the hospital. Detectives from Mount Clemens PD determined that the suspect living at the home was estranged from his wife and very upset about their impending divorce. His wife, who had recently moved out, arrived at the house on this day to collect some of her belongings and brought her sister and brother-in-law along to help. The dead man was identified at the hospital as the woman's brother-in-law.

That news did not bode well for the outlook of our mission, but we tried to establish contact with the suspect to bring the incident to a peaceful conclusion. If we could contact the suspect by phone then our hostage negotiators would, hopefully, be able to reason with him. Unfortunately, that was not to be.

There was no response from inside the home when the negotiators tried calling, and nothing else they did elicited any response from the suspect, including using a loud public address system from one of our armored vehicles. The decision was made to insert a "throw phone" into the home, in case other forms of communication weren't available to the suspect. This was a normal looking landline phone encased in a padded nylon box. Rather than being a wireless unit, this phone had a long cord attached, which allowed it to be used without dialing. A hidden microphone also allowed negotiators to hear voices inside the home, even when the phone wasn't being used. This instrument was generally thrown through a window or other opening, hence its unique name. How the phone was to be delivered was left to me, as leader of one of the two entry elements. I consulted with my trusted teammate Officer Mark Bratton, who was beside me at the rear of the home.

Bratton was a Mount Clemens police officer and had been on the Team for a couple years. He had served in the United States Marine Corps prior to becoming a Detroit police officer, just like his dad. When he arrived at Mount Clemens PD, we clicked immediately. Bratton wouldn't just help me solve a problem on paper; he was always willing to jump in the fire with me and take action, regardless of the consequences. "Hell with it, let's go" was a phrase we used many times over the years.

We decided to insert the device via the entry door on the back side of the home. We knew that there was a landing just inside the door with a stairwell that led to the basement. A short three-step climb to the left led to the kitchen. The negotiators and observers believed the suspect was probably in the basement, so down the stairwell is where I would throw the phone. As Bratton and I approached, we would have the over-watch of a sniper unit behind us and cover from the other members of our entry element.

After communicating this plan to the command post, Bratton and I made our way to the back door. Once there we didn't waste any time. After a quick check of the device and the long spooled cord attached to it, I made eye contact with Bratton, and he pulled back the outer door. The inner door had been left wide open, so I reached back and stepped into my throw as I entered the threshold.

It was just at that moment I saw the suspect inside. He was seated upright on the basement floor with a massive gunshot wound to the side of his head. He was clearly deceased. Sitting in front of him, leaning back against his chest, was his wife. She, too, was mortally wounded and it appeared that the suspect had shot her first, before positioning her body and then taking his own life. The suspect's large-caliber handgun was on the tile floor beside them.

Unfortunately, I couldn't stop my throwing motion in time to avoid sending the phone down the stairway, and with a fair amount of velocity. The phone struck the suspect's body on the left shoulder before bouncing across the floor. Bratton had seen the entire episode and pulled me backward out of the doorway. We both knew that there was at least one person, the sister, still unaccounted for and we needed to make entry immediately.

Crouched up against the back side of the house, we radioed the command post of what we'd seen and stood by while the rest of our entry element joined us near the back door. At the same time the other entry element, led by Sergeant Darren Bondy, lined up on the opposite side of the house near the front door. When both units were ready we made simultaneous entry into the home. My team went downstairs while Bondy's group cleared the main floor.

Reaching the bottom of the stairs, we had to step over the deceased couple to continue moving forward into the wood-paneled room. To describe the blood-soaked scene as gruesome would be a gross understatement. As we proceeded I saw some bloody footprints leading away from a door on the right side of the room.

Bratton and I headed that way and button-hooked into a room containing a laundry and storage area. Lying in front of the washer and dryer was a woman later identified as the wife's sister. Like the others, she had been shot and killed by the suspect. Evidence technicians and detectives would later surmise that the suspect chased the two women into the laundry area and shot them both there, before dragging his wife out to the area where we found her.

All three murders and the suicide had most likely occurred prior to the arrival of the Team and were probably happening while the police officers were trying to rescue the man in the front yard. It was a brutal and sad situation which required an intense debrief afterward. A few cold beers were part of that session, if I recall correctly.

The city of Mount Clemens is almost 200 years old and contains much amazing history. It was the hideout of the notorious Purple Gang from Detroit during Prohibition, and John F. Kennedy gave a famous speech downtown during the 1960 presidential campaign. The incident on Canfield Street must rank among the most violent days in the city's long history.

Summer Morning Stickup

As the sun broke over the eastern horizon of Lake St. Clair on an early Tuesday morning, a woman eased her car to a stop in a freshly painted parking space behind a bank branch in Clinton Township, Michigan. She was alone, and tired from the overnight shift she'd just completed at a nearby 24-hour business. She had one more task before she slept, though, so she retrieved a zipper-locked canvas bag from inside her over-sized purse.

The building was a two-story regional office of Michigan National Bank, and it stood on the southwest corner of Gratiot Avenue and 15 Mile Road. The red brick structure featured a shingled overhang attached to the south side covering a three-lane drive through banking center. The first lane adjoined the south wall of the building and offered customers several options; an ATM, a teller window, and a night depository drop box.

The woman pulled the release handle of the driver door, elbowed it open, and stepped out onto the asphalt. The air was still cool but already starting to warm in the first light of day. With the locked bag in her left hand and a bank key in her right, she stepped quickly from her car to the drop box, as she'd done dozens of times before. Though she relished the thought of sleep, she was proud to be trusted by her employer to make the daily deposits.

As she reached the brick wall and raised the brass key, she felt someone emerge from around the corner to her right. The woman turned her head to see a Black man clad in blue sweatpants with a thick white stripe, black Nike shoes, and a floppy bucket hat. He was no taller than she but looked strong and athletic. The gun in his right hand was pointed directly at her.

"Check it in, bitch" he snarled.

The woman froze, her hand still raised. Whether she didn't comprehend his command or was paralyzed by fear, she remained momentarily motionless.

"Gimme the fuckin' bag!" he snapped, this time louder.

She extended the bag to him as far away from her body as possible, terrified of the gun and the man's menacing presence. He snatched the bag from her hand, tucked the gun into his waistband, and sprinted westbound away from the woman, across the blacktop parking lot.

An alley ran along the bank's west wall connecting 15 Mile Road to Sharkey Street, the first block south. Quickly reaching the alley the man turned left and continued running. As he approached Sharkey Street he slowed, looking right and left. A silver Ford Crown Victoria, striped in the colors of the Clinton Township Police Department, passed by northbound on Gratiot Avenue just 100 yards away. The police officer inside had not yet been dispatched to the robbery call and didn't see him, but the man panicked.

When the police car was out of sight, he took off again at a dead run. This time he ran westbound down the sidewalk on the north side of Sharkey Street. As he ran diagonally across

Sharkey Street to the south side, the man made another bad decision.

Before him was a small rectangular ranch house, measuring no more than 1,000 square feet in total size. Faded yellow vinyl siding covered the outside walls of the home, and a concrete driveway led from the street to a carport overhang on one side, where a red Pontiac sedan was visible. There was no garage. A small brown wooden porch was attached to the home's foundation beneath the front door. Three skinny decorative iron posts, each painted white, supported an aluminum awning over the porch. Behind the dark outer storm door, the main entry door stood open.

Wanting desperately to hide from the cops, the man sprinted over the curb and across the lawn in front of the house, then up the steps and onto the small porch. Yanking the storm door open, he entered the home and slammed the main entry door closed behind him. Inside was a grandmother feeding breakfast to her toddler grandson. And just like that, an armed robbery morphed into a barricaded gunman with hostages; or so we thought.

"*All Team members acknowledge this message and report immediately to the SWAT office. We will respond to a barricaded gunman in Clinton Township. Situation actual, this is not a drill.*"

So read the text message transmitted that morning by Sergeant Darren Bondy, Assistant Commander of the Macomb County SWAT Team. The Clinton Township Police Department had reacted swiftly and expertly upon receiving the 911 call of an armed robbery. By canvassing the working-class neighborhood door-to-door, they quickly determined that the suspect was possibly hiding in the little yellow house in the middle of the block. The patrol supervisor called for SWAT when she learned who else was inside.

Twenty-five minutes after receiving Bondy's message, I was seated on a bench in front of my locker blousing my BDU trousers over a pair of black Hi-Tec Magnum boots. When all my gear was properly donned, I unlocked my Pelican hard case and retrieved the Heckler & Koch Model 53 rifle inside. Together with a Glock Model 22 sidearm it completed my standard loadout, though we had other available options.

Bondy and Lieutenant Craig Sparks, the Team commander, were efficient in the briefing that followed. Using a whiteboard, they mapped out the scene and detailed our assignments. Four members of our sniper element had been sent out immediately to survey the scene from all sides and lock it down. They would provide overwatch as our two entry elements, one led by myself, approached and relieved uniformed cops on the inner perimeter.

When the briefing was finished both entry teams filed out and headed north down the hallway, through the steel door and out to the concrete parking area which was surrounded by a 10-foot fence topped with razor wire. Some newer members of the team hefted hard cases and canvas bags into the back of our black 24-foot converted transport van. They contained specialized gear and equipment such as Arwen 40-millimeter launchers to deliver tear gas, a portable cell phone signal jammer, ballistic shields, spare flash bang and smoke grenades, and lots of other items that SWAT teams justify to bean counters in budget offices.

Prior to stepping onboard, I made sure my group was locked and loaded, weapons on safe, and conducted a radio check. Nearby my counterpart, Sergeant Brian Kozlowski, did the same with his entry crew.

The scene was a mere five miles from the SWAT office so when all the operators and command cadre were loaded up, we proceeded due south on Groesbeck Highway to 15 Mile Road, then hung a left for the short journey to Gratiot Avenue. One block before that crossroad we turned into a commercial parking lot across from Lowe's Home Improvement Warehouse. The black asphalt lot was ringed by a white brick half wall; it served customers of Studio 15 Hair Salon and Roseann's Kitchen Café, located on either side of the property.

The crisis negotiation unit, which was a separate entity from the Team at that time, was on scene and had established a makeshift command post in the parking lot, out of the suspect's line-of-sight in the house. They were attempting to contact him by calling the landline inside the home, having determined the number by researching the address.

The primary negotiator that day was Lieutenant Ron Krueger, a highly trained and experienced cop who was an expert at observing a suspect's mannerisms, attitude and emotions to create a rough psychological profile. Compiling that knowledge helped Krueger determine the suspect's motivations, mental state, and propensity for violence; all of which assisted in crafting a peaceful resolution. But the attribute that made Krueger such a great negotiator was his personal demeanor. He possessed the natural ability to make people feel valued and appreciated, and he did it with everyone. Krueger was another in the long line of strong positive role models I had during my police career, and his presence at critical incidents was always an asset.

When the wheels on the SWAT transport stopped turning, we stepped out ready to go. My entry element was already assembled and after a quick thumbs up from Bondy, we set out on foot. My point man that day was Officer Patrick Carson. He was a tough kid from Detroit who had grown up idolizing the cops who policed his neighborhood. He boxed in the Golden Gloves tournaments as a boy, stayed out of trouble, and later joined the Detroit Police Department, where he served in the Tactical Services Section before being hired away by Mount Clemens PD. Next in line was his cover man Officer Mark Bratton, followed by myself in the third (team leader) position, with five more operators behind me in the stack.

We moved south across the parking lot to Sharkey Street, crossed it and then continued west past two houses. We turned up the second driveway, quickly moved past the home into the back yard and paused briefly. Our goal was to proceed to the east, hugging the rear side of neighboring houses as we went, then arrive at the southwest corner of the home containing the suspect. The movement would put us at the back end of the driveway and afford us the ability to cover the west and south sides of the house, including two entry doors: one from the driveway and the other from the small deck at the rear of the home. Kozlowski's element would be making a similar approach from the other direction, ultimately arriving at the northeast corner to cover the front and east sides of the home. It was an extremely close perimeter, but necessary if we were eventually tasked with making an entry with innocents inside.

We traveled in a closely stacked line through the yards quickly and quietly. We encountered a couple uniformed cops along the way, so I gave them thumbs up and a quick nod to fall back from their positions. I always tried to be cool and show appreciation when doing this on SWAT calls because I'd been in their shoes. The occasions as a young cop when I'd been relieved of my position by SWAT officers made me frustrated; I wanted to be in on the action. But it was necessary, and I didn't have time to explain it to them, so we just kept moving.

Our arrival near the southwest corner of the home was almost simultaneous to the other entry team's appearance at the northeast corner. I assigned two officers from my stack to cover the south side of the home, including the door leading inside from the deck. Two more were tasked with covering the door accessed from the driveway. That left Carson, Bratton, myself, and Officer Rick Rhein to plan our next moves in conjunction with the command post and crisis negotiation team, while staying ready to move rapidly if necessary.

Rhein was a good-natured, quiet guy who we affectionately called 'Scooby' because, honestly, he bore some resemblance to the canine cartoon character. If you get a nickname when assigned to a special unit, it's a sign that you belong and your teammates like you. You cannot pick your own nickname; that is strictly forbidden. You just roll with it, and Rhein always did so admirably. Some nicknames are easy. Friends had called me 'Diss' since the eighth grade, just as Kozlowski had always been 'Koz'. Bratton's recent ancestors hailed from Kentucky, and he liked to eat the potted meat known as Spam, so 'Hillbilly' was a natural fit. Some nicknames were even more colorful.

Once settled, I radioed the command post that we were in our assigned position. As we received sporadic updates over the encrypted SWAT radio frequency from the command post concerning Krueger's progress negotiating with the suspect, I noticed a growing racket above our heads. The engine moan and 'whump-whump-whump' of helicopter blades were not uncommon sounds at a scene such as this, but the volume was a bit unusual. Kneeling on the white concrete, I looked into the blue sky and saw three news helicopters carving circles at different altitudes. Local channels 2 (FOX), 4 (NBC), and 7 (ABC) had their respective choppers peering down on us in high definition.

Into our earpieces just then came a transmission from Sparks.

"Entry teams be advised," he said. "Krueger can hear the television on inside the house. If the suspect turns to a news channel he's probably going to be able to see our positions from the helicopters overhead."

That would not do.

I had recently attended a tactical training course in Detroit and learned of a rule established by the Federal Aviation Administration (FAA) that allowed law enforcement to clear the airspace above a critical incident. I withdrew the Nextel Motorola iDEN i1000 mobile phone from a Velcro pocket on my tactical vest and dialed the Detroit Field Office of the Federal Bureau of Investigation (FBI).

As one would hope on a weekday morning, my call was answered quickly. The receptionist must have been away because the person who picked up was a Special Agent. After introducing myself via name, rank, and department, I explained our predicament to the agent as efficiently as I could.

"Sir," I said. "This may be the strangest call you receive all day, but I'm currently at the scene of a barricaded gunman who may be holding a woman and child hostage. We have entry teams and snipers surrounding the house, and our crisis negotiation team has the suspect on the phone trying to talk him out."

The pause that followed was finally broken when the agent asked, "What can I do for you, Sergeant?"

With a chuckle I continued, "Well, sir, we have multiple news helicopters circling above us, and we're worried that the suspect will be able to see us on a television inside the house. We'd like to invoke the FAA regulation that allows us to clear airspace above a critical incident."

Fortunately for us, this Special Agent must have been at the top of his class at Quantico because he knew exactly which rule I was referencing.

"No problem," he replied. "I can't make any promises, but I'd be happy to call the air traffic control center at Selfridge Air Base and see what they say."

Truth be told, if I had thought it through better, I could've called there myself. We were close enough to Selfridge that the controllers inside the tower might be able to visually see the helicopters over our position. They would certainly have them on their radar.

"That would be fantastic," I told him. "Thank you very much, we sure do appreciate it."

I snapped the phone shut and returned it to its secure berth, then got back to business. I wasn't sure if the call would do any good, but it had been worth a shot. The agent had seemed positive about the idea but, like most local cops, I had my reservations when it came to the FBI. I've worked with a few great agents; usually they'd been street cops or soldiers before becoming G-men. But the general rule was that the FBI would take all your information and give you absolutely nothing in return. Not the case in this instance, it turned out.

Ten minutes after I hung up with that Special Agent, the sky above us was vacant but for birds and bright sunshine. The helicopter pilots had bugged out after being informed that the SWAT team beneath them had requested the FBI to make it so. The phone call was the source of some high-fives and fist bumps at the debriefing that followed, but we still had work to do.

About 30 minutes after the sky was cleared of aircraft, Sparks again spoke across our encrypted frequency.

"Listen up, fellas," Sparks said. "Kreuger advises the suspect is about to surrender."

There were some raised eyebrows (including my own) because that was an unusually quick resolution of a very critical incident, relative to most that we'd encountered. But it wasn't completely surprising, given that Krueger was the negotiator.

Sparks informed everyone that the suspect was being instructed to exit through the front door. He directed Kozlowski's element alone to give all commands to the suspect once he cleared the house. They would cover down on the man while directing him to lay prone on the grass in the front yard.

Once that was accomplished, per Sparks' plan, my crew would advance from the west side of the home and secure the suspect in handcuffs. Our snipers would, as always, provide overwatch of the entire movement. There was just one twist in the plot. When the man emerged slowly through front door onto the porch, his left hand held the cordless phone through which Krueger was still communicating. In his right hand was the gun.

As our snipers calmly relayed that observation over the radio to the command post and Kozlowski's crew started giving clear directions to the man, Krueger asked him incredulously, "Dude did you bring that gun outside with you?"

"Yeah," he replied.

At that moment there were more crosshairs and reticles focused on the suspect than he could have imagined. The caliber of the projectiles pointed at him covered .40, .223, and .308. It was truly an instance in which one wrong move would cost the man his life.

"Buddy, put that gun down immediately. And do it slowly!" Krueger said over the telephone line.

The man looked to his left, then right. He seemed to shrug his shoulders slightly before tossing the pistol into bushes beside him. I'm sure a collective sigh of relief was heard at the command post just then.

The man followed directions the rest of the way, finally finding himself face down on the green grass in the front yard. When it was appropriate to do so, my unit advanced. Carson and Bratton provided cover as Rhein and I handcuffed the man, patted him down, and stood him up. We walked him a short distance away from the house before turning him over to Clinton Township police officers and detectives.

During their interviews and interrogation, investigators determined that the suspect was known to the woman inside the home. Krueger later confirmed that she did not seem hysterical or even fearful during the time he was negotiating with the man. He was a distant relative or otherwise known to her and may have been at the home prior to the robbery.

Whatever their affiliation, a genuine bad guy was arrested and charged with armed robbery and other crimes that day. And a young but experienced SWAT team did its job well, assisted by expert crisis negotiation.

Insane Number 9

At the time of my initial assignment to COMET, I had been the detective sergeant in charge of a Mount Clemens Police Department (MCPD) team called Special Investigations Unit (SIU). It consisted of myself and two detectives: my friends Mark Berger and Mark Bratton. They were amazing to work with, both having come from the Detroit Police Department and each the son of Detroit cops.

SIU did a lot of good work in town; buying some dope with confidential informants, executing search warrants, doing surveillance and grabbing wanted fugitives, among lots of other things. But as a small city unit, we didn't have jurisdiction outside our borders unless we were working with other agencies, and our hits weren't very big. Berger had previously been assigned to COMET, the Michigan State Police drug task force in our county that was comprised of city, county, state, and federal agencies. They had no jurisdiction issues and were extraordinarily well-funded from federal tax dollars and their own case forfeitures, which often reached into the millions of dollars each year.

The truth was that our new Chief of Police was all about civil forfeiture, the legal process that allows police agencies to seize cash, vehicles, even real estate if we can show that it is proceeds from dealing drugs. Instead of splitting the forfeiture funds equally with the other agencies who participated in COMET, our Chief had formed his own unit so that we could keep it all. It just wasn't realistic. The downtrodden neighborhoods we operated in and the houses we raided usually didn't have suitcases full of money laying around, and that wasn't likely to change soon. I also didn't like being motivated by forfeiture proceeds; I just wanted to catch bad guys. Taking the ill-gotten gains of drug dealers was intended hit them where it hurt the most, not substitute for properly funded police budgets. So, I went into the Chief's office one day and had a conversation.

I had already spoken to Rich Margosian, the Michigan State Police (MSP) Lieutenant in charge of the Street Narcotics Team, one of COMET's four divisions. He assured me that MCPD would be welcomed back into the fold and any political waves caused by our Chief's previous withdrawal would be forgiven. So it was with full confidence that I sat down with the Chief and sold him on all the benefits of our participation in COMET. The best training, tactics, and techniques. Statewide jurisdiction. Take-home undercover vehicles paid for by the state (with fuel cards), MSP cellphones and radios. He finally agreed when I explained that our portion of the forfeiture money we'd split in COMET would probably exceed what we could accumulate on our own.

Berger and I were immediately assigned to COMET, while Bratton went back to road patrol. Having been in COMET for two years previously, Berger had completed the mandatory MSP training such as Basic and Advanced Narcotics Investigation (each one a 40-hour class). Margosian explained to me that as a detective sergeant on his crew I would be expected to serve as an assistant team leader along with Detective Sergeant Brian Kozlowski, assigned to

COMET from the Macomb County Sheriff's Department. Together we would supervise a team of eight undercover (UC) narcotics investigators, but that could not happen until I had the proper training and experience.

The goal for COMET detectives was to buy dope directly from a dealer in a transaction commonly referred to as a 'hand-to-hand'. That was preferable because delivery of drugs directly to a police officer was a felony crime punishable by up to 20 years in state prison. The alternative was sending a confidential informant (CI) into a drug house with state police money to make the purchase and return with the dope. After three such transactions (fewer if the CI had good credibility), we could swear out a search warrant and raid the place hoping that the dealer had recently 're-upped' and was sitting on a large quantity of drugs. It's not a bad technique and we did it frequently, but a hand-to-hand deal made a much better case.

Initially this was usually done during an introduction of a UC police detective to a drug dealer made by a confidential informant, which is known as a 'dirty buy' because it can't be used to prosecute the dealer. If that buy was prosecuted, the informant would have to be listed in the report and potentially called as a trial witness; generally not good for their health.

We'd complete the dirty buy, write an incident report, and put the drugs into evidence. Since it couldn't be prosecuted, any money we spent on a dirty buy was 'in the wind' and wouldn't be recovered, so we tried to keep the initial purchase small. But the UC detective would soon hit the dealer up again and arrange another buy, this time without the CI.

This was appropriately referred to as a 'clean buy' and if that was successful, we were really in business. The next step would be to introduce another UC detective from the team during a clean buy, then have that second detective purchase drugs from the dealer alone. This technique was called a 'double-clean' and it was intended to protect the CI. When the bust went down and the dealer wondered who had introduced him to the undercover cop, the likely culprit in the dealer's eyes would be the first detective. It didn't always go like that, but we tried to protect informants and we never had a CI injured or killed during my time in COMET.

As you can imagine, supervising all that action could be a nightmare. Each deal had to be properly vetted; we needed to know where we were going and who we were meeting, if possible. A briefing for the team was always held in the COMET office prior to the operation, with addresses and suspects detailed on the large whiteboard in our meeting room. The locations varied from working class neighborhoods in Mount Clemens or Warren, to trap houses along the 7 Mile corridor in Detroit; one of the most dangerous neighborhoods in America. Surveillance on a venue had to be established by team members prior to arrival of the UC, and that wasn't always easy in the tough areas. Many dealers had scouts on the street who would whistle loudly or otherwise communicate to a dealer if they spotted the drug police. The UC always wore a wire, and it was the supervisor's responsibility to listen and recognize any signs of trouble. If the boss heard the UC utter a predetermined word or phrase indicating they were in extreme danger, it was his responsibility to lead the team inside and rescue the UC at any cost. And when it came time for search warrant executions, the boss's list of responsibilities only got longer.

For all those reasons and more, Margosian explained that I wouldn't be supervising any operations until after I'd spent the next six months to a year shadowing him and conducting my own undercover investigations just like the rest of my teammates. During that time, I would also complete the mandatory MSP classes and some additional training like the Reid School of Interview and Interrogation.

During my first week in COMET, I got a taste of the chaos that accompanies undercover operations in the city of Detroit. One of our crew had made some buys with a CI from a house in the Ninth Precinct, and the time had come to knock down the door. After briefing, we loaded up and headed south on Gratiot Avenue. I was in the front passenger seat of Margosian's car, listening and learning as he communicated with our team over the radio and offered me pieces of wisdom along the way.

Prior to leaving the office on a mission to buy drugs or execute a search warrant anywhere, we always notified the local HIDTA Office (High Intensity Drug Trafficking Area) of the address or area where we would be operating. This was to avoid hitting the same place at the same time as another law enforcement agency, a process known as 'deconfliction'. Over the years that had happened more than once, including a terrible day in 1986 when undercover Detroit Police Department (DPD) Officer Giacomo Buffa was shot and killed by friendly fire, along with a uniformed patrolman named Mark Radden, at a drug house on Euclid Street between Woodward Avenue and I-75.

As an added measure of safety and courtesy when we were executing a search warrant inside the Detroit city limits, we'd also notify DPD Control Center, a unit staffed by police officers attached to their central dispatch. As we crossed 8 Mile Road and entered the city, Margosian gave me a nod and told me to make the call. I dialed the number and put the cell phone on speaker.

"Detroit Control Center," answered a female cop on the second ring. She had a warm voice and demeanor that just made you believe she was smiling, not a common trait in our profession. I told her who we were and the address on Sanford Avenue where we were headed.

"And what is your radio call sign, sir?"

"I-462, ma'am" I replied.

"Ok, I-462, let's look at what we have for you. Hmm, we have a report of a man on the front porch of a house on that street brandishing a shotgun. But he's two blocks down from your target, he prolly won't be bothering y'all."

I turned and looked at Margosian deadpan. He just shook his head, smiled, and kept driving. As our caravan turned onto Sanford and headed southwest, she continued.

"And we did just have a carjacking in the parking lot of the CVS drug store at Gratiot and Conner," she said. "Cars in number 9 are chasing the vehicle at this time. They should be coming your way!"

It was a warm spring evening and Margosian's window was cracked. We could literally hear the patrol car sirens chasing that stolen car on Conner Street, northbound alongside Detroit City Airport. Just life in the 'D' on an average Tuesday night.

We made it to the crib, piled out of our cars, and lined up to breach the door. It was a small brick ranch-style house on a street dotted sparsely with homes well-kept by defiant owners who refused to be chased away by the criminals or advancing blight and decay. The remainder were either burned out shells, overgrown vacant lots where houses once stood, or abandoned homes like this one, converted to a drug den by the neighborhood's latest aspiring dealer.

No one answered when we knocked, so we had to use our key; otherwise known as a battering ram. The interior of the house was decrepit. The wet plaster walls and leaded glass windows, so common in Detroit architecture from the city's heyday, were damaged far beyond repair. Where there was carpet, it was black with years of stains and mildew. The hardwood portions of the floor were destroyed and, in some spots, unstable from leaks in the ceiling above. The moldy smell of garbage and sweat was a punch to the senses. Unfortunately, it was a typical trap house, not much different from those found in every American city.

The team moved carefully but swiftly through the structure and found it empty except for one person. When I saw her, the image was etched into my memory where it remains today. Seated cross-legged on the bare floor behind the door we had just breached was a rail-thin Black woman wearing a tattered hooded sweatshirt and jeans. Her left wrist was handcuffed to an eyebolt sunk into the floorboards, and she was sipping cheap red wine called Mad Dog 20/20 from an old Campbell's Soup can. She wasn't unhappy to see us. Her drunken smile and sunken eyeballs reminded me of character from a zombie movie.

The woman's sole purpose for being in the house was to receive money through the mail slot in the door in exchange for the crack cocaine she would hand back through it. At regular intervals she'd turn over the money when the dealer showed up, then be resupplied with dope and (hopefully) allowed to use the bathroom. She was almost out of inventory, so we seized the money and small quantity of crack cocaine, then turned her loose.

Since we hadn't arrested anyone or recovered a significant amount of drugs, it was the type of raid we referred to as a 'dry hole'. But it certainly provided some lasting memories for me during the first week of my new assignment.

My kid sister, Aimee, and me with our dad and his police dog named Hogan.

With my dad after being sworn in at the Mount Clemens Police Department.

Lance A. Folson, my friend and mentor.

Patrol car 57, following my crash involving a drunk driver.

Wedding day misbehavior with my dad and Jim Grasel.

Skirmish line at the Mound Road facility during the Detroit Newspaper strike, Labor Day 1995. Photo courtesy of Damon J. Hartley (Detroit Free Press)

SWAT training at Fort Custer with Brian Kozlowski and Mark Bratton.

Taking an armed robbery suspect into custody with my teammate Rick Rhein, aka 'Scooby', after a standoff in Clinton Township, MI. (Photo credit: Macomb Daily Newspaper)

Three years assigned to COMET went by in a flash. We stayed busy!

Thanks to my teammate Jeffrey 'Bud' Budzynowski, we took an extra look inside the Cadillac Escalade driven by our Vietnamese drug trafficking suspects and found a surprise!

The COMET Street Narcotics Team just before I rotated back to patrol. They'll always feel like family to me, and there's not much I wouldn't do for any of them.

MSP D/Trooper Brenda Hoffmann (right) with a Detroit Police Department detective, during one of many COMET prostitution enforcement operations.

With Officer John Stover, after seizing 120 pounds of 'BC Bud' on a traffic stop in Marysville.

Oakland County SWAT officers take murderer Doug Ball into custody following an intense Major Crimes Unit investigation.

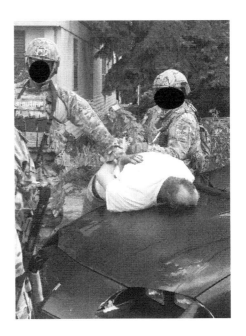

Assigning duties during a Major Crimes Unit briefing, prior to a human trafficking enforcement operation.

News helicopter view of the crime scene where Jonathan Stahl murdered his poor father; inset is Stahl's booking photo from the St Clair County Jail (Photo Credit www.clickondetroit.com)

With my Major Crimes Unit brothers at Christmas. Not surprisingly, the team was called away from this party for an armed robbery!

Friday Phone Call

Fridays in COMET were usually called 'paperwork' days. Instead of working a normal shift (usually 1500-2300 hours or something similar), detectives would start out at Rosie's Diner on 15 Mile Road for breakfast and then go back to the office. During the week there was always a large amount of office work generated; reports to file, evidence to catalog, phone calls to return, and lots of other follow up to do on your caseload of investigations. Friday was usually the day you had a chance to catch up.

One typical Friday the Street Narcotics team was in the office after breakfast getting our work done, when the phone rang. The call was answered by Detective Sergeant Brian "Koz" Kozlowski from the Macomb County Sheriff's Department. Kozlowski was a linebacker during his college football career and looked a bit like Opie Winston from the TV show 'Sons of Anarchy', which came a few years later. Kozlowski is a loyal friend and, without a doubt, the finest undercover detective I ever worked with. We had a lot of fun over the years and caught a ton of bad guys.

On the other end of the call was an officer from LAWNET (Livingston and Washtenaw Narcotics Enforcement Team), another Michigan State Police task force like COMET. A man had called LAWNET and told them that he wanted to confess to crimes he committed and provide information about a major drug ring. The man had a heavy foreign accent, but the detective was able to determine that the man was calling from Mount Clemens. Apparently, the man looked in a phone book and got the number for LAWNET, headquartered near Ann Arbor about 65 miles away. The caller, named Hanh, was put through to COMET, and so began an 18-month investigation into an international drug smuggling and money laundering network.

Hanh was a Vietnamese citizen who had been in the United States for almost 20 years. He was brought to the US by criminals from his country who were moving narcotics into Canada and then across the border into the United States. During his time here, he met a woman with whom he had children. Their daughter had recently been accepted into a prestigious university and Hanh was afraid that his own life choices would ruin the young woman's chances of success. For that reason, Hanh wanted out of the criminal network but knew that he would be murdered for even suggesting it. The only choice, Hanh knew, was to turn informer.

Almost immediately we knew that this case would exceed our capabilities and that we needed additional resources. Meetings were held and manpower gathered, along with intelligence and technical equipment. The federal Drug Enforcement Administration (DEA) became a full partner in the investigation, bringing all the assets of the world's premiere narcotics enforcement agency and providing nationwide jurisdiction. An apartment was acquired for Hanh, and it was hard-wired to record high-definition audio and video by the MSP Technical Services Unit, which helped us gather valuable information whenever Hahn's criminal bosses and associates visited him.

We learned that the drugs were brought into Vancouver, British Columbia, where the organization would also purchase large amounts of high-grade marijuana referred to as 'BC Bud'. All the drugs were then transported in vehicles across Canada to Windsor, Ontario, a journey of about 3,000 miles. Once there, they would be smuggled across the border into Detroit and eventually stored in a residence in the nearby suburbs. From there, members of the organization would transport the dope to cities throughout the United States including Atlanta, Baltimore, Minneapolis, New York, and others. When the drugs were sold in those cities, the money would be brought back and stored in a different house in metropolitan Detroit before being smuggled across to Windsor, and then delivered all the way to Vancouver and eventually to Vietnam.

We began to follow the drugs as they were transported away from the Detroit area by members of the criminal network, all of whom were Vietnamese citizens. Some of the suspects, male and female, didn't speak English and this was by design. The leaders of the gang didn't want them to be able to communicate with police if they were caught. On more than one occasion we had civilian interpreters (provided by the DEA) working with us to translate intercepted conversations.

It was tough to watch the large shipments of drugs be transferred from one courier to the next without swooping in and arresting them, but each time we did more intelligence was gathered. We'd record the license plate of the next car and follow it as far as possible to learn about residences and businesses that were part of the network.

The meetings, surveillance, long days and planning went on for many months, all while we continued to work other active, unrelated cases. Eventually the investigation began to reach its conclusion. Dozens of suspects and locations had been identified and it was time to wrap up the case and make arrests. On a sunny spring weekday my Street Narcotics crew was directed to relieve the Surveillance team, which was watching the 'money house' where proceeds of all those shipments of drugs were kept prior to being transported out of the country. Those cops had been on the location all night and were due to head home for some rest.

As my teammates took up positions in the blocks surrounding the residence, I settled into a spot on the street with a direct eye on the house. On the encrypted police radio, I let the Surveillance team know that they could bug out, and then settled in for what I thought would be a long day sitting in my unmarked black Dodge. There were detectives from other units nearby, including the Violent Crimes team which was set up on nearby Interstate 75 to intercept any bad guys traveling north or south.

In the driveway of the house were two identical Cadillac Escalades, both white with chrome rims and tinted windows. I was surprised when, only a few minutes after we arrived, five Asians males walked out of the house and loaded up in one of the Escalades. They immediately backed out of the driveway and headed around the block and out of my sight. My teammates stationed throughout the neighborhood verified that the suspects were heading for the freeway, and that they entered the on-ramp for southbound I-75.

The first thing I did was radio the Violent Crimes guys who were up on the freeway. I didn't receive an instant reply, but I thought that might be due to them scrambling for position as the Escalade merged with the traffic flowing toward downtown Detroit. I then called my boss, D/Lt. Rich Margosian, who had left the area a short while before to take care of some other business. I wanted to know his intentions for the five Asians, so that I could relay the information to the Violent Crimes team.

While I was on the phone, I noticed I hadn't heard any reply from the Violent Crimes guys, so I tried to raise them again on the radio. Perhaps it was the digital encryption mode, which can sometimes be troublesome, but for some reason we were not communicating, and the bad guys were heading for an international border with Canada: the Detroit-Windsor Tunnel.

I explained to my boss that the suspect vehicle was southbound on I-75, and I'd received no response from the cops who were supposed to be following it. Margosian's voice took on a certain tone I recognized, and he said "You get up there on the freeway and get that vehicle stopped. Whatever happens, don't let that vehicle cross the border!" At that moment I realized that stopping the five suspects who'd left the house might initiate all the other agencies moving to take down the whole network.

I radioed my teammates that I was heading for the freeway and for them to keep their current positions, with one officer moving to my spot with a direct eye on the house. There was still another vehicle in the driveway and an unknown number of people inside. Also, if we planned to later execute a search warrant on that house (we did), the law required that we maintain surveillance if we wanted to criminally charge the five suspects who'd left.

As I entered the southbound lanes of I-75 the traffic wasn't too heavy, since it was early afternoon on a weekday. I pushed the speedometer in my UC car to triple digits as I again tried to raise anyone from the Violent Crimes team on the radio. Finally, I received a reply. At some point they'd heard me and had started to follow the vehicle, though they hadn't quite caught up to it yet. They were a couple miles ahead and it was going to be difficult for me to reach them before they all arrived at the international border.

I contacted the Detroit Police Department and MSP to ask if either agency had a marked patrol unit available to stop the vehicle. We didn't have any uniform cops with us, except for a dog handler who was way out of position. Unfortunately, the answer was a unanimous "NO", so I did what must be done in those situations; I carried on. Sometimes you just have faith that things will work out.

As I rapidly approached the exits for downtown Detroit, an officer from the Violent Crimes team radioed the suspect vehicle was on Jefferson Avenue and headed for the tunnel to Canada. I simply told him and his teammates to stop it, suggesting they block the tunnel while being careful to ensure their badges and police identification were visible. We could always explain ourselves to U.S. Customs, and I've often said that sometimes it's better to apologize then ask permission. That philosophy was about to be put to the ultimate test.

I was still southbound with the hammer down as I-75 became I-375 and then merged up onto Jefferson Avenue at the foot of the General Motors Renaissance Center. I had a clear shot westbound to the tunnel entrance as I heard the radio report; the suspects had made it into the tunnel and were about to enter the city of Windsor, Ontario.

While telling the detectives from Violent Crimes over the radio to stop the suspect vehicle, I had been very adamant. I may have even used some profanities, but the situation was intense. Perhaps it was that energy or enthusiasm in my voice which caused them all to follow the vehicle into the tunnel, crossing the international border and exiting directly onto the tunnel plaza near the inspection booths belonging to the Canada Border Services Agency (CBSA). I admire that type of dedication to duty, but Canadians have some hard and fast rules regarding firearms, not to mention arrest authority (or the lack thereof).

I had no choice but to follow my guys down this wormhole, so I badged my way past US Customs at the tunnel entrance and came out on the Canadian side. When I did, I immediately saw all five Asian drug trafficking suspects lying face down on the concrete at gunpoint. This was not good.

As the guys handcuffed and secured the suspects, they holstered their guns and I tried to find someone in charge with whom I could have a conversation. That wasn't difficult. An initial calm, probably from pure shock, had evaporated and there were now Canadian border cops moving in every direction. I saw a kindly-looking woman dressed in a white uniform shirt with a gold badge and captain's bars on her collar. As I began to explain who we were and why we were causing such a spectacle, she held up her hand with a wry smile and told me to stop talking.

"You're going to have to speak with the Chief of the Port of Windsor," she said.

The good Captain directed me to the second floor of the office building behind her, so I told the Violent Crimes team to secure the vehicle and stand by as I headed inside. I passed through a bustling office area, getting more than a few sideways looks, and boarded the elevator to the next level. The second floor appeared to be deserted and it was a long walk down a polished tile floor to the Chief's office. The door was open, so I stepped in to see an older man in a short-sleeved shirt and tie, seated behind a desk and looking out over the commotion outside. He pointed at a chair in front of his desk, so I sat down.

He was quiet as I introduced myself, offering my police identification and badge for his inspection. I told him all about COMET and our investigation into an international drug smuggling ring, including the details concerning the five suspects currently detained downstairs. I made sure to explain our partnership with the DEA on the investigation, hoping that might assuage some of his concern, and generally included more specifics about the case than I would have normally revealed to anyone else.

When I thought I had summarized the situation well, I said "Sir, if you'll allow us to turn these folks around, we'll head back to the States and get out of your hair!"

That statement, comical in retrospect, was met with dead silence. There was an old Seth Thomas clock high on the wall to my left, the kind you saw in schools and churches, and I heard the second hand click 10 times before he exhaled a deep breath and answered.

"Son," he said. "That's not going to happen. You have absolutely no authority to detain anyone here, and any contraband in that vehicle now belongs to Canadian Customs. As for the guns your men are carrying, I don't know what's going to happen. But it probably won't be good."

I stood up, thanked him for his time, and got the hell out of there. In addition to the concealed 40-caliber Glock on my hip, there was a padlocked Pelican hard case in the trunk of my car which held a Heckler & Koch Model 53 assault rifle and a Benelli M1 Super 90 tactical shotgun. Fortunately, that bit of information was never discovered. Walking back down the lonely hallway, I punched Margosian's number from my contacts list.

Thankfully he answered on the first ring. I detailed my chilling conversation with the crotchety old 'Chief of the Port', and asked Margosian to come get us. The situation was becoming too deep for a Detective Sergeant like me, and I needed some of our own gold badges to arrive and join the fray. As I spoke with Margosian, I heard a 'ding' and turned to see the elevator doors open.

Out of the elevator stepped two men I recognized immediately, and I couldn't have been happier to see them. Special Agents Brian Kelly and Alejandro 'Alex' Torres were partners at the DEA with whom I'd worked on previous cases.

Apparently, they heard some of the radio traffic and surmised what happened.

Torres smiled as a cheerful Kelly said "Hey, Jimmy! Heard you were having some trouble?"

With the phone still to my ear I pointed to the office I had just left, and while shaking my head whispered, "Not good!"

Kelly told me that he and Alex would talk to the old man and said, "Don't worry, I was INS!"

It was a reference to his service with the defunct Immigration and Naturalization Service prior to DEA. I wasn't sure that would carry much weight, but Torres gave me a fist bump and told me to go take care of my guys while they tried to smooth matters on the second floor.

When I reached the first floor, I headed for the parking lot where I had last seen the Violent Crimes team. As I approached the exit, I passed a holding cell which had clear Plexiglas walls and a heavy steel door which was wide open. Inside the cell were the five Asian suspects seated on a long concrete bench. They didn't look up as I passed by because they were each busy eating sandwiches and drinking coffee from Tim Horton's. Someone from the CBSA had made a run to the famous Canadian coffee franchise to get them some grub. I exited and found my guys gathered in the lot near their vehicles, which were parked alongside each other in the shade of a metal awning. There wasn't a Tim Horton's wrapper or coffee cup anywhere in sight.

The men told me that while I was inside their badges and police identification cards had been confiscated by CBSA agents. For me, this kicked the intensity up a notch. I understood the ramifications of the situation but believed that we were all still on the same team; or should be. I told the guys to stick together right there by their UC cars and to not say a word to anyone, and to call me immediately if anyone gave them the slightest bit of trouble.

I then set off to find the Cadillac Escalade and I located it a short distance away in the 'Secondary Inspection' area. As I approached, a Canadian Customs canine handler was walking around the vehicle, directing his dog to give it a good sniff. I spent some time watching closely as the dog worked its way around the SUV in the late afternoon sun. I'm no expert in police dogs but I swear I saw that dog 'indicate' on an area near the driver door. The handler missed it though, and after finishing his inspection he took the dog away to other duties.

Just then I noticed MSP Detective First Lieutenant Charles 'Chuck' Schumacher walking toward me from the area near the CBSA office. Schumacher was my boss's boss, essentially what the State Police called a 'Post Commander', and he oversaw all the units and staff that comprised COMET. He had made it from the COMET office to our location in about 30 minutes flat, after receiving the call from Margosian. I'd never had much contact with him, but I knew that he treated his troops fairly. He ran some major interference for me that day.

Schumacher informed me that he had reclaimed the badges and identification cards from CBSA agents, after each was photographed, and returned them to the Violent Crimes team.

He told me that he was going to take everyone else back to the US and then said, "Get that Escalade and those suspects back on our side of the border!"

I gave him the only acceptable reply to such an order, "Yes, sir!" But it was tough for me to imagine that happening.

It was just about 1600 hours, about 2 hours since the COMET 'invasion' of our fine sovereign neighbor to the north, though our position in Windsor was actually to the east. (Fun fact: part of Canada is south of Detroit. Google it!) I found myself with some time to kill as the CBSA staff took the Escalade to another inspection area. I checked on the Asians to make sure they were still in the cell and made sure that my UC vehicle was locked, especially the trunk. Just then I saw two uniformed police officers climb out of a Windsor Police Department patrol car and head my way.

As they walked up, they seemed friendly enough. The older of the two was a veteran cop with salt-and-pepper hair who asked me if I was the American narcotics detective in charge of all the excitement. I told him I was and showed him my identification, then gave them an abbreviated rundown of the information I had previously explained to the Chief of the Port of Windsor. They listened closely and took a few notes. When I finished, the younger Black cop explained that the Chief had called the local police to file a firearms complaint against me and my guys. I just shrugged. I knew at that point it just was going to work out however it worked out and we weren't the bad guys in this situation, regardless of how the Chief felt about it.

To my pleasant surprise the two city cops told me that they were going to make a note of the incident on their log sheet and then proceed to the closest coffee shop (probably Tim Horton's) and have a cup. Translation: they weren't going to proceed any further with the Chief's complaint.

After they departed, I received another such inquiry from a smartly dressed detective from the Royal Canadian Mounted Police (RCMP), who arrived in an official-looking unmarked burgundy Ford Crown Victoria. He recorded all my information and wrote down all the same details that I was becoming accustomed to reciting. He must have arrived at the same conclusion as the two street cops, because I never heard from that detective again.

I learned the Chief of the Port of Windsor had personally called Windsor PD and RCMP to report us, and he then called Canadian Customs headquarters in Ottawa, Ontario. They, in turn, called US Customs in Washington DC, who called Michigan State Police Headquarters in Lansing, MI. By the time the higher-ups at MSP headquarters reached Schumacher, he was back on US soil with all his officers. Well, except me. It was quite the international incident we'd caused! I'm not sure if the old Chief still walks the earth but, if he does, I'd wager he's still pissed off.

The Cadillac Escalade was now a bit farther away from the Secondary Inspection area, down the striped concrete driveway near a large white building that reminded me of an aircraft hangar. Next to the Escalade was a big flatbed vehicle called a VACIS truck, which had a large boom extending out away from it and enveloping the Escalade on three sides. I watched as the truck slowly drove past the Escalade, using the boom to create a detailed x-ray image of the interior.

When the operator of the VACIS truck had finished, I walked inside the big white building. I wanted to get a look at the x-ray image to see if it revealed any contraband like drugs or money. The area inside wasn't well-lit and I didn't immediately see anyone. Exploring farther into the space, I turned a corner and found a young woman sitting at a desk. She was a civilian analyst for CBSA. The computer monitors in front of her displayed exactly what I'd been looking for, an x-ray image of the Escalade's interior.

I introduced myself but her smile and nod made it seem like she already knew who I was. She wasn't surprised or upset that I had walked in uninvited and couldn't have been nicer to me. This is a common theme among the many Canadians I've known over the years, especially in Ontario. They are usually friendly, helpful people whose company I enjoy very much.

I asked if I could see the image on the monitor, but she did me one better by printing for me an 8.5" x 11" glossy color photo of the image on the screen. Not being an x-ray technician, I was unable to make heads or tails of the image, but the friendly clerk explained that there were no anomalies visible on the x-ray. I was disappointed to hear that news, but I didn't give up hope that we'd still discover something.

Sometime around 6pm the CBSA officials decided to release the vehicle and the five Asians. I was relieved and happy to learn of their decision and started to plan for a tow truck and a prisoner transport vehicle to come over from Detroit. No such luck.

It was explained to me by CBSA that the suspects were free to drive their own vehicle back across the border and I could lead them or follow them, but they were not to be detained in any way. Fortunately, my DEA friends Kelly and Torres were still with me, and we improvised a plan.

I would lead the procession back across the border with the five suspects in the Escalade following. Agents Kelly and Torres would follow the Escalade in their DEA vehicle, and I arranged for a trooper in an MSP marked police car to be waiting for us on the other side.

As the Asians loaded up in their Escalade (it wouldn't be theirs for much longer), I leaned into the driver's space so the message I was about to deliver would be heard clearly. He had implied during the entire episode that he didn't speak or understand English, but I had my doubts. I spoke plainly as I told him to follow me closely with no deviation to the other side. When I pointed to Kelly and Torres in the green Ford Taurus behind the Escalade, the driver turned to see them waving and surely understood they would follow him.

I threw a salute to some CBSA guys and then we set off into the tunnel and back across the international border. We made it through without any issues and as we came up on the other side, I expected to see the state police car waiting near the inspection booths of US Customs. No, sir! The MSP cruiser was nowhere in sight as our little entourage was stopped again, this time by US inspectors. They'd been made aware of the brouhaha on the Canadian side and now wanted their turn at putting our investigation through the wringer.

Ahead of me was a short, stout Black woman in a US Customs uniform with her own gold badge and set of captain's bars. Clearly, she was in charge of the situation and walked past my car to the Escalade behind me. I exited and walked slowly toward her with my badge clearly visible on a chain around my neck.

I didn't want to startle her from behind, so as I drew closer, I cleared my throat and said, "Good evening, ma'am".

Before I could introduce myself or give any explanation she spun around and pointed at me saying, without a drop of geniality, "Step away from the vehicle!"

Dreading yet another border incident, I rolled my eyes and did as I was told. The angry captain directed all three vehicles to an area behind the Detroit-Windsor Tunnel Toll Plaza as US Customs officers began their inspection.

The five Asians were again placed in a holding cell with clear Plexiglas walls and the suspect vehicle was taken to the Secondary Inspection area. After a US Customs canine handler ran his dog around the vehicle without success, preparations were made to use a VACIS truck for yet another x-ray examination. When it was completed, they didn't present me with a glossy color photo of the x-ray, but neither did they find any contraband.

Another four hours passed in the course of the US inspection and during that time a delightful woman who worked inside the Toll Plaza brought us, but not the five suspects, bags of potato chips, chocolate chip cookies, and cans of Sprite on ice in a cooler. Finally, at 2200 hours we were told that the inspection was over and we were free to carry on with our investigation. I had been correct in my guess that detaining the Escalade and its occupants would trigger a domino effect of movement by other involved teams and law enforcement agencies.

During our time at the border, search warrants had been served by COMET on the 'money house' (where we started that day) and the nearby 'stash house' where the drugs were stored after being smuggled into the United States. Simultaneously DEA began to move against the criminal network spread across the country, arresting individuals and raiding other locations. Hundreds of thousands of dollars in cash and pounds of drugs had been seized at the two houses in Metropolitan Detroit, and our five suspects would now join some of their comrades who were lodged at the Macomb County Jail in Mount Clemens, MI.

I called the jail and requested a prisoner transport van to come downtown and pick up our suspects, who were now arrestees. Just then I got another surprise. The angry captain I had first encountered on the US side of the border had overheard my call as she walked into the detention area.

She pointed at the floor and said, "This here? This is Customs. You have no authority here." Pointing through the window, she continued, "If you wanna walk these boys up the ramp to Jefferson Avenue, you can arrest them up there!"

She ascended the nearby stairs to her office, queen of her little domain, and I watched her disappear behind the door. Part of me really wanted to unload on that lady right at that moment. She had been rude and acted like we were the enemy. But I was too tired, and I knew it wouldn't help.

Luckily, the perpetually upbeat Kelly jumped into action yet again. He headed for the stairs and told me, "Don't worry, bud. I'll talk to her. Remember, I used to be INS!" The captain, it turned out, had also worked for INS prior to the agency's assimilation into US Customs and Border Protection, and Kelly convinced her to leave us alone.

As the transport van was pulling up outside, I searched each of the five Asians before putting them onboard. Every one of them had large amounts of US currency in their pockets. When it was totaled, I had taken about $17,000 in cash out of their collective pockets.

Just as the transport van drove away with our bad guys, it started to rain. When I say it started to rain, I mean the lightning flashed and the thunder crashed during a downpour that lasted more than an hour.

Before we left the border with Kelly driving the Escalade and Torres in the DEA car, we were visited by the Special Agent in Charge of DEA Detroit Group 6, the division where Kelly and Torres were assigned. I'd met him previously and knew him to be a highly accomplished DEA agent who was revered by his own men and women as a thoughtful and trustworthy leader. He reminded me of a younger version of NFL head coach Tony Dungy, and I was humbled that he remembered my name. After our quick debrief he gave us a thumbs up and we headed onto Interstate 94 toward the COMET office, located in a non-descript industrial complex just north of Detroit on the east side.

It was still raining and nearing midnight when we pulled into the parking lot and I unlocked the gate of the COMET impound yard, an area surrounded by tall, barbed wire fencing that could hold about 25 vehicles. Kelly parked the Escalade next to a cream-colored BMW 5 Series which had been seized a few weeks before. I then locked up the gate, thanked Kelly and Torres profusely for their vital assistance, and we all headed home for some rest.

The next morning, I woke up early because I had an absolute mountain of paperwork to complete. My wife was working that day and it was too short notice to get a babysitter, so I brought my two kids, Travis and Jenna, with me to the COMET office. It was highly unusual, but I had no choice. When we arrived at 0900 hours, the secretaries made a fuss over them both and I plopped them down on a big soft couch in our briefing area. There was a 50-inch high-definition TV in the room, one of many we had seized from drug house raids. I turned the channel to Nickelodeon, and they were more than happy to watch Sponge Bob Square Pants for the next couple of hours.

As I fired up the computer on my desk and got busy, my teammate Jeff Budzynowski came around the corner from his cubicle. 'Bud' was a Macomb County Sheriff's deputy who also served with me on the county-wide SWAT team. Here was another cop who was always optimistic and unwilling to give up without a fight. I'm lucky to have worked with so many enthusiastic cops like Budzynowski.

He gave me his trademark grin and said, "Hey Diss, let's go take a look inside that truck!"

I told him that two separate nations had given it their best shot and come up empty.

"Bullshit," he said. "I've got a killer tool set, bro. Let's go!"

I checked on the kids and found them to be just fine, so we walked out the side door of the office directly into the gated impound lot. The overnight rain had passed through our area, and it was another beautiful day. I told Budzynowski about the Canadian police dog that I thought had hit on the driver door, so that's where he started.

It didn't take him long to unscrew the big single bolt on the Escalade's driver-side door panel and peel it back away from the frame. I knew something was up when Budzynowski started chuckling.

"Look at that, brother," he said, as I leaned in over his shoulder.

Looking straight down into the space between the panels I could see multiple stacks of rectangular objects wrapped in aluminum foil. They were each the size and density of a Hershey's chocolate bar and there were dozens of them. We ripped the interior panel off that door as fast as we could and removed the foil-wrapped packages, laying them on a nearby picnic table.

Before we destroyed the rest of the Escalade's door panels, we took a quick peek inside one of the 'candy bars'. It was filled with crisp 100-dollar bills, as were all the rest of them. We eventually recovered more tall stacks of identical items from the passenger-side door and brought all our new-found treasure inside the office.

On the long briefing table in the center of the office we laid out the packages and started to remove the foil from them. We stopped and asked our MSP property officer to help us so that every dollar was accounted for, and nothing was missed. We started to attract attention as the word spread about our recovery. It was a lot of money.

After an hour of counting and re-counting the bills using automated currency counters, the total from the Cadillac Escalade was $265,000; a damn nice hit, especially when combined with the money we'd taken from the suspects at the border. That seizure paled in comparison, however, to the total amount seized and forfeited by the DEA and United States Attorney General's Office at the conclusion of the case.

Millions of dollars in cash, drugs and property were lawfully taken and repurposed to fight future battles against drug traffickers. The Vietnamese group had been laundering money for years, so the federal government reached out for those assets, too. Among the businesses they rolled up were laundromats in the Midwest and a shrimp boat in Gulfport, Mississippi.

The federal government eventually indicted 42 members of the Vietnamese drug trafficking organization on a myriad of federal narcotics charges. The only member of the outfit who suffered no repercussions was a Vietnamese Army general at the top of the hierarchy, who had never left his home country and was essentially untouchable.

I kept the glossy color x-ray image of the Escalade pinned to my cubicle wall for the remainder of my time in COMET, and I probably still have it in a box somewhere. The entire investigation was an amazing exercise in cooperation and teamwork between many police agencies at the federal, state, and local levels.

And it all started with a phone call.

Chicago Blues

Most successful investigations at COMET started with a confidential informant, what we called a 'CI'. Sometimes a CI worked for money, but usually they were working off charges. In exchange for introducing an undercover detective to a supplier, the CI could have their charges reduced or dismissed. Each time we'd make the next arrest we would try to "flip" that person and create another CI, unless that person was so heinous that helping them evade prison time crossed the line of decency. We didn't always get to the top, but it was fun to climb the ladder.

The Conspiracy team at COMET arrested a man who insisted he could order up 50 pounds of high-grade marijuana from a connection in Chicago. Since the deal had to be made that same day and they were short-handed, Conspiracy requested help from my Street Narcotics crew. Our boss, Detective Lieutenant Rich Margosian, requested that we put whatever deals we had on hold and show up for a briefing at 1600 hours.

At the briefing we learned that the Chicago suspects would arrive at the M-59 Motel, a roadside dive on the corner of Gratiot Avenue and Hall Road. Its location just a block from Interstate 94 would allow the suspects to hop off the freeway, do the deal, and hit the road back to the Windy City. That last bit, of course, wouldn't actually happen.

When the Conspiracy unit supervisor asked for an undercover officer (UC) from our team to conduct the transaction, I volunteered. The assignment was simple; roll up to the motel with the money and walk into the room. Once I saw the dope, I just had to give the signal and my team would enter the room and make the arrests. I had to be mindful of weapons and the potential for robbery, so I was definitely armed, and any red flags would be communicated to my team over the wire. But the deal was not complicated. I didn't have to convince the bad guys to sell me drugs or prove to them that I wasn't a cop. They trusted their associate (our CI), so we weren't expecting anything difficult. In the history of undercover drug deals, this was not one for the record books.

The agreed upon price for the 50 pounds of weed was $50,000, so we found a bag with a shoulder strap that looked like a piece of carry-on luggage. I could walk up to the motel with the money and make it appear that I was just another traveler checking into my room; and there was a bonus. For months I had asked Margosian if I could drive the Alpine White BMW 325xi that was parked in the storage area behind our office. It had been forfeited during an unrelated investigation and had yet to be sold at auction. He had always denied my request, since the car was out of place for our usual investigations. But this deal was different; a buyer showing up with that kind of money would be expected to drive something nice.

After our briefing, the Conspiracy unit directed the CI to make the call. The arrangement was quickly made, and the suspects said they were on the way. A trip to Detroit was normally a four or five hour drive, but the suspects encountered Chicago rush hour traffic and didn't arrive until almost midnight. The Conspiracy team members conducting surveillance on the motel watched as a dark green Chrysler 300M entered the lot and parked near the office. Two white men were inside, and the driver exited the car. He walked into the office and returned a minute later, after checking in and receiving a room key. They drove around to the north side of the building and parked in front of room 112. While the driver keyed open the motel room door, his partner retrieved a large suitcase from the trunk and carried it inside; it looked heavy.

The CI almost immediately received a call from one of the bad guys. He told the CI they had arrived and to send the buyer (yours truly). They were in a hurry and wanted to drive back to Chicago that same night. We didn't rush to show up, since that would be unusual for a dope deal. Most dealers and buyers operate on what cops call "doper time", and deals almost never happen promptly.

After an appropriate delay, my teammates from the Street Narcotics team arrived and parked in a used car lot south of the motel. They walked north to the hotel property and stacked up on the east side of the building, where it was completely dark and out of sight to anyone near room 112. Since the motel room was small and about to be crowded, my guys carried handguns instead of rifles or shotguns. When Margosian called to tell me they were in position and ready, I pointed the BMW towards the motel and arrived a few minutes later.

I parked the sports car two spots down from the green Chrysler 300M, threw the bag over my shoulder and headed for the door. Though my teammates were completely out of sight, knowing they were just a few feet away gave me a good feeling. I knocked on the door, just below the placard that said 112. The suspects had placed a 'Do Not Disturb' sign on the handle, which turned as the door was pulled back about 12 inches. The door stopped and hung there, so I pushed it the rest of the way open and walked in, closing it behind me.

"What's up, fellas", I said to the two middle aged men. They looked harmless, but I knew better than to assume that was true.

"How ya doin'," replied the one with a shock of premature white hair and bright blue eyes. He had the Irish American working man look I'd seen a million times; this guy could have been one of my uncles. The other man, tall and thin, leaned silently in the corner against the wall to my left.

The man who'd greeted me stood between the only bed in the room and an old wooden wardrobe positioned against the wall to my right. On the floor next to the man lay the suitcase seen before by the detectives working surveillance; it was now empty. Atop the old wardrobe were two huge, compressed bricks of marijuana. Each was tightly shrink wrapped in plastic, so completely that the smell of the weed was negligible. The bricks later weighed in at exactly 25 pounds each.

Displaying the drugs in the open like that eliminated the need for us to play show and tell, so I slipped the bag off my shoulder and tossed it on the bed.

"Damn, I like the way you guys roll. Looks like a good deal to me," I said. Margosian knew that if he heard me say the words 'good deal' over the wire at any point, it was go time.

With almost no delay the door was opened by Margosian with a motel master key and my teammates stormed inside.

I took a sidestep as they flowed past and watched as the two men were roughly placed face down on the bed. They offered no resistance and were handcuffed easily.

I grabbed my bag off the bed; the two men hadn't even had time to examine the contents. Good thing, because it was full of newspapers. We didn't have fifty grand lying around the office that day, unfortunately. Placing it in the trunk of the BMW I waited outside for a while, giving my teammates time and room to operate and to make sure no one else approached the room. A sheriff's department patrol car arrived after about 20 minutes, having been called to transport our bad guys the short distance to the Macomb County Jail.

After photographing the room and its contents, the marijuana was loaded up and transported to the COMET office by members of the Conspiracy team. My Street Narcotics teammates went home for the night, but I headed to the county jail with one other detective to interview our two arrestees.

The man who had been silent in the motel room remained so at the jail, which was his right to do. He had been recruited by the other man to ride along but wasn't a real player in the deal. He figured that he didn't have anything to gain by talking to us, and he may have been right; not so for his friend.

The man who looked so familiar to me gave me an idea; since he reminded me of family, I'd talk to him as if he was. I could tell he was really stressed out and I soon found out why. As soon as I confirmed that he understood his rights, he started talking.

The man owned a small mechanic's garage in a tough Chicago neighborhood, doing oil changes and tune ups for people in the community. It was the kind of area where people still went to work, but crime was common, and gangs were visible. In his neighborhood, that meant the Southside Gangster Disciples.

The man had always managed to scrape by, providing food for his family and a roof over their heads. But as his daughters approached college age, he made a bad decision. To finance their education past high school, the man started selling marijuana. In a neighborhood where the Gangster Disciples controlled the criminal activity, you didn't just need their approval; they supplied the weed and received a cut of your proceeds. Failure to operate in that prescribed manner might result in your mechanic garage business going up in flames, or worse.

Drugs distributed by the Gangster Disciples arrived directly from Mexico and their connections to cartels in Sinaloa, Michoacán, and Jalisco were well-documented. To become partners with the Gangster Disciples is a dangerous business, and a tough one from which to extricate yourself. Fortunately, we were about to offer him that opportunity.

To exacerbate his situation even further, the 50 pounds of marijuana the man delivered to us had been fronted to him personally by the leader of Gangster Disciples clique (chapter) that controlled his neighborhood. Forget cutting the gang a percentage of sales, he owed them for the entire 50 pounds.

I continued to empathize with the man and express my concern for his family's safety, just as if they were my own family. When I asked how this transgression against the gang might affect his daughters' future, the man burst into tears. I didn't need to ask if their lives were in danger, we both knew they were. Was I manipulating the man's emotions during this interrogation? Of course, I was. Don't like it? Don't put yourself in that position.

I had some genuine empathy and a true understanding of the man's plight, but my job was to enforce the law. Clearly the man had been successful moving Gangster Disciple weed over an extended period, hence the large amount of credit he'd been extended. I didn't feel too sorry for him, but I made him believe that I did.

The time came during our conversation when I turned off the video camera and offered him the chance to become a confidential informant. It didn't take long for him to think that equation through. Returning empty handed to face the Gangster Disciples simply wasn't an option. He may have considered going on the run if he had been a single man, but he wasn't. He was a family man. He truly loved his wife and kids and was terrified for their safety.

I made sure he had a bunk for the night away from other prisoners in the jail. I didn't want him to say a word, even accidentally, about our agreement and it was better if no one knew he was there.

I got to drive the BMW home that night, but it was short-lived. There was faint light in the eastern sky as I parked that beautiful car in my driveway and went inside to grab a few hours' sleep. I was back at the COMET office by 10:00 AM.

I explained my conversation with the man to Margosian and Detective First Lieutenant Charles Schumacher, the commander of all four divisions of COMET. Clearly we would need the Drug Enforcement Administration (DEA) to take the man on as a confidential informant, since the scope of the investigation and its geography was beyond our immediate capability. Since I had both bosses in the same room at the same time, I took my shot at escorting the man back to Chicago and assisting DEA with the continuing investigation. Why, I could even drive the BMW.

"Zip it, Disser." Schumacher said. "You're not going anywhere."

I was disappointed but happy to flip a potentially great CI to the DEA. We later learned that the man provided intelligence and conducted transactions that led to the arrest of the some of the Gangster Disciple leadership in south Chicago. From there, the DEA climbed the ladder to a high-level drug kingpin in Miami, Florida, seizing his million-dollar yacht and other assets.

It would have been fun to be part of that operation, but I had to settle for getting to drive the BMW for a couple days. I didn't complain about it.

Chateau Macomb

My first 'double clean' didn't involve a ton of drugs, but it was fun, nonetheless. A man who purchased crack cocaine from a street corner dealer near the housing projects in Mount Clemens' northeast end was stopped and arrested by a patrolman named Daryn Santini. I always reminded the uniformed cops to offer their arrestees a chance to work off criminal charges by becoming confidential informants (CIs) and provided them my business cards to hand out to those who showed interest. Some people are more motivated than others, and a motivated CI is a wonderful thing. When Santini offered the chance to avoid a felony drug charge, this guy jumped at it.

I was on duty with my COMET crew that day and not far away when Santini called me. I met him at MCPD, and he showed me the twisted-up corner of a plastic bag containing 3 rocks of crack cocaine which he'd recovered while searching the man's vehicle. It was a good bust for a young cop. I followed Santini as he walked past the old holding cell toward the booking area; to describe it as spartan would be an understatement.

The cinderblock walls painted off-white enclosed a room floored with grey-on-gray checkerboard tiles, stained from the occasional spill of blood and faded from a thousand moppings. On a large metal desk sat an electric typewriter and a stack of report forms; next to the desk a chest-high station for rolling fingerprints. Bolted into the far wall was a cold iron bench painted dark brown; handcuffed to that bench was my newest CI.

The first rule of handling informants is to never, ever trust them. Assume that everything coming out of their mouth is bullshit mixed with some truth, then try to mine for those little nuggets of reality. I never spent any time trying to convince them that they should do something for us. It had to be completely their decision, or they might hesitate in the big moment and fail. Failure could lead to the CI (or worse, one of us) being injured or killed. If they weren't sufficiently motivated by money or eliminating their own criminal charges, there were plenty more where they came from. Informants are a dime a dozen.

"Are you Sergeant Disser?" he asked.

"Yep. What can I do for you, boss?" I replied.

"That cop said if I helped you guys, you could make my charges go away. Is that true?"

"Yeah, man. That's the basic idea," I said. "What you got for me?"

This was a skinny white guy 30 years old with some hard miles on him, but he was clearly street smart. His penchant for partying had cost him a few jobs but he was the type who kept grinding. He'd just landed a legitimate sales job with a heavy equipment company and was making decent money. But another criminal conviction, especially a felony drug charge, would send him tumbling back down the ladder he'd just managed to climb.

"I got a guy I can buy coke from right now."

Those are words uttered by almost every potential CI and the key term is 'right now'. They all want to be released right then and there, regardless of how potentially awesome their hook up might be (or not). They don't want to be in jail. He doesn't want his wife to find out, she doesn't want to lose her job, he wants to get the car out of impound, she's dope sick; the list of reasons is endless. But the risk you take by releasing them immediately, obviously, is that they'll ghost you and never be seen again. Then you must issue an arrest warrant for the original charge and hope to find them down the road. The alternative is locking them up and charging them with their crime, then making contact once they've been arraigned and released on bond.

The most important thing to do is whatever benefits our team the most in its mission; screw anything the informant wants.

Sometimes putting the CI on the street right away was advantageous. If the person seemed relatively squared away, not drunk or blown out on drugs, and their information was solid, we could put them to work. If a CI held up their end of the bargain, then the report would be closed and criminal charges against them would simply never be filed. That allowed us to bypass the criminal justice system altogether; we didn't have to explain to prosecuting attorneys why we wanted certain charges dropped or risk a defense lawyer divulging his client's status as an informant to other criminals. Correctly judging when to employ that tactic was a fine line to walk but paid big dividends when you got it right.

I decided to take the risk with this one. Since he owned a house, had a job and paid child support, I knew where to find him if the deal didn't pan out. I debriefed him about his source then completed all the necessary paperwork to officially make him a confidential informant of the Michigan State Police. Even though I wasn't in a hurry, my new CI insisted we could make an introduction and buy some dope the same day. I checked with my boss to see what else was on the schedule that evening, then took the CI out to the parking lot and told him to make the call.

His supplier agreed to meet us in the parking lot of the 'Babies-R-Us', just a few miles west on Hall Road in Sterling Heights. It was a big box store with a huge parking lot in the shadow of the M-53 expressway, surrounded by other busy places like sporting goods stores and restaurants. I'll forever be suspicious of parking lots, not to mention hotels, because I know how much criminal activity happens on a daily basis in those places, and this would be no different; well, technically our drug deal would be legal.

Three undercover (UC) detectives from my crew left the COMET office and headed out ahead of us. Since we wouldn't be arresting anyone and it was unlikely to be a robbery, we didn't need the whole team. Two of the guys set up in positions with a wide view of the parking lot and its ingress/egress, the other in a spot near where I would park, just in case I needed quick assistance. The CI hopped in my unmarked police car, a blacked out Dodge Intrepid, and we headed west at about 1800 hours.

The warm sun was getting low in the sky when I parked in a space out away from the building. There were some cars sitting empty nearby, their owners inside shopping, that provided good cover for our deal. I checked with my three teammates on our encrypted frequency and learned they were all on scene and ready to go. I told them I'd be "off the air", then spun the volume knob on the Motorola counterclockwise until it clicked. I tucked the radio under the driver seat just as one the UC cars came to a stop half a dozen parking spots away with a clear line-of-sight to us.

I had told the CI to order up an 'eight ball' of powder cocaine. It was street language for an eighth of an ounce, about 3.5 grams. The price of cocaine varies depending on where you are, its purity, and how much you're buying. In Macomb County at that time, the going rate for a gram was about a hundred bucks. When the suspect told my CI the price was $300 for an eighth, I knew that was about right given the slight volume discount. I also knew it would probably be 'stepped on' or, in other words, reduced in purity to increase profit. If you start with an ounce of pure cocaine and mix it equally with baking soda, you've just doubled your money. Most cocaine that reaches end users isn't anywhere near 100 percent pure. It's often cut with other substances like quinine or Epsom salts and may even contain additive drugs such as lidocaine or caffeine to mimic the effects at lower cost.

The CI's cell phone rang then, and he put the call on speaker after answering.

"Hey, bro." the CI said.

"What's up man, you guys good?" the suspect asked.

"Yeah, we're here, dude. Is that your car that's turning in right now?"

The suspect replied "Yep, where you at?"

"Just keep coming straight back. We're in a black Intrepid. You see us?"

The line went dead as a silver Oldsmobile Cutlass Supreme drove south through the parking lot from the entrance off eastbound Hall Road. It was one of the older body styles we called a 'ghetto sled'; I had always thought they were sweet back in the day. I saw only the driver as the car approached, a skinny white male in his mid-twenties with curly hair that was slicked back. Our little drug deal wasn't going to be worthy of a Hollywood movie script, but my heart was pounding, nonetheless. The suspect 'doored up' on my side, so that he and I were just a couple feet apart. I powered down the dark tinted window on my car's driver side.

"Hey, Patrick, this is my buddy Jim" the CI leaned over and said, pointing to me.

"Dude, that car's fucking sick" I said with a nod. "I always liked those."

"Aw thanks, man. It's an '88. That's the last year before they started making them so damn ugly."

The guy wasn't wasting any time. He reached across the space between us and plopped a knotted plastic baggie on my lap. The weight of the white powder inside felt correct. I placed it on a small digital scale which I kept in the center console; 3.5 grams on the nose. I handed over six prerecorded fifty-dollar bills, folded twice into a green paper rectangle that I held below the window line. As he took the money, he asked the question I'd hoped to hear.

"So hey, dude. Will you be looking to get some more of this shit?"

"Hell yeah, man" I replied. "If it's good, me and my buddy got the perfect place to move it. The factory where we work."

I purposely kept it vague, but the factory scenario was my backstory. There are factories everywhere in metropolitan Detroit. From the giant stamping and assembly plants of the Big Three car makers to all the smaller shops that support the automotive industry, you can't drive a mile without seeing one. If he pressed for details to test me, I could describe my uncle's tool and die shop on the east side. He didn't.

"Awesome, dude." Pointing at my CI, he said "He's got my number. Hit me up."

My new suspect drove away then, as suddenly as he had arrived, and just like that our deal was done. It was smart to not linger and risk some soccer mom calling the police about three suspicious dudes lurking near her minivan. I got up on the radio and told my teammates that the deal was good and asked them to 'trip' the suspect. It was the term we used for conducting moving surveillance to follow a vehicle, and I hoped that Patrick would lead them back to wherever he lived.

Tailing a car without being noticed is harder than it sounds if the suspect is an experienced criminal. It's an acquired and depreciable skill that requires practice, and three follow cars is the minimum number needed to do it professionally. The crew needs to switch off the lead car frequently to give the suspect a different 'look' in his rearview mirror and still cover any turns he might make. In this instance my teammates had recorded the suspect's license plate while he was in the parking lot, and they tripped Patrick all the way back to his humble abode in a lovely development called Chateau Macomb.

That name always cracked me up. Chateau Macomb was a 1,400-lot trailer park encompassing a full square mile north of Hall Road, not far from Mount Clemens. It was a constant source of 911 calls for the sheriff's department: domestic disputes, drunks being disorderly, car crashes, the occasional trailer fire. There was even a homicide or two over the years. Giving that place a fancy French name was like putting lipstick on a pig.

The following day I stopped by Mount Clemens PD for a few minutes, prior to making roll call at the COMET office at 1600 hours. I planned to call Patrick later in the afternoon to set up another deal, this time without my CI, but it wasn't necessary. When my phone started to vibrate and play its customized Iron Maiden ring tone, I looked at the screen and saw 'Patrick' on the Caller ID. Answering his call inside the police department's squad room was not an option; the sound of police radios and cops yapping at each other might leave a bad impression. I stepped quickly out the back door and walked behind the police station to the edge of the Clinton River, which meandered lazily through downtown on its way to Lake St. Clair.

"Patrick," I said. "Whazzup man?"

"Hey, dude," he replied. "How did that work out for you?"

"Good, bro," I told him. "My partner worked third shift and got rid of it real quick last night. I mean, it wasn't much. We stepped on it again, but it still only added up to a quarter."

I told Patrick that my business partner, whom he had yet to meet, and I had doubled the amount of cocaine from an 'eight ball', or eighth of an ounce, to a quarter ounce by adding inert ingredients.

"I need to get some more," I said.

"I got you, bro," Patrick answered. We were definitely becoming bros.

"Sweet," I said. "Can I get a couple O-Z's?"

Pushing to buy two ounces that soon was risky. Some dealers (most, in fact) would be suspicious of someone they just recently met asking for that weight. But this guy was foolish. He wanted to be a mid-level drug dealer in the worst way and was pushing our relationship harder than I was. This was going to be a 'clean buy' and delivery of two ounces would put him over the 50-gram statutory threshold, resulting in a more serious penalty. From there I hoped to take him to kilo country; unfortunately, it was not to be.

"Nah, bro," he said. "Not today but soon! I got a couple more 8 balls though, if you're interested?"

Buying 7 grams did me no better than buying 3.5, and my boss wouldn't be thrilled when I put the extra money 'in the wind' unnecessarily, but I had opened the door and now I couldn't say no.

"Sounds good, dude," I told him. "I'll come get 'em both. When you wanna hook up?"

"I'll be home around 7," he said. "You can just come by my crib! I'll be partying, bro! "Are you cool with six hundred?"

Having someone you don't know come to your house to buy cocaine is stupid. Getting robbed or arrested are just two of the possible consequences of such foolishness. It was becoming clear that my guy's entrepreneurial spirit exceeded his intelligence. Also, I would normally negotiate a decent discount for doubling my order, but I agreed to the price since it didn't seem that my case would lead to bigger and better things. I told him to text me his address (which I already knew, thanks to my skilled teammates) and said I would see him in a few hours.

At the end of the daily COMET briefings our boss, Detective Lieutenant Rich Margosian, would go around the room and ask each detective what they wanted to put on the agenda for that day. It would occasionally get testy. Every cop in the room was proactive and usually had deals lined up. Since every operation required at least a portion, if not all, of the team to safely accomplish, Margosian had to prioritize our agenda each day. Sometimes guys (and gals) would be pissed off when their deal got put on a back burner. It had happened to me, so I knew the feeling.

"Whattaya got, Dis?" Margosian asked me.

I detailed my investigation to that point. I had positively established Patrick's full identity from the intelligence we'd gathered. I told the boss how much I wanted to purchase, along with the location and approximate time for the 'clean' buy I had set up.

The deal was uncomplicated and wouldn't take long, so Margosian put it first on the schedule for that evening. Following the briefing everyone got something to eat, then a couple of my guys headed for Chateau Macomb to set up surveillance on Patrick's trailer prior to my arrival. I picked out a wireless transmitter before leaving the office. Together Margosian and I made sure it was working properly and that he could hear it clearly over the digital radio frequency dedicated for that purpose. On the way to the deal, I stopped at Harbors Market across the road from the trailer park and picked up a six-pack of Bud Light.

As I turned into the park, I told Margosian and the team that I was approaching and would be off the air, then tucked the radio under my seat. Patrick's place was an old double-wide that sat on a cul-de-sac just off the main drag to my left. I stopped at the dead end and parked near some overgrown Box Elder trees, then grabbed my still-cold beers and headed for the trailer.

"What's up, bro?" Patrick asked, as he propped open the old screen door for me.

The entryway led into the kitchen, where Patrick had his product packaged up next to a digital scale on the tabletop. Along with my two eight balls there were two fat lines of powder cocaine laying on a handheld mirror. That was precisely why I had brought along the beer.

"Get you some of that, bro," Patrick said, pointing at the lines. "You'll see how fuckin' great that shit is!"

"Wish I could, bud," I replied. "But if I piss dirty again, they're gonna lock me up for sure."

This was a reference to being on probation for a criminal conviction and having to give a urine sample as a condition of being released. It was another part of my undercover backstory for use in situations such as this.

"But that don't mean we can't party, bro" I said. I peeled one of the cans out of the plastic ring and handed to Patrick. "They don't test me for alcohol," I said with a laugh.

We sat down at Patrick's kitchen table, and I opened another one of the beers for myself. He noticed my Metallica t-shirt, so we talked about thrash metal music while Patrick snorted both white lines on that mirror. He got real fired up then, and we talked about how much money we were going to make providing cocaine to all the factory workers I knew. After a little while I handed over $600 in prerecorded MSP buy funds, and Patrick slid the dope across the table into my waiting hands. And at that moment, we owned him.

I stood up from my chair and leaned for the door. Patrick gave me the high-five into the handshake and 'bro hug', and I told him I'd see him soon. Once loaded up into my UC vehicle, I headed south out of the trailer park and back to the COMET office. The surveillance team did the same, one by one rolling out of the park without being noticed by anyone except some dirty-faced kids playing near a garbage can.

After tagging the drugs and placing them into an evidence locker, I sat down with Margosian and discussed how the investigation would proceed. I wished that Patrick had the potential to be a big-time coke dealer who could deliver some serious weight, but I couldn't see that happening. Margosian agreed. We decided to not prolong the case and spend money unnecessarily. I would make another buy soon, but this time bring along my teammate Mark Berger, callsign 'Cheese'. He would play the role of my partner with whom I was identifying new customers at the factory. Berger would then make one more purchase from Patrick, this time without me, meaning we'd have a successful 'double clean' to protect our original CI from suspicion. At that point I would prepare an arrest warrant for Patrick and a search warrant for his trailer home, to be executed and served by our team.

And that is exactly how we proceeded. A few days later Patrick hit me up to see if I wanted to 're-up' with another purchase. Of course, I did! I showed up with Berger and Patrick didn't even blink. On that occasion Patrick's brother drove over from his house in the city of Utica to deliver the drugs for Patrick to sell to us, which was a bonus since we now had an additional suspect.

The next week I gave Patrick's phone number to Berger and asked him to arrange the final buy. I was part of the surveillance team that provided cover as Berger rolled up solo and purchased the final installment. Patrick told Berger he'd have plenty more the next day when his brother made another drop, so that would be the day we'd knock down his door.

Twenty-four hours later I had arrest warrants for Patrick and his brother, charging them each with Delivery of Cocaine, and a search warrant for Patrick's trailer, each one signed by a judge and ready to serve. We had researched Patrick's brother and sent three UC officers to Utica mid-afternoon. They waited for him to leave his house on that city's tough north side and then followed him all the way to Patrick's crib. The surveillance allowed us to later serve a second search warrant at the brother's house, since we could show that the cocaine originated there and was transported to our target.

Thirty minutes after Patrick's brother arrived, our unmarked dark blue Chevy Express 3500 raid van turned into the cul-de-sac and stopped near the trailer. We piled quickly out and formed a single-file line, then moved to the entrance of the trailer. We found the main door propped open, but the outer screen door locked shut.

"POLICE! Search Warrant!" Detective Sergeant Brian Kozlowski shouted.

Koz used his left hand to rip the door open, while gripping a Heckler & Koch MP-5/40 submachine gun with his right. Patrick and his brother, both seated at the kitchen table, wore shocked expressions as the team moved swiftly into the home and handcuffed them face down on the kitchen floor without resistance.

Berger and I both wore black balaclavas and ballcaps, hiding our faces from view. We didn't speak inside the trailer until our two suspects had been walked outside to waiting patrol cars for transport to the county jail. Patrick and his brother never knew we were part of the team that had stormed in to arrest them. In fact, we never saw them again; they each decided to avoid trial and plead guilty, so no court appearances were necessary for us.

A nice quantity of powder cocaine was recovered that day during our search, along with money and a gun. Vehicles belonging to both brothers were seized and forfeited; we even took the mobile home. It wasn't the biggest drug bust in the annals of law enforcement, but it was a great example of a motivated informant's effectiveness and the techniques used to protect him from suspicion.

Two Birds

"What up, doe!" said the confidential informant into his cell phone.

It was Detroit slang for hello, and the suspect on the other end had just answered his call. I'll call the informant 'Jesse' because he looked like the character Jesse Pinkman from the television series *Breaking Bad.* Talked just like him, too.

"Yeah, dog ... it's like I said. These dudes are ready to deal you up."

Jesse was Detective Mark Grammatico's informant. Like all the undercover cops assigned to COMET Grammatico had a 'call sign', or nickname, assigned to him by his teammates. Intended for use over encrypted police radios, the moniker usually became the preferred handle for all communications including face-to-face. Grammatico's call sign was 'Chachi' due to his alleged resemblance to the *Happy Days* character. I always thought Grammatico looked a lot tougher than Chachi Arcola, even though he was one of the nicest guys I'd ever met.

"Yup, double birds for 20 apiece, yo" said Jesse. "These motherfuckers don't play, neither."

Jesse had a contact who had recently expressed to him that he wanted to get in the dope game and had the money to do so. That was a mistake. Jesse didn't know the young man well but saw that he was serious and not kidding about having the money. Knowing he could make some easy money himself, Jesse called up his handler Grammatico, and here we were. Jesse had just told the man that his connections (that would be us) had two kilos of cocaine available for $20,000 each, and that we were serious about doing business.

"Aight, den. I'll let 'em know and then holler at you, dog. Peace."

Jesse was in the back seat of Lieutenant Rich Margosian's undercover SUV parked in the lot of a Warren grocery store but leaning forward so that he was almost between Margosian and Grammatico in the front seats as he spoke on the phone. After searching him thoroughly, to the point Jesse had complained about me about molesting his junk, I'd slid into the rear seat next to him. He was unarmed.

As he snapped his cell phone shut Jesse told us, "He's good to go, y'all."

The suspect had agreed to the weight and price, all we had to do was set up the time and place. Oh, and we had to acquire two kilos of cocaine. Fortunately, since COMET was a Michigan State Police (MSP) drug task force, that wasn't terribly difficult. MSP had amazing resources available to its personnel. It did require some highly placed permissions, though, along with a lot of paperwork.

About a week later, on a Tuesday midafternoon, First Lieutenant Charles "Chuck" Schumacher keyed open the front door of the COMET office, walked past the secretaries' desks, and arrived in the section of the converted factory building that housed the street narcotics team. He looked haggard. Beads of sweat were visible on his brow as he plopped a black nylon gym bag on Margosian's desk. Judging by Schumacher's stress level, the bag seemed to weigh a thousand pounds. In fact, it weighed about two kilos.

"There you go," Schumacher said to Margosian. "Anything happens to that … well, let's just say my career is in your hands."

"Don't worry, boss," Margosian replied with a grin. "We got your back. It'll be safe and sound with us."

"It better be," Schumacher said, trudging back to his office without a word to the rest of us. He couldn't wait to get that dope back where it came from.

As commander of the entire COMET task force, which included three other teams in addition to our own, Schumacher oversaw about 40 cops and millions of dollars of vehicles, equipment, evidence, and other property. According to MSP policy, it took an officer of his rank to sign for the two kilos of cocaine and ensure its safe return after the operation. Schumacher had driven to regional MSP headquarters, about an hour away in daytime traffic, which housed the Southeast Criminal Investigation Division (SECID). SECID was the command to which COMET and all other MSP task forces in southeast Michigan reported. SECID had lots of capabilities, to include providing material support to its drug teams. It was funny to think about Schumacher driving back to the COMET office alone with two kilos of Columbian bam-bam in the trunk.

Naturally, a few of us couldn't wait to get our paws on it. As we approached Margosian's desk to investigate, he held up a hand to stem the tide.

"Simmer down, boys" he said.

The bag bore the familiar Nike swoosh in white on both sides. Margosian hefted the bag by its canvas handles, also black, and placed it on a nearby conference table which held digital police radios, flashlights, and charging docks. With three swift pulls on the zipper tab, Margosian pushed back the bag's top flap, exposing its contents. A kilo of cocaine, sometimes called a 'bird', 'key', or 'brick', weighs 2.2 pounds. These two were each pressed into sharp rectangles and wrapped in brown butcher paper. They had been seized in a prior drug bust somewhere and since that case had been adjudicated in court, they were awaiting destruction.

We'd previously instructed Jesse to tell his connection that the price was $20,000 per kilo. The price of cocaine, like everything else, rises and falls according to supply and demand. Geography can also play a role, as can the quantity purchased and its purity. At that time in metropolitan Detroit our price point was reasonable, but not too low that it would raise suspicion. After a team conversation about meeting spots that would be advantageous for us, Margosian called Jesse and told him to set the deal for the following day at noon.

Doing the deal on a weekday at noon made sense. There are other legitimate times and places for undercover drug deals, and good rationale for them, but hiding in plain sight worked well. Most people are oblivious to the people and places around them. They're usually focused on where they are going and concerned only with circumstances that affect them. Half the time they have their faces buried in cell phones sending text messages or counting their 'likes' on Facebook, so a crowded area with lots of vehicle traffic favored us. If the deal went so far south that it resulted in a shootout with the wannabe dealer, well … some might then disagree with my philosophy.

An eternal truth of drug deals is that they almost never happen on time. Another is that narcotics traffickers, if the deal involves a lot of dope and money, will often try to change the location of the deal at the last minute. The goal of this tactic is to flush out undercover cops. A smart bad guy will have his own surveillance on the meeting spot prior to the deal. If the location is changed and a bunch of unmarked cars start bailing out of the area towards the new spot, that dealer will be in the wind immediately and never heard from again. And the informant who set up the deal could be in grave danger. If the undercover team refuses to change locations, that also will be a red flag to bad guys.

For these reasons it's important to expect the last-minute call and have a plan to accommodate it. It's unwise to just agree to whatever venue they demand; if you make that your default setting, it won't be long before your undercover officer is robbed at gunpoint. A decent strategy is to feign some mild anger at the sudden change and then present a viable third option. It should be nearby, so that traveling the distance doesn't present any unnecessary obstacles and marked units or tactical teams can remain at their staging point or close to it. And, of course, the location should also be scouted ahead of time and undercover surveillance officers placed there in advance. If the suspects refuse to budge and demand the deal be done at their new location or not at all, a good team leader won't get sucked in by the temptation to make a big bust. No matter how hard the undercover cops protest, their leader must let it ride and live to fight another day. These transactions are dangerous enough without taking stupid risks and endangering police officers unnecessarily. It's just dope, after all.

Our 2-kilo reverse drug deal on that springtime Wednesday was all set and ready to go. Until it wasn't. Originally planned near a giant parking lot that served a shopping mall called the Gibralter Trade Center, it wasn't long before noon that the bad guy called Jessie and wanted to change the location of the deal. But that was just another day at the office for Margosian. As he would sometimes say, "I was born at night but not last night, baby!" Margosian let an appropriate amount of time lapse and then directed our deal to the parking lot behind a nearby Burger King restaurant. The suspect agreed, and the deal was back on track.

This particular Burger King was a new franchise which stood along North River Road, near an exit ramp from westbound Interstate 94. Even though our meeting wouldn't occur at high noon as originally planned, there would be plenty of cover from the mid-afternoon lunch crowd. Margosian directed our team to move slowly from the original venue, just one car at a time, to join the undercover cops already conducting surveillance on the Burger King. If there was counter-surveillance from the bad guys, we didn't see it and they didn't detect our movement.

Sometime around 1400 hours that sunny afternoon, Jessie's contact rolled into the Burger King parking lot in a dark red Cadillac Escalade. He drove slowly once through the lot, then selected a spot all the way in back between empty parking spaces. After watching him look around for a moment, I saw him punch digits into a cell phone and place it to his ear.

"Hey crew, looks like S-1 is here," I said over the encrypted radio frequency, using terminology to describe our primary suspect. "Red Escalade all the way in back. Just picked up his phone, so he might be making the call."

"Copy that," Margosian replied. "We just got the call, that's our guy. Chachi will be inbound momentarily."

A few moments later Grammatico turned into the lot from North River Road and eased his undercover vehicle past the cars lined up in the drive-thru lanes. After crossing another 100 feet of black asphalt he came to rest in a space next to the Escalade, killed the engine and exited with the black Nike gym bag.

The good citizens coming and going all around us could not feel the tension at that moment, but for us it was palpable. As Grammatico hopped into the passenger seat of the Escalade, we all recognized the moment of truth. In a very short time, we'd know if the deal was legitimate or if this guy had showed up to steal our dope at gunpoint, an all-too-frequent action called a "rip". Even though Grammatico had a gun and was surrounded by heavily armed teammates who could get to him swiftly, things could potentially go bad just as fast.

After an eternity that was only a minute or two, Margosian's voice came across the radio. He'd been listening intently to the conversation inside the Escalade via Grammatico's concealed wireless transmitter.

"All right boys, it sounds like a good deal. Get ready to take him down as soon as Chachi is out of there. Do it quickly, I don't want him to make it to the road and end up in a chase."

A moment later, Grammatico pushed open the passenger door and stepped out carrying a different bag. This one was smaller and made of brown paper. It contained $40,000 cash in several denominations, each wrapped in color coded paper bands. I imagine the suspect had a fist pump or other celebratory gesture as Grammatico backed out of his parking space and disappeared into the afternoon traffic, but it was short lived.

Several ordinary-looking cars, including my own black Dodge Intrepid, which just a moment earlier had glided through the parking lot looking like they contained hungry Burger King customers, suddenly accelerated as we crossed the blacktop toward the red Escalade.

I stopped my UC car quickly near the front quarter panel on the passenger side of the Cadillac and exited with my Heckler & Koch Model 53 rifle pointed directly at the driver. I got a good sight picture on him as my teammates surrounded the suspect vehicle and blocked his path to potential escape. It was another tense moment. The driver's eyes were wide as he surveyed the scene, his heart no doubt racing and head spinning. Would he hit the gas and try to ram his way through the blockade, or reach for a gun to fight his way out? Fortunately, he made the only smart decision and raised his hands to surrender.

I continued to cover the suspect as several teammates opened the driver door and removed him from behind the steering wheel. He was a man in his mid-20's and this dude was large; about 6'5" tall and 275 pounds. He really wasn't overweight, either. Just a great big, athletic guy who chose not to fight with us or offer any resistance. Thank goodness.

As the suspect was placed roughly on the ground outside the car and handcuffed, two of my teammates quickly cleared the interior of the big SUV and found no one else inside. Standing on the hot pavement next to the Cadillac I used my digital Motorola Saber radio, issued to all COMET detectives, to notify Margosian that the suspect was in custody, and that we were all good. After switching frequencies to request a marked patrol car to transport the suspect, I flipped open my Nextel phone and called Chief Joe Macksoud of the Mount Clemens Police Department. He answered on the second ring.

"Hey, Jimmy. What's up?"

"Afternoon, Chief," I said. "Listen, I wanted to give you a heads up that we just did a 2-kilo reverse at the Burger King on North River Road."

"That's great!" Macksoud said. "Everybody OK?"

"Yep," I replied. "Everyone is just fine including the bad guy."

"That's good news," he said. "Attaboy, kid! Really nice job."

There was a pause before he asked, "Is that all?"

I stifled a laugh. I was expecting him to tell me he was on the way out to the scene, or that he was sending someone in his stead. But Macksoud was a different cat. Our first chief of police hired from outside the ranks, he'd come to MCPD from the Detroit Police Department, where he'd been a precinct commander after years of working the streets in uniform and undercover. A 2-kilo reverse wasn't that big of a deal to him.

"Well, Chief" I said. "I feel like in the very near future there's gonna be some MSP brass out here on your turf, maybe even the sheriff. It is an election year, after all. Just didn't want you to hear about it from them."

"Oh," he replied. "Yeah, you're probably right, kid. I was about to head home, so I'll slide by there on my way."

I didn't wait for him to arrive.

While Grammatico and Margosian left to meet the transport car at the Macomb County Jail and interview the suspect, I helped with getting the Cadillac impounded and securing evidence back at the COMET office, then assisted in serving a search warrant at the suspect's home in another Detroit suburb on the other side of town. I couldn't wait to hear the results of the interview; if they could get this guy to flip, we might be onto something big.

When an arrestee agreed to become a confidential informant for COMET, he or she was usually required to do three felony deals to 'work off' their own felony charge. In other words, three people had to go to jail for the confidential informant to have their charges dismissed. If they flipped immediately upon being arrested, that usually that meant their charges would never be filed. The case would be quietly and confidentially closed without any public record, as if it never happened. It didn't always work out perfectly, but it did in this case.

Our suspect in the red Escalade turned out to be highly motivated. He'd recently graduated from a large university where he'd been a star athlete. His short-lived foray into professional sports hadn't worked out but he'd still been paid a decent amount of money in that time, hence his wish to parlay it into something bigger via drug dealing. Even though that idea was stupid, he was smart enough to realize his mistake immediately. He knew his future was bright and that the only way to protect it was to get out from under the dope charges as fast as he could. He also had connections in the narcotics world and the gift of gab; it turned out this guy could sell ice cubes to Eskimos. He was someone toward whom others naturally gravitated; they just wanted to be around him and be involved with whatever he was doing. He was a leader. It meant that some people were about to get pulled into our world against their wishes.

Before we all went home that night, Grammatico and Margosian gave us the breakdown of their interview with the man I'll call Hoss (because he was big, like Hoss Cartwright on the TV show *Bonanza)*. Hoss was ready to work. He wanted no part of prison or even the county jail. He spelled out a deal he could put together immediately, in which our undercover officer (Grammatico) could buy Afghani heroin. The description and details were enough to convince Margosian to release Hoss from the jail without going through the booking process and creating a legal record of his presence there. It was a risk, since Hoss could have disappeared in the wind, but one that paid off handsomely.

Over the next few days our team started to plot and plan the deal that Hoss was putting together. There were a lot of details to work out, but the gist was that Hoss would introduce Grammatico to some bad guys willing to sell 500 grams of heroin for $60,000; that's half of a kilo, or about 1.1 pounds. The price seemed outrageous but, because the United States military had recently invaded Afghanistan in the aftermath of 9/11, supply was short while demand had not abated; in fact, it was increasing.

The deal would go down at a chain hotel just north of M-59, near its intersection with the M-53 Expressway. A room was reserved on the second floor under a fictitious identity, with an adjoining room next door. At our request, special surveillance technology was placed in the room by the MSP Technical Services Unit so that we could remotely monitor video and audio in high definition. This included a completely normal looking 44-ounce drink cup with actual soda pop and ice inside. The only difference being the fiber optic camera inside the drinking straw, which would send a live feed to the laptop computer in the adjoining room.

We closely examined the L-shaped hotel and surrounding property, with overhead maps and in-person inspections, to determine where to place our human assets. All four COMET teams would be needed to properly secure the deal. Every hotel room in the place was accessed from the outside, either adjacent to the parking lot or from the outdoor walkway on the second floor. Inside the adjoining room would be our Street Narcotics team. Grammatico was our teammate, and we would enter the room when it was time to make the bust, or to rescue him if it became necessary before then. The Surveillance, Conspiracy, and Fugitive teams would combine to create an inner perimeter on the ground floor and an outer perimeter covering the parking lot and its egress to M-59. Finally, we'd have uniformed state troopers in marked police cars, which we referred to as 'rollers', tucked away out of sight near the northbound and southbound on-ramps to M-53, to assist us on the hotel property if needed or to engage in pursuit of the suspects if they breached our perimeters. We tried our best to keep it simple, but there was a lot of ground to cover and many variables. It was essential that everyone knew their assignment and completed it successfully.

A week later, the day had arrived. A briefing was held in the COMET office and assignments were detailed on a large white grease board attached to the wall in the spacious briefing area of the former factory building. Some of the cops slouched on the big comfy couches, while others sat at the long table or stood nearby. Friendly insults and replies were traded among the group until Margosian called everyone to order. A detailed map of the property and surrounding area, carefully drawn in several shades of dry-erase markers, showed all the points of ingress and egress to the hotel, it's parking lot, and the nearby highways. Also on the board was a color photo of Hoss, our newest confidential informant, so that no one from the other COMET teams would mistake him for one of the newest bad guys.

When the briefing ended, we headed out to the hotel in stages. The Street Narcotics Team went first, but even then we arrived separately so as not to raise suspicion entering the room. Next came detectives assigned to the inner perimeter, then the outer perimeter. Finally, our rollers arrived and made themselves invisible nearby. We double-checked all the surveillance equipment inside the room and ensured that the door between the two rooms appeared to be locked from the bad guys' side but was easily accessible for us to make entry when the time came. When all was found to be well, Margosian placed the call.

"Chachi," Margosian said when his call was answered. "You guys good to go?"

Grammatico reported that he and Hoss were ready to roll from the coffee shop where they were waiting, so Margosian told him to head for the hotel and get settled in the room. Upon their arrival 15 minutes later, they were a sight to see. Hoss possessed his usual intimidating presence and

Grammatico looked the part, too. Wearing a three-quarter length black leather jacket over fitted slacks with a collared white shirt and sporting his thick black hair in a stylish cut, Chachi couldn't have looked more "mobbed up" then he did that day. He reminded me of Christopher Moltisanti from *The Sopranos*.

Inside the adjoining room our team stacked up in a line behind our point man, Trooper Dave "Dutch" Vansingel. He would be the first person through the door separating the two rooms when we made entry to take down the bad guys. He wore body armor in a dark blue vest carrier with Velcro placards front and back that said, "State Police", and he carried an MSP-issued Sig Sauer P226 chambered in 9mm. I was immediately behind him with a Benelli M1 Super 90 12-gauge shotgun. As Vansingel knelt on the threadbare carpet next to the door and I crouched over his shoulder, we watched and listened as the laptop computer quietly displayed the feed from the surveillance equipment inside the main room.

Margosian called Grammatico again once he and Hoss were established in the room and told him to have Hoss put in the call to the bad guys. Half an hour later, they arrived.

Three raps on the hotel room door announced the presence of three Black male suspects waiting outside. As Hoss turned the handle and pulled open the door, his huge frame filled the space. When the three tried to enter, Hoss placed one of his giant paws against the first man's chest to stop him.

"Gotta pat you down, bruh", Hoss told him.

It must have been a practice the man was accustomed to when selling drugs, because he immediately raised both hands and stood peacefully while Hoss checked his waistband and pant legs for weapons. The process was repeated on the second man after Hoss allowed the first one to enter. As the third man crossed the threshold of the doorway, Hoss motioned for him to raise his hands.

"Nah, man" he told Hoss. "I got my shit."

That man then lifted his white oversized RocaWear t-shirt, exposing the black knurled grip of a Glock semiautomatic pistol. Hoss looked in the man's eyes for a brief moment before letting him enter. There wasn't really another option. It wasn't crazy to think a group of dope dealers would have an armed enforcer when they showed up with half a kilo of heroin and expected to leave with sixty grand.

I turned my head toward Vansingel and made eye contact. Dutch nodded to me, acknowledging that he saw the gunman and heard what he'd said. He was still visible on the laptop monitor, standing close to the door away from the others, and would be to our immediate left when we burst into the room. I turned to my teammates in the stack behind us and held up three fingers, then made a pistol shape with my thumb and index finger and held it in front of my belt buckle. Each of them understood that the third man had a gun in the front of his waistband.

Good cops always presume bad guys could be armed and prepare for that eventuality but seeing that gun definitely cranked up the suspense a few notches. It wouldn't be long now.

Grammatico silently leaned against the back wall of the hotel room, near the small bathroom, playing his role of 'money man' while Hoss coordinated the transaction. The second man who'd entered the room produced from his jacket a large resealable plastic bag; the kind made by Ziploc called a 1-gallon 'freezer bag'. Light brown powder speckled with white filled the bottom third of the clear container. Afghanistan's finest.

When the dope was placed on the king-sized bed, Grammatico followed suit with the money in a folded brown paper bag. When the first man who'd entered the room picked up the cash, Margosian said, "Let's go".

The door between the two adjoining rooms was yanked back and our team barreled through. As our teammates shouted "Police! Hands up!", Vansingel and I made an immediate hard left turn towards the dude with the Glock. We expected an armed confrontation but instead got a surprise. He was gone.

As soon as the door between the rooms was cracked, the man with the gun had bolted outside and down the second-floor elevated walkway. Vansingel quickly followed but almost as quickly turned back to remain with our team. The inner and outer perimeter units were there for just such an occurrence and Vansingel radioed them immediately to advise of the fleeing gunman. Each of the cops on both perimeter units had seen the group of suspects approach and enter the room, so they recognized the man who was trying to escape. They caught him in the parking lot and took him down hard as he ran toward a vehicle with a female in the driver seat. It was she who'd driven the trio to our drug deal.

Back in the hotel room there was some brief resistance from the other two suspects, but the team had overwhelmed them. Soon they were face down on the bed and floor, respectively, and no one was any worse for wear. The mission was a success.

The two rollers we'd hidden away near the freeway now came forward into the parking lot to separately transport the pair of suspects from inside the room to the Macomb County Jail.

A third police car was called to transport the gunman, following some short-lived excitement. After handcuffing the man face down in the parking lot, the detectives assigned to the outer perimeter checked his body and clothing for the gun but came up empty. He was now unarmed. The entire scene was scoured for the gun, and it was finally located underneath dirty linens in a wheeled laundry cart used by housekeeping staff. It had been standing next to a second-floor room a few doors down, and the man had pitched the gun in there while sprinting past.

If a casual observer were to believe this deal was a pretty great effort by our newest confidential informant, they would be correct. But there were factors that made this one unique. Usually, we took pains to separate a confidential informant from the suspicion of the bad guys. In this case, Hoss had no such protection, and he didn't want it. He knew he could put the deal together and that it would go a long way toward getting him out from under the weight of criminal charges that could ruin his life. It was a courageous move to make, and it worked. Hoss went on to set up several more high-profile drug deals which were all successful and got some serious bad guys off the street. In the end, criminal charges were never filed against Hoss, and he lives a successful life today like it never happened.

Donuts and Armor Guard

In Detroit, you're either on the East side or the West side. It all depends on your position relevant to the dividing line, which is Woodward Avenue. Despite that famous line sung by Steve Perry in the classic Journey song, there exists no "South Detroit". There is an area in the southwest part of the city called Mexicantown which has the most authentic restaurants north of the Rio Grande, but I digress.

Detroit's northern border is 8 Mile Road, made famous by another great artist (and movie). A mile to the south is 7 Mile, then 6 Mile. On the far east side of town these streets become Vernier Road, Moross Road, and Cadieux Road, respectively, as they cross into an area which was designed according to the French Colonial "long lot" system hundreds of years ago, prior to the Northwest Ordinance survey grid.

At the intersection of Moross Road and Interstate 94, for decades, stood a Dawn Donuts shop. Immediately adjacent to the exit ramp, it was a small building with a big asphalt parking lot on the southeast corner. Bigger still was the sign that towered above it, plainly visible to travelers on the freeway. It featured a smiling, chubby-cheeked cartoon chef dressed all in white, with a puffy baker's hat, holding a big tray of donuts and standing on a red rectangular box. On both sides of the red box were the words 'Dawn Donuts, Drive In' in white block letters, highlighted with neon tubes.

As a little kid, sitting in the back seat of my parents' car, I'd see the Dawn Donuts sign and know that was our exit as we drove to see my grandparents at Thanksgiving and Christmas. As an adult, flying around the east side doing deals with my COMET crew, the sign remained. The little donut chef was always smiling at me, a friendly beacon in a neighborhood that wasn't always so. He's gone now. The chain was bought up by Dunkin Donuts and the property at Moross Road and I-94 sold to someone who plopped a cruddy cell phone business there. The building is covered in advertisements; 'Free Phones! Fast Repairs!'. The new sign is purple and sticks out like a sore thumb; perhaps that was the idea.

It was in the shadow of that little chef, however, that I met with a confidential informant (CI) named Candace on a late weekday afternoon in autumn just before rush hour. My teammate Mark Berger, aka Cheese, sat in his undercover car a just few spaces away, watching closely. We almost never met with female informants alone, lest one of them get the bright idea to cozy up to her handler in exchange for cash or other considerations. Doing so would get them fired as confidential informants and if they chose to make a false claim of harassment in return, we always had a witness.

Candace was used up. Her thin body, thinning blonde hair and hollow eyes spoke of the difficult life she'd led; a life made harder by the drugs she used to ease her pain. Candace had been referred to me by a uniformed patrol officer who'd arrested her on a traffic stop for possession of cocaine. She had several prior felony convictions for drugs and if she didn't work off her current charges, a lengthy prison sentence was likely.

Wearing a short-sleeved purple t-shirt with Prince and the Revolution on the front, blue jeans which were tight and ripped several times, and dirty white Reeboks, Candace sat in the front passenger seat of my black Dodge Intrepid as I went over the same rules and instructions she'd heard before. It was to be our third controlled purchase of crack cocaine from a dealer she knew only as 'Prophet', a buy that would establish Candace as a reliable informant in the eyes of the court. If successful, we'd serve a search warrant on Prophet's house later that night.

"Here's another fifty bucks," I said, handing her two twenty-dollar bills and a ten spot. Each had been dutifully recorded before I left the COMET office. "Have you been over there since the last buy?"

"Yeah," she confessed. As she cast her gaze away from me she admitted, "I was there last night."

I wasn't foolish enough to think that confidential informants didn't continue to smoke dope on their own time. It would have been better for Candace if she stayed away from people like Prophet altogether, but it was advantageous for us that she didn't.

"How did he seem?" I asked. "Did you notice anything different, anything that might be useful for us?"

"I sure fucking did," she replied. "He keeps the dope in the freezer. And that ain't all!"

Like many good informants I employed over the years, Candace wasn't stupid. She'd made many bad choices in her life, but she was observant and street smart; two qualities that kept her alive in 'The D', as Detroit is often called.

"What else?" I asked, eyebrows raised.

"He's got a gun. A big gun, like that one cop on Miami Vice," she said.

"Crockett or Tubbs?" I asked, half-jokingly.

"The white guy," she replied.

In my mind I filed away an image of the Smith & Wesson Model 4506 that Sonny Crockett carried back in the day, the show having ended many years before, and asked her where the gun was kept.

"I saw it when I sat on the couch in the living room, right by the front door. It was shoved down between the cushions."

"Ok, that's good shit," I told Candace. "Let's get rolling. Remember, straight there and then straight back here. And don't forget the golden rule."

"I know, man. I know," she said, referring to her understanding that if she were to smoke any of the crack cocaine she was about to purchase with our marked money, her whole arrangement would disappear. She'd no longer be a confidential informant and she'd have to face the consequences of her original arrest and certain felony conviction.

Candace pulled the handle and threw her right shoulder into the passenger door to push it open. She clambered out and hopped in her ancient two-door Pontiac Grand Am with teal metallic paint and two missing hub caps, one on each side. As she fired the engine to life and pulled out of the parking lot, I keyed my encrypted Motorola digital radio and waited for the chirp while holding it out of sight below the window level.

"Ok crew, CI is out and away," I said. "She's 9-bound and down on the 4 by 3, crossing the ditch now."

I'd let my teammates know that the confidential informant was traveling westbound on 7 Mile (Moross Road) and

crossing Interstate 94. Surveillance terminology was initially confusing, but once you learned it was like being fluent in another language that protected you from anyone who might possess your radio frequency and encryption key.

The route was simple. My CI was going to travel 10 blocks due west, then turn left in the shadow of St. Jude Catholic Church onto Kelly Road. From there it was a short distance to Prophet's house in the 18000 block of Kelly, just north of Saratoga.

"I got her, Diss," said Jeff Pintal, callsign 'Mini'. "She's in my trunk."

Pintal was letting me know that the CI was behind him, not actually in the trunk of his car. While Pintal led the way, unbeknownst to Candace, Berger would follow. A third teammate, Ron Lehman aka 'Chief', was stationary in the middle of the block on Kelly Road and would watch the CI enter and leave the premises, a key component in securing a search warrant. I would remain stationary to meet Candace when she returned. As far as she knew, I was the only cop present. If there were any complications along the way, I was close enough to be there in two minutes or less.

Just a minute or two later Candace approached the intersection at Kelly Road and Pintal keyed up on the radio, "Ok she's set up for a 6-bound shot on the main. Lights flipped and she's away, I'm ten. You got her, Chief?"

"Yep," Lehman replied. "She's curbing it in front of the crib right now. Ok, she's out of the ride, up and inside through the front door."

After just a short while, Candace exited the dope house. The rolling surveillance was repeated in reverse, and she pulled alongside my undercover car in the Dawn Donuts parking lot about five minutes later. This time she stayed in her own car and rolled down her driver door window, as Berger eased into a parking space nearby.

"He's fat right now," Candace said as she reached across into my car and dropped a plastic baggie containing three big white chunks of crack cocaine onto my lap. I picked up the bag and looked at it closely. Each rock was easily worth twenty dollars or more, but apparently she'd received a discount as a regular customer. In her streetwise manner, she had just informed me that Prophet was holding a large quantity of drugs. That was good news for us. I wanted to hustle back to the office and get the search warrant written and signed, then brief up the team and hit the door before he sold all his inventory.

"Where's the kitchen located inside the house?" I asked. "Is he still keeping the dope in the freezer?".

"Yeah, he told me to come into the kitchen with him," she said. "It's in the rear, by the back door. The fridge is next to a big window looking out at the back yard. That's when I saw the fat sack that he pulled out of the freezer."

"All right, cool." I replied. "Nice work."

"Am I good now?" she asked. "Are you gonna get my charges dropped?"

"We'll see," I said. "It depends how much dope we get when we raid his place. Maybe we'll do it next week. Hit the road and I'll call you later."

Candace rolled her eyes and her shoulders slumped. She looked sad as she put her ghetto sled in reverse and backed out of her space, then pulled out of the lot and disappeared down the ramp and onto the freeway. The truth was that she had done a great job and we had more than enough probable cause to get a search warrant signed by a judge, which I was going to do immediately so that we could knock down Prophet's door that night. But the first rule of handling informants is that you do not, under any circumstances, trust an informant. Allowing Candace to know when we would raid Prophet's house could have bad consequences. At very least the dope might disappear, and we'd hit a dry hole; at worst, someone could get killed.

"Ok, crew," I said over our radio frequency. "That was a good deal. Well done, thanks for the help! Sounds like Prophet is sitting fat, so let's head for the office. I'll get a search warrant signed and we can pay him a visit."

Like a pack of hungry wolves sprinting after prey, we all shot down the freeway ramp and jumped into the far left lane. Pedal to the metal, we each made it back to the industrial park which housed the COMET office in about 10 minutes. Routinely blasting through posted speed limits was simply part of working narcotics. I'm not justifying it, exactly, but the team always had a dozen deals lined up and there were only so many hours in the day. It was a practice that my lovely bride did not enjoy when I was off duty and forgot to slow the hell down.

After keying open the dead bolt on the former factory's glass front door, I walked quickly through the carpeted office space occupied by our two secretaries, Claudine and Patty. They worked the dayshift, so we didn't see them too often except on Fridays. I always respected and admired them for their dedication to the team's success. They would bust your chops in a heartbeat if you were failing in your administrative duties or writing crap reports, but they wanted us to succeed. Each of them assisted me countless times with their expertise pertaining to state police reporting rules, case management, accounting for cash expenditures, and many other issues. And they both possessed great humor, an essential ingredient for success in a high-stress environment.

I strode through an intersection with the hallway on my right, which led to executive offices, and into the large open portion of the building once occupied by tool and die molds or plastic injection presses; I never knew which. Perhaps it had held something altogether different, inventory or other machinery. The high-ceilinged room now housed a catacomb of bland office cubicles divided into four distinct jurisdictions.

Way back in the far left corner, almost out of sight, was the Violent Crimes (Fugitive) team's little village. If you made an immediate right turn, you'd cross into Surveillance team territory and then the kitchen and dining area. Straight ahead was Conspiracy, smallest of the four COMET teams as it was essentially a couple of state troopers who were our liaisons with DEA. Beyond the Conspiracy cubbyholes was our open briefing area with whiteboards, couches, a long table and a big screen TV.

Past that, along the far wall, was a combination-locked vault door that opened into the evidence and property room; it was a strict 'no-go' zone. A female state police sergeant, whom we affectionately called 'the Property Nazi', oversaw all COMET evidence and was the only human on the premises who possessed the combination to the former bank vault lock. It was a necessary arrangement. Protecting the chain of custody in criminal cases is very important, lest a defense attorney challenge its integrity in court. Once we processed our drugs, guns, and money, we secured them in nearby temporary evidence lockers. The good sergeant would retrieve those packages the following morning, catalog them officially, then lodge each one inside her domain until it was needed for trial or marked for destruction. I can tell you that when she cracked open that vault, the aroma from pounds of weed, cocaine, and heroin infiltrated the entire building.

On this day, however, I turned quickly left into the Street Narcotics sector. We had the most cubicles because we had the most detectives; on average, 8 or 10 total. Walking past them, each desk usually featured a computer monitor adorned with yellow sticky notes, surrounded by court subpoenas and calendars pinned to corkboards on the wall. There were also personal touches. Pintal was a Star Wars junkie, and his many photos and figurines left no doubt about that fact. Berger listened to gangster rap music just to figure out what they were saying, so that he could speak the language on the street. Passing my workstation, you were likely to see a poster of Eddie, the iconic mascot of my favorite band Iron Maiden. And across the way my counterpart, Detective Sergeant Brian Kozlowski, displayed sobering quotes from Ernest Hemingway and a life-sized cardboard cutout of Brooke Burke.

Finally, all the way in back, was the expansive lair of the lieutenant. MSP Detective Lieutenant Rich Margosian, that is; callsign 'Deak'. Margosian deserved and needed that space, though, as his was a tough assignment. Managing almost a dozen 'Type A' hard chargers and their often-times complex investigations required patience and attention to detail. Sometimes it was supremely stressful, and Margosian's reliever was chocolate peanut M&M's. There was always a bag in his desk somewhere, and not the size you received while trick-or-treating as a kid on Halloween. Ironically, the large packages of chocolate peanut M&M's came in packages weighing 2.2 pounds, or exactly 1 kilo. If you pissed off the boss for an offense which wasn't too terrible, he was likely to cast his gaze your way and say, "You owe me a kilo."

"Hey, boss," I said. "You got a second?"

"Sure, Diss," he replied. "Your buy go OK?"

I caught Margosian up on my Kelly Road case as efficiently as I could. He was a busy guy and I wanted to get the search warrant affidavit started as soon as possible. When I'd given him the complete rundown, I asked him if we could fit the search warrant execution in that evening after the warrant was signed.

"Yep, the schedule is clear," Margosian declared. "Get it done and let me know when you're ready to go. We'll brief it up with the crew here and then roll out."

"Thanks, L-T," I replied, already moving toward my desk nearby.

I sat down on my wheeled office chair and opened the file on my computer desktop which contained search warrant templates. They were affidavits I'd successfully written in the past for various people, places, and things. The idea was to save time by inserting the relevant data for an upcoming search warrant execution into an existing document that contained the necessary legal framework, so I didn't have to retype all of it each time. The file contained past affidavits for searching houses, apartments, businesses, vehicles, boats, mobile phones, call data records, even human bodies for blood and DNA. Once sworn to before a judge and signed, the affidavits officially became search warrants.

I selected the basic template for a residential structure. Into the affidavit I entered the details of Prophet's house, having taken several photos of it during prior surveillance. Then I described all three of the controlled purchases we made from the home using our confidential informant.

Candace was only ever referred to in official documents by her 'CI Number', never her name. The CI Number was a designation which an informant received after being signed up, vetted according to MSP guidelines, and recorded at MSP headquarters in Lansing. I never received any legal challenges from defense attorneys to reveal an informant's actual name. But if a judge had ordered me to do so, I wouldn't have complied. I would have simply requested the criminal charges against the defendant be dropped and moved on to my next case. No dope case is worth getting an informant killed. It also makes it tough to get new informants if they know your agency can't be trusted.

After about 30 minutes of typing, my newest affidavit was complete; now, I just needed a judge to sign it. It was almost dinner time and the courts had closed for the day. I'd have to contact a jurist who was assigned to be on-call after hours for that week. I'd awakened many judges in the middle of the night for such purposes. I even met the Honorable Judge Linda Davis on a golf course as she made the turn to play her back nine holes one sunny afternoon. The rest of her foursome had a chuckle as she read and signed my affidavit on the 10th tee box.

I had in mind a particular person on this day, however. I'll call him Stan. He was a magistrate of the 41st District Court and mostly handled disputed traffic tickets. Although his position was appointed, rather than elected, Stan still possessed the same legal authority as a sitting judge. Since all judges in Michigan have statewide jurisdiction, it didn't matter that we were leaving Macomb County to execute a search warrant in Detroit. If my affidavit was deserving, Stan could sign it.

Best of all, Stan was just a good guy. He was smart and loved a good laugh. He was a socially adept person who could talk to anyone about anything but was also capable of being quite serious when required. He answered my call on the second ring and I requested to meet him for a review of my affidavit.

"Sure thing," Stan said. "Meet me at my office."

"In the court building?" I asked.

"Nah, bro," he replied. "My other office!"

I knew what he meant. Fifteen minutes after hanging up, I walked into Johnny G's Bar & Grill through the back door off the parking lot. Seeing Stan seated at the bar having a burger and beer, I settled onto the high-top barstool next to his.

"Hey, Jimmy," he greeted me. "Want a cold one?"

I told Stan that I'd love one, but unfortunately my day was far from over. I needed to cross the T's, dot the I's, and hit the road.

"Ok, ok," he said. "Let me see what ya got."

I made sure the bar top wasn't wet, then placed the three-page affidavit and search warrant in front of him. He scanned it quickly and completely. As he reached into his jacket pocket for something to sign his name with, I held a black Sharpie S-Gel pen in front him cocked and locked.

"Thanks, buddy," Stan said, making the document official with his looping and completely illegible autograph. "You sure I can't get you something?"

"Next time!" I said, already off the stool and heading for the door. "Thanks, Stan!"

When I walked back into the COMET office, I could hear the team talking and laughing over near the briefing area. Margosian had them assembled and ready for the raid briefing.

"Hey, Diss," Margosian said as I approached. "We good to go?"

"Roger that, boss," I said, holding up my black leather binder which contained the signed search warrant as I walked to the large white board on the wall.

I had previously drawn a rudimentary map of the Kelly Road house and property on the whiteboard using dry erase markers in several colors, including the driveway and location of the main entry door. Next to the map I'd listed our personnel and their respective assignments.

I would 'shotgun the door', as I usually did when we executed search warrants using the MSP-mandated method of dynamic building entry. That simply meant that I was first through the door and employed a shotgun as my primary weapon; an all-black Benelli M1 Super 90 12-gauge semi-automatic model, with a pistol grip, extended magazine tube, and Surefire tactical light, to be exact. My cover man, number two in the stack, was Kozlowski. Koz, also an operator and leader on the Macomb County SWAT Team, was perfect for that role because he was a few inches taller than me and could easily see what was ahead of us inside a hostile environment. He could also be plenty hostile himself when the situation called for it, and there was no one in the world I trusted more than Koz to have my back. His left hand was usually on my right shoulder so that we didn't get separated, and together we'd move through any structure efficiently and confront anyone we encountered.

In the lineup behind us would be the rest of the team in close single-file formation. As Koz and I encountered bad guys and ordered them to the floor, the next person in the stack would be responsible for handcuffing them and making sure they didn't try to escape. Our team would move through the building in that manner, like a long heavily armed snake, until the entire place was cleared. This method differed greatly from the technique we employed during SWAT Team entries, but it was still effective and worthwhile.

After assigning duties for the entry, I described the approach. The front door, through which we would enter, featured armor guard. Designed to keep out intruders, an armor guard outer door was like a screen door except that it was made of iron bars and had a large locking latch. Fortunately, we had a special type of key and plenty of practice using it. Last in the stack were the breachers, in this instance Berger and Brian Dowell, nicknamed Guido for his resemblance to Father Guido Sarducci of Saturday Night Live fame. They acted as a rear guard while we were moving and would be called upon to defeat the armor guard if necessary.

Finally, I told my team what Candace had said about the gun and where the crack cocaine was located, describing the couch near the front door and the location of the refrigerator with an up top freezer toward the back of the house.

It was at that point that Margosian spoke up.

"If the gun is in the front room and you're planning to go through the front door," he said, "then I will cover the rear. If he's up front, you guys will deal with him. If he heads for the back, I got a little something for him." Margosian coached high school baseball and had been a fair player himself. It turned out that he still swung the bat quite well.

"Thanks, boss," I said, as the briefing ended. "Let's get our gear together and roll out in 10 minutes."

Just then, across the open briefing area, I saw MSP Trooper Sarah Krebs entering the room. Krebs frequently volunteered to be our uniformed patrol presence, just as I had done in Mount Clemens 10 years earlier. Since troopers had statewide jurisdiction, accompanying us to Detroit was not a problem. Her presence, in her marked MSP patrol car, would ensure that no one mistook us for us for a home invasion crew, and she could also transport our suspect directly to jail when all was said and done. Years later, Krebs would become a world-renowned forensic artist who created lifelike drawings and sculptures of missing persons, while also advancing through the MSP command ranks.

"Hi, Sarah," I said. "Glad you could make it!"

"Hey, Diss," she replied with a smile. "You know I wouldn't miss this. Beats the hell out of writing traffic tickets, right?"

"My philosophy exactly," I replied.

Across the office was heard the sound of Velcro as everyone donned their Kevlar vests and secured weapons. A few minutes later we loaded into the dark blue, windowless Chevy panel van used by COMET for raids. Today it was driven by Dowell. Margosian was in the front passenger seat as Dowell pulled out of the lot behind Krebs in her blue goose, the name given by cops to MSP patrol cars, and soon we were flying up the ramp onto Interstate 94 from Shook Road.

Ten minutes later we exited at Moross Road and made a right turn.

"About two minutes out, fellas," I said.

That was the point at which I always silently said a quick prayer for the safety of our team and success of the mission. It must have done some good, because we never had a serious incident in all my years with COMET, SWAT, and MCU. I was involved in over 400 search warrant executions, by conservative estimate, and personally never suffered more than a dislocated shoulder. Of course, there were other reasons; proper training, high-quality teammates, speed, surprise, and violence of action all played a role.

Soon we made the left turn onto Kelly Road and Margosian said, "Here we go, boys!'

As Dowell and Krebs killed their headlights and glided to a stop in front of Prophet's house, Kozlowski ripped open the sliding side door and we quickly piled out, already lined up in proper order for the assault. Krebs drove her scout car over the curb and onto the front yard as we approached the door. At the moment the front door was breached and entry was made, but not before, she would briefly activate the overhead light and siren of her police car to make sure everyone knew it was the cops coming through the door.

Our stack quickly ascended three steps onto the home's front stoop as Margosian made his way around a corner, disappearing behind the house. Dowell placed the adze, or bladed edge, of his Halligan tool into the space between the strike plate of the armor guard door and its iron frame. Berger then drove the blade deep into that gap by striking it with a wicked blow from his hand-held battering ram.

"POLICE!" I yelled. "Search warrant!"

Using his body weight, Dowell then pulled backward with all his might and the armor guard door popped open. It was a coordinated move they'd practiced many times. As the iron door swung around on its hinges, Berger reared back again and struck the interior wooden door with his battering ram just in front of the knob. Berger was also an ex-ballplayer and athlete; that door was no match for him. It almost flew off its hinges and, just like that, we were inside.

Momentarily bathed in the red glow of Krebs's patrol car bubble light, I moved through the threshold and into the foyer. With my Benelli raised and pointed downrange, Koz's big paw on my shoulder, I saw Prophet turn into the hallway. He'd come from the kitchen and was walking purposefully when he looked up at us; what a sight it must have been.

"POLICE!" I yelled.

"AAAHHGG!" said Prophet, eyes wide as he spun around and sprinted for the kitchen.

As one unit we continued forward toward him quickly but efficiently, not chasing or running. Even if he was trying to get to the dope before we did, which he undoubtedly was, we didn't break from our disciplined advance. My first concern had been the living room near the front door and its couch that might contain a gun. But the small room was clearly empty, so we bypassed it for the moment and kept moving.

Rounding the corner from hallway into kitchen, we saw and heard the big plate glass window along the back wall near the fridge explode and rain shards down onto the dirty vinyl-covered floor.

"AAAHHGG!" said Prophet, again, this time spinning to run away but having nowhere to go except directly at us. Hands up, he surrendered.

Margosian had anticipated Prophet trying to retrieve his crack cocaine and was waiting in the back yard next to the window, a 34-inch Louisville Slugger metal baseball bat in hand. When he saw Prophet round the corner at high speed heading for the fridge, Margosian stepped into the pitch and hit a bomb. Miguel Cabrera couldn't have struck that window any harder.

The first two detectives in our stack secured Prophet. The raid team continued throughout the house, but we found no one else inside. As Krebs marched Prophet outside and then transported him to Macomb County Jail, we broke up the stack and stowed our weapons and equipment before beginning our search of the premises.

The first place checked was the top-shelf freezer of the fridge. A knotted plastic bag concealed inside a purple Crown Royal pouch contained about three ounces of crack cocaine, and several thousand dollars in cash money was later found rubber-banded in the top shelf of a bedroom dresser. Tucked in between couch cushions, just as Candace has said, was a fully loaded semi-automatic handgun. It was chambered in .45 ACP caliber, just like Sonny Crockett's, but this was a Colt Model 1911 with a faded nickel satin finish. When I later queried the serial number through the National Crime Information Center, we learned that it had been reported stolen in the city of Chicago, Illinois.

It was a good day. Busting dope dealers in metropolitan Detroit was a lot like playing Whac-A-Mole, but it was a worthy endeavor, nonetheless. Candace earned her shot at staying out of prison, though I lost contact with her not long afterward. Hopefully she made the most of it. And our boss demonstrated once again that low-tech solutions to tactical challenges are sometimes the best.

River Rats

Working a midnight patrol shift in Marysville could be challenging. Not in the traditional way that I was accustomed to at Mount Clemens PD, encountering felons on a nightly basis, but trying to stay awake and focused when there was literally nothing happening. I tried to remember that while it wasn't the target-rich environment I longed for, it was important to stay vigilant for when something serious did arise. The reason for the slow pace was due to the good people who lived in Marysville; they worked hard, paid their taxes, and generally obeyed the law. It's the same reason Cyndi and I chose to move there and raise our children. So, I felt an obligation to be observant and attentive, no matter how bored I frequently was in the small hours.

On a particularly lonely summer night I was working the road in patrol car 676. My friend John Stover was in car 677, and around 0300 hours we were dispatched to a private boat dock in front of a home along the St Clair River. The homeowner reported that there were two men on her property, possibly trying to steal her fishing equipment. She was looking through the living room window of her waterfront home from a distance of about 100 yards but could see shadows moving on the dock.

This was a typical call for service in Marysville, so I wasn't too excited, but I was very close to the woman's home when the call went out. The city has a 4.5 mile shoreline along the big river, which is also an international border with the province of Ontario, Canada. With a single turn onto River Road from the nearby highway I found myself approaching the home.

As I traveled south along the river's edge my headlights illuminated a burgundy-colored Ford Explorer near the woman's dock. The SUV was facing me with its headlights extinguished. I drove past slowly and in the shadows near the water I could see two Black males walking from the dock toward the parked vehicle. When they saw the patrol car they each froze just for an instant, then continued walking with the objects they were carrying; large canvas duffel packs that I recognized as hockey equipment bags.

They didn't run or freak out, just continued as if their actions were perfectly normal. I didn't stop either. I kept driving south right past them for about 200 yards until I reached an entrance to the city park. I kept it casual as I watched them in the patrol car's side view mirror, using my turn signal as I entered the park. Nothing to see here, boys! Just a small-town cop with no idea why you might be loading hockey bags from a boat dock into an SUV on an international border at three in the morning.

I was pretty sure they weren't on their way to a hockey game, so when I entered the park I immediately killed my headlights, spun around to a spot where I could keep an eye on them, and called Stover on my mobile phone. Stover was an excellent young police officer who, like most cops hired at Marysville PD, had started out at with a larger police force in metropolitan Detroit. He was someone I trusted completely, and I was glad he was on duty to help me with the high-risk traffic stop that was about to take place.

I briefed Stover on my observations, and he positioned himself about halfway between my location and Interstate 94, since that was the most likely direction for the suspects to move their suspicious cargo. After another minute, the SUV's rear deck lights lit up when the driver stepped on the brake and shifted into gear. The headlights came on and the Explorer was northbound. I switched my digital police radio over to the car-to-car frequency, so that I could call out the vehicle's direction to Stover without the county-wide dispatch hearing our transmissions.

I followed the vehicle but stayed a good distance behind them, hoping they wouldn't identify the Dodge Charger in their rearview mirror as a police car. The driver carefully obeyed the speed limit and used turn signals properly at each intersection. From my training and prior experience working undercover narcotics, I knew that I had probable cause to stop and investigate the two men. Their suspicious actions along an international border in the middle of the night, combined with the frightened 911 call of the property owner, was more than enough to stop the car. A judge later agreed with that assessment when the suspects' lawyers challenged my motives in court, insisting that I stopped them only because they were Black.

As the suspects turned from State Highway 29 onto Huron Avenue, they traveled west past Marysville High School. This area was a wide, well-illuminated four lane roadway and a good place to conduct a 'felony stop', which occurs when the suspects or circumstances are potentially more dangerous than usual. The procedure calls for officers to remain back near their patrol cars and give loud verbal commands for the occupants to slowly exit, rather than walking up to the car and asking, '*May I see your driver's license, registration, and insurance please?*'

Stover fell in beside me as we closed distance on the suspect vehicle, so I switched over to the main radio frequency and called out our location and intentions. The dispatcher issued a county-wide order to "hold the air" so the radio frequency would remain available to us if things went sideways. We activated our overhead lights and the vehicle slowly pulled to the curb. We stopped a safe distance behind it, aiming our patrol car spotlights at the vehicle's interior.

As Stover began to call out commands such as 'Turn off the vehicle!' and 'Toss the keys out the window', I covered down on the vehicle and its occupants with my .223 caliber Colt M4 Carbine from behind the driver side front pillar of my patrol car. From that angle I could look over the top of my EOTech holographic gunsight and see the driver looking right back at me in his side view mirror.

Ignoring Stover's commands he shouted at me, "Why you stopping us?"

The midst of a felony traffic stop is not the time to question the legal justification of cops who clearly have the tactical advantage, and we were not about to start answering them. As Stover continued to give calm clear directions, I watched the driver pick up his cell phone and make a call.

"676 and 677, what is your status?" the dispatcher asked over the digital radio.

I informed her that we were still engaged with the felony stop, but that the suspects were refusing to exit the vehicle. I requested that she send some reinforcements our way. That didn't take long. State troopers, county sheriff's deputies, and cops from neighboring cities started to arrive, along with a couple Border Patrol agents for good measure. Pretty soon it looked like a scene from the movie *Blues Brothers* as we had more flashing red and blue lights than I could count. Like I said, it was a slow night.

I asked two of the nearby officers to cover the suspects while Stover and I fell to the back of the police cars to formulate a plan. The standoff was approaching 30 minutes and we were going to have to think of some way to bring it to a successful conclusion. Just as we got together, the passenger side front door opened, and the second suspect got out. He wasn't moving slowly and deliberately like he was told, so a whole bunch of guns were quickly pointed in his general direction. But he eventually complied, did exactly as he was told, and was taken into custody peacefully.

Not long after, the driver also decided his best option was surrender. At that point the suspects were under arrest for failure to obey the lawful direction of police officers, so the car would be impounded. That's an important detail because we could then conduct an inventory search of the car, which didn't require a search warrant, and it was the content of those hockey bags that intrigued me. Inside the SUV we found three identical hockey bags, all zippered shut and padlocked. Rather than try to defeat the locks, I unfolded the blade of my Benchmade pocketknife and opened one of the canvas bags from end to end. I was elated, but not surprised, by what was inside.

Each canvas pack contained 40 vacuum-sealed clear plastic bags with high-grade marijuana called 'BC Bud' inside. The bags were all one pound each, for a total of 120 pounds. At that time 'BC Bud' sold for $3,000 per pound, so we were happy to take well over a quarter million dollars' worth of illegal drugs off the quiet streets of Marysville. Marijuana is now legal in Michigan for both medicinal and recreational use, and I don't have any qualms with that fact. Police officers don't make the law; we just enforce it. We had intercepted a couple dope runners bringing illegal drugs across an international border because that was our job.

We logged some overtime hours and were still at the police station well into the day shift cataloging and securing all that pot as evidence in the property room. By the time we'd finished the entire police station smelled like powerful weed. The gentleman who was the Chief of Police at that time was a good man and he congratulated us on the bust, but I honestly think he was a bit shocked that a shipment of drugs that large had been moving through his town.

Since this case had a clear nexus to the border with Canada, I called my good friend Dennis Rulli from the US Border Patrol and filled him in on all the details. Rulli was assigned to a DEA task force in Detroit at the time, so he'd be able to follow up on the investigation easier and more thoroughly than we ever could.

Rulli is a true character and whenever we get together we have a blast. Born and raised in Youngstown, Ohio, Rulli had been a phenomenal baseball player who went from the college ranks to tryouts with several Major League baseball teams. When that didn't work out he decided to become a rodeo cowboy and chose to be a bull rider. He competed in rodeos from Ohio to Texas and, after placing first at one event, had to spend the entire $5,000 grand prize to have his broken arm surgically repaired after the bull smashed it. Compared to that circuit, the Border Patrol was a less risky career option.

Rulli determined that the marijuana had come from a man in Canada whose huge grow operation had been financed by his former career as a professional football player. Suspects with First Nations status had transported the drugs up the St Clair River from Walpole Island on the Canadian side and waited offshore until they saw our suspects arrive at the dock. They then zipped across with their fast boat, dropped off the hockey bags full of dope and high-tailed it back to the other side.

The driver of the Ford Explorer was out on bond after being arrested by state troopers on a Detroit freeway with 50 pounds of the same high-quality weed in the trunk of his car a few months prior. In exchange for a couple hundred dollars, he had recruited a friend to help him deliver the 120 pounds to Baltimore, Maryland. The driver ended up doing a year in the county jail on our case. His passenger, who had no criminal record, received probation.

This case was a reminder to always stay vigilant, no matter how serene and quiet our community normally seemed to be.

Human Trafficking

When I started on the job, there were always prostitutes walking Gratiot Avenue on the north end of Mount Clemens. They weren't fancy looking or 'dressed to kill'. Most normal citizens wouldn't notice anything but a woman walking down the street. But if you watched closely you could see telltale signs, such as an over-the-shoulder look given to vehicles as they passed by.

These young women usually came from some other place; often a rural area or a drug rehabilitation center where they'd been sent by a judge. They were almost always addicted to crack cocaine and would turn a trick for twenty dollars, then immediately exchange the money for a hit from a local drug dealer. In my experience, they very rarely had pimps controlling their lives.

In the 30+ years since, the problem of prostitution has become exponentially worse. What's truly terrible is the rise of human trafficking. Human sex trafficking occurs when a person is engaged in prostitution through the force, fraud, or coercion of someone else. There are still many young women selling themselves for sex in exchange for money to purchase drugs, and those drugs now include crystal methamphetamine and heroin, usually mixed with fentanyl.

The difference now is that there are predators lurking everywhere who spot those girls as addicts and try to exploit them. They often approach a female in a friendly way and offer to party with them, even to provide the drugs and a hotel room. After a few days, during which the victim thinks she's made a friend, the trafficker will flip the script and say something like *"you know this room wasn't free, neither were the drugs. You owe me!"*

At that point, the conversation becomes very threatening. The victim is now forced to give the trafficker some or all of the money she earns through prostitution. If she refuses, she might be beaten or the trafficker may threaten to hurt her family. Another tactic is for a trafficker to withhold drugs as punishment or to coerce compliance. If the girl is not yet a drug addict, the trafficker will make sure that she becomes one.

The three most common ways, in my experience, that young women are victimized by human traffickers are by suffering from a drug addiction, experiencing extreme poverty, or by being a runaway juvenile. Each of these situations has something in common: vulnerability. If a person has an extreme need for money, either for drugs or basic survival, predators will swoop in offer a solution to her problem. And if a young girl is a runaway, she is in danger almost immediately due to her lack of life experience and ignorance to potential threats.

A major aggravating factor has been the advent of the Internet and social media. Even though notorious websites like Backpage have been taken down, new ones pop up every day. The websites are in foreign countries now, but that makes no difference at all.

The result is that you don't see prostitutes walking the street anymore, except in certain big city neighborhoods, like the 7 Mile & John R area of Detroit. If you did see them all, it would look like a parade going down the street. But the nature of online prostitution and human trafficking now makes these girls invisible.

Although prostitution and 'pimping' has been around forever, the problem in the United States is worse than ever before. The terms 'pimp' and 'human trafficker' are definitely synonymous! Just as drug traffickers sell drugs and gun traffickers sell guns, human traffickers sell humans. And stop to think that human sex traffickers don't have to grow their commodity, smuggle it across a border, or buy it from a cartel. They merely recruit a person and, if she is taken away, go find another one.

Some may ask, *"Why doesn't she just leave when she is alone, or ask one of her clients for help?"*

The answer is not that simple. Besides desperation and addiction, there can be horrible acts of violence threatened or committed against her. If a trafficker is holding her baby hostage when he tells her to go earn $1000 per day, she's going to do it and return to him. I've heard examples of traffickers sending associates to pose as customers and tell the victim that they are law enforcement officers. If the victim accepts their fraudulent offers to help, she is beaten severely. If she later encounters actual cops who offer real assistance, she's likely to not believe them. Instead, she'll think to herself, *"Right, I know how this story ends."*

Of course, victims of human sex trafficking can also be male, particularly juvenile boys recruited by various means including online gaming, but the overwhelming majority of victims are female.

Similarly, there are female traffickers, but most are male. They come in all colors, races, and backgrounds, and it's important to never have preconceived notions about the appearance of traffickers or where they're from.

It happens everywhere.

Push-Offs

In the battle against human trafficking, it's necessary to attack the demand side of the equation. Just as with narcotics or any other illicit trade, there would be no supply without that demand. This translates to reverse prostitution stings, commonly called 'push-offs' by cops.

During my three-year assignment to COMET I was part of many push-offs that involved having a female undercover (UC) officer on the street, walking alone under the watchful eye of our street narcotics team. The female officer always wore a wire, a hidden microphone, which transmitted her conversations to the team leader, usually me or Detective Lieutenant Rich Margosian. When potential customers approached, the officer would talk with them briefly as they drove up and stopped their cars in the street. It usually didn't take long for that person to say what they wanted and how much they were willing to pay for it. At that point the officer would tell the suspect to drive into an alley or a nearby parking lot to meet her, and she'd walk in that direction. Never did she get into the suspect's vehicle, as that would be too risky and completely unnecessary. The suspect would be stopped and arrested by other members of the team, usually assisted by a uniformed cop in a marked police car.

The Internet was definitely a thing during my time working dope, but the advent of widespread prostitution websites was still a few years away. Doing push-offs the 'old fashioned way' was a lot of fun and an interesting study of human nature. We became adept at spotting vehicles which had circled our UC more than once and figured out that the drivers (often referred to as 'johns') were usually working up their courage to approach her, although that wasn't always the case.

On one occasion, a small pickup truck driven by a shirtless male had circled the intersection of Gratiot Avenue and Scott Street in Mount Clemens several times before coming to a stop along the curb. It was a high traffic area north of downtown and our UC on that day was a city cop named Michelle Ryder. She was small in physical stature but wasn't the least bit scared to mix it up with bad guys. Combined with her good tactics and talent with firearms, she was a good fit for this operation. As she approached the parked truck in the street, she saw the suspect smiling at her and noticed that he didn't say anything, even after she greeted him. When she got close enough, Ryder could see the guy wasn't just shirtless.

He was buck naked and masturbating while watching her walk up and down the block. Ryder had been narrating her movements over the wire during her approach, so I immediately knew what the suspect was doing as she moved quickly away from him. I radioed for our team to move in and make the arrest. The crew appeared from their surveillance hiding spots instantly and arrested the man for Indecent Exposure and Lewd Conduct. We joked later that he had been trying to "get one on the house", using someone he thought to be a prostitute for his sick pleasure without paying her. Gallows humor aside, I hope that we prevented this man from progressing on to even scarier sexual crimes. I have my doubts.

Another operation, with a different UC, resulted in the successful arrest of a man who had been on his way home from work when he stopped and solicited our female officer. She was a Michigan State Trooper named Brenda Hoffmann and was a member of our Street Narcotics team at COMET, unlike the female officers we borrowed from other departments just for the enforcement details. Hoffmann was an experienced law enforcer with a great sense of humor. I've always thought her greatest strength was determination, because she would always see a project through to completion and not miss a single detail. In later years Hoffmann was promoted within the MSP ranks and at one point oversaw the sex offender registry for the entire state.

The takedown went smoothly so I was a little surprised when Hoffmann told me I needed to come forward to where the suspect was detained. When I got there I saw that the man was a United States Marine. His uniform that day was the "Dress Blue Delta" which features a khaki short-sleeved shirt over red-striped, blue trousers; all sharply creased. The stripes on the Marine's sleeves told me he held the rank of Staff Sergeant, and the ribbons on his chest bore witness to his many years of service.

The man worked at the recruiting station in town and the sky blue Dodge Spirit he was driving belonged to the federal government. Cars involved in prostitution arrests were generally forfeited by our unit, and I was sure the US General Accounting Office wouldn't be pleased about that. This man had made a terrible decision that day, and now I had to make one of my own.

I directed one of our team members to drive the Marine's car to One Crocker Boulevard, home of the Mount Clemens Police Department, while a uniformed cop transported him there. We gathered up Hoffmann and left quickly so that we didn't 'heat up' the area by standing around, potentially scaring away other johns. I wanted to return later and continue the operation. When we arrived at the police station, I interviewed the Marine in the booking room where he was handcuffed to an iron bench. I learned that he was assigned to the Marine Corps Recruiting Station on Groesbeck Highway. Without hesitation, he told me the truth and accepted responsibility for his actions that day.

After considering my options I called Selfridge Air National Guard Base, a nearby military installation, and spoke with the senior Non Commissioned Officer (NCO) in charge of staff at the recruiting station. He arrived quickly and he wasn't happy. A Gunnery Sergeant who was also in full uniform, this dude was seriously squared away. He was the strong silent type and he listened closely as I described every detail of our operation and how his Marine had come to be in our custody. I wanted him to know that the arrest had been legitimate and when I had finished, he knew that it was.

I handed him the keys to the government car and said, "Here's your vehicle, Gunny."

As one of my guys brought the man out from the booking area, I said, "And here is your Marine."

The man was visibly cowed in the presence of his senior NCO and remained silent. I opened the back door of the police station and told them they were free to leave; that no record of the incident would exist, not even a police report or a notation on a log sheet. They left together and I kept my word; we moved on to the next operation as if it hadn't happened.

Some people might think my actions were unfair, and they'd be right. But neither is life fair, and I wasn't under any legal obligation to arrest that Marine. I was taking a personal risk that I might be admonished by higher-ups in the department for deviating from procedure, but it was a risk I was willing to take. The man's service to our country was way above and beyond that of a normal citizen and I was sure he'd receive harsh internal discipline from his command. He likely would have been dishonorably discharged with a conviction for soliciting prostitution, whereas the average Joe's employer wouldn't have even been notified. I still believe that my judgement was sound in that circumstance, but I was wrong about that Marine.

One year later, almost to the day, we conducted yet another prostitution sting with yet another UC officer walking the streets at the same intersection. She had no idea who that Marine was when he pulled up because she'd never seen him before, but it was the same man. This time he was in civilian clothing and a car personally owned by him (and his wife). During their conversation, which I listened to over the wire, that same Marine told our UC what he wanted and how much he was willing to pay for it. She gave the prearranged signal and walked away as the COMET team swooped in and arrested him.

I didn't realize who it was until after the arrest but when I did, I was angry and let him know it. He had the audacity to beg me to let him go, saying that it would ruin his career and marriage. I was quiet and let him blather on for a while, seething inside while he did.

"You must think you're special or that I'm a punk," I said. "Either way, you're wrong".

His vehicle was impounded, and we dropped him off at the county jail. The case never went to trial, so he must have pled guilty. I have no idea how the Marine Corps dealt with him. Hopefully, he solved some of his personal problems.

Since the growth of prostitution websites and the human sex trafficking trade, we've changed tactics when we do 'push-offs'. We create fictitious advertisements for prostitution which include a phone number that is linked to law enforcement software. The software records the calls, texts, and photos, then preserves them as digital evidence.

Prior to the first such advertisement, I worded the message carefully and had it reviewed by one of the prosecuting attorneys assigned to work MCU cases, so that we avoided any claims of police entrapment. The suspects in these investigations still must say what they want and how much they're willing to pay for it.

Prior to uploading the advertisement to an online prostitution site, several members of MCU were positioned inside a local motel room as an arrest team, often with a female detective outside the room to greet 'customers' when they arrive and lead them inside. Other MCU officers were dispersed in the area conducting surveillance. I generally remained in the MCU office during the operation, where I could answer the text messages with a female officer present to answer voice calls.

Once the fictitious prostitution ad went 'live', it didn't take long for the messages from potential 'johns' to start rolling in. Sometimes we had an office pool to guess how quickly the first call or text message would hit. The record was 4 minutes. Just like the old school prostitution stings, the new operations brought in people from all walks of life. We had firemen, prison guards, parolees, people with felony arrest warrants, and plenty who possessed drugs. A few even carried concealed guns (some legally, others not).

After I'd communicated with a potential 'john' and the legal burden had been met, establishing probable cause to make an arrest, I radioed the surveillance and arrest teams that a suspect was inbound. When he arrived and saw our female detective out front, he'd believe she was the person with whom he'd been communicating. She didn't have to say a word; just a wink and a smile as she walked into the room, and he'd follow her like a zombie on *The Walking Dead*. It was generally at that point that the suspect got the surprise of his life from the arrest team, and people had differing reactions to that kind of stress. Sometimes the person would freeze up from the shock; others were completely cooperative and submitted without any incident.

One suspect who did not have a peaceful reaction was a local family physician who had arrived to have sexual intercourse with our imaginary prostitute in exchange for $200. This man reacted violently and assaulted two of the cops on the arrest team while he tried to run away. He probably was having his professional life flash before his eyes as he fought to escape, and one of those eyes got rightfully dotted by the cops he was fighting with.

After he was handcuffed and convinced to calm down he was transported to the police station by a uniformed patrol officer who, awkwardly, was one of the good doctor's regular patients. I'm sure that cop switched to a different health care provider soon after. At the police station he didn't completely confess to his involvement but made some critical admissions. Among them was that he had arrived at the motel to spend time with a female whom he had been texting. He also admitted ownership of the condoms and $600 cash in his pocket. That money was forfeited along with his vehicle, which was eventually sold back to the doctor's wife. As she handed me several thousand dollars to reclaim the car, I noticed the wife's disheveled and shocked appearance and felt empathy for her. Clearly it was the first time she realized what her husband was involved with, though it wasn't the doctor's first encounter with prostitution and human sex trafficking.

The criminal charge of Accosting & Soliciting an Act of Prostitution is a simple 90-day misdemeanor in Michigan. I honestly believe it should be a felony and when people ask me how they can help, I encourage them to contact their elected representatives to insist upon it. Anytime someone says that prostitution is a victimless crime because a woman has the right to sell her body, they are simply mistaken. My belief is not based on morality; I just know from experience that prostitution enables the worst predators and opportunists to victimize women and children, and to profit from their suffering. Whether they know it or not, anyone who regularly engages the services of a prostitute has almost certainly lined the pockets of human traffickers with their money.

Mariah

ariah came to my attention the way most of the girls did at the Major Crimes Unit (MCU), via an online advertisement for prostitution. This particular ad was placed on Backpage, a website notorious for facilitating prostitution and human trafficking, just a month or two before it was shut down by the federal government. Using special software that records texts, images and voice calls and saves them as digital evidence, I contacted the number in her advertisement.

We texted and exchanged photos and eventually agreed on a price for her services, which is to say sexual intercourse. This is critical because a price and an act to be performed must be stated by the suspect before an arrest can be made. The police aren't allowed to entrap people, and MCU was always careful to never do so.

Once a prostitution arrest was made, we immediately tried to determine if the prostitute was conducting her business because of the force, fraud or coercion of someone else. In other words, was she being trafficked? If she was, we never prosecuted her for the crime of prostitution. The charges were simply not filed, and we tried to get her to a safe place where she could receive any help she needed. That would prove to be the case in our contact with Mariah.

We agreed to meet at a seedy roadside motel called the El Rancho, where Mariah had rented a room. Prior to my arrival, my MCU teammates established a perimeter around the motel and conducted surveillance. Mariah asked me to pick up some Crown Royal and Newports for her, so I did that as part of the undercover operation. Upon my arrival, I walked up to Room One and knocked. When Mariah opened the door, I could immediately see that she was the same girl whose photo appeared in the advertisement. Mariah was a brown-eyed blonde whose body had not yet suffered the ravages of her drug abuse, unlike many of the girls we encounter.

"Hey, baby," she said.

"What's up, kid?" I replied, handing her the whiskey and smokes.

"Nothing much, come inside," she replied.

She locked the door as she closed it behind me, but I unlocked it as she walked toward the bed. When I did so, my teammate Grafton Sharp immediately entered, in accordance with our tactical plan. Sharp is one of the best street cops I've ever worked with. He combines intelligence and experience with common sense and old school instincts. We told Mariah she was under arrest and to sit on the bed. She was calm and cooperative as we quickly checked the room for anyone hiding; clearly she'd dealt with police before.

A few more MCU team members came in while a couple of them maintained surveillance outside. I noticed that Mariah's iPhone was blowing up, so I asked for her permission to examine it. She agreed and I saw that another customer who had answered her advertisement was texting her, wanting to come to the motel room. I saw on the text string that they had agreed to a price and sex act so, posing as Mariah, I told him to come over.

I alerted the MCU cops outside, and they stopped a man who drove into the motel lot and parked near the room. Upon being contacted the man was extremely nervous. I went outside and joined my teammate who was speaking with him. MCU Detective Erik Krikorian, a veteran cop with a wealth of experience and a sharp eye, pointed out to me that there were two $100 bills sitting in the center console. I knew from seeing the text string that the price they had agreed to was $200. I asked the man what his cellular phone number was, and it was the same as the phone number in the text string. At that point Krikorian and I arrested him for Accosting & Soliciting an Act of Prostitution.

When we impounded his car, I saw that there was a baby's car seat in the back. I learned later from an agent at Child Protective Services that the man had left his 5 year old in charge of an infant so that he could go have sex with a prostitute while his wife was at work.

Mariah was transported to the police department for an interview. Prior to speaking with her, I did a 'work up' which included a request for her computerized criminal history and inquiries into other databases. I found a report from a police department in metropolitan Detroit which listed Mariah as an acquaintance of a man named Andre who was suspected of being a human trafficker.

During the interview, I asked Mariah about Andre. I must have caught her at the right moment, because she gave me the whole story on him. In fact, she was angry at Andre because he had recently beaten her. The man, who had four to six prostitutes under his control at any given time, had become enraged when Mariah purchased a used BMW with money she had earned on the side.

Andre had an associate call Mariah's number and pose as a customer willing to pay for sex. When she arrived at a house in Detroit to meet him, Andre appeared from a hiding place. He snatched her out of the car, punched her to the ground and kicked her, then took the keys and drove away in the car. Andre later forged Mariah's signature on the title and registered the BMW in his own name. She never got the car back.

I learned a lot about Mariah's life, including how she had been trafficked as a prostitute since the age of 15 (she was 27 at this time). She was a wild child and ran away from home a few times. On one of those occasions, she met a man who drove her to Detroit. When they got there the man told her that if she had sex with his friend, that person would provide them with a bunch of marijuana, and they could have a party. She did have sex with that man in exchange for the weed, and that was her first time being trafficked as a prostitute. She was in the game from that day forward.

Mariah was released without criminal charges and Andre, the man who had most recently trafficked her and stolen her car, became the focus of our investigation. I called my friend Kellen O'Boyle, an FBI Special Agent at the Detroit Field Office. O'Boyle had been an ordnance disposal expert in the US Army and served in Afghanistan. I was fortunate to have worked a bank robbery case with O'Boyle the year before and knew that he would help us any way that he could. It was quickly determined that our suspect was already the target of a federal investigation by the FBI human trafficking task force in Detroit.

O'Boyle hooked me up with an investigator on that task force, who called me a few days later. He told me that they had identified a 15 year old female trafficking victim who was featured in a prostitution advertisement placed online by the suspect. The task force had geo-located Andre's phone using the number in the advertisement and had a general area of the suspect's house but couldn't determine the exact address. The investigator wondered if my informant (Mariah) would know the address.

I contacted Mariah and then quickly called the federal investigator back with the address she provided. They then called the number provided in the advertisement, set up a date with the juvenile victim, and sent an Uber driver to the house to pick her up. Of course, the Uber driver was actually an FBI agent. After rescuing that young girl, they executed a search warrant at the house and arrested Andre.

Inside the house, they rescued four other girls who, while not juveniles, were also victims of human trafficking at the hand of the same suspect. Andre was charged and convicted in federal court of numerous human trafficking charges and sent to prison. During the trial, his victims testified to his horrific physical abuse and the fact that he forcefully injected heroin into the neck of a girl, in order to create an addict whom he could then control.

A few months later, Mariah went to a drug rehabilitation center and got clean and sober. Tragically, she relapsed and died within a year from an overdose of heroin laced with fentanyl. Although she led a troubled life, Mariah made a huge impact on the lives of others by helping us apprehend a brutal human trafficker.

Trailer Park Trouble

Whenever MCU did a human trafficking operation, we were almost certain to come across other types of crimes. It could be guns or drugs or fugitives, almost anything, since prostitution is so often linked to other crimes. As with narcotics investigations, we also had to be conscious of other threats like robbery.

During one such investigation, I contacted a number listed in an online advertisement for prostitution and an agreement was reached. The female listed in the ad called herself Charlotte and said she would provide sex for 30 minutes in exchange for $100. During our conversation I asked if she had any rules.

This type of question usually draws a response that assists in proving a criminal case. For example, in this case the response was "no anal, no bareback, and no cops!" It's tough to make a judge or jury believe that you weren't involved in prostitution when you specifically say that you don't allow anal sex or sex without a condom, and you don't want any contact with police.

We set up a time to meet and she gave me the address. It was in a huge trailer park called Minnesota Lakes just outside of town. We discovered later that the trailer belonged to someone else, a woman who let other people use it for nefarious purposes. That person had paid for a year's rent at the trailer park with welfare benefits she received from the state. Not a great use of taxpayer dollars.

My MCU teammates got into position and conducted surveillance before I arrived. On this day the team was led by Detective Sergeant Chris Frazier. Frazier was a tall, squarejawed, no-nonsense guy who had a reserved and calm demeanor, but he wasn't a person you'd ever want to tangle with. He was a great cop but, more importantly, Frazier was a great leader and I enjoyed being on the team with him.

As I arrived it was just after sundown and Charlotte was waiting in the driveway. She was thin and looked sullen. She was wearing faded jeans and a green zip-up hoodie over her white t-shirt. As she turned to lead me to the door, I noticed she had a bad tattoo on her neck. We went inside and immediately there was a strong smell of marijuana. Not the smell of burning weed but marijuana plants, which I couldn't see. I noticed there really wasn't any furniture in the place, except for a couple metal folding chairs and some wooden barstools over by the kitchen.

On the floor in the empty living room there was a blanket laid out with a couple pillows and a candle burning. It wasn't exactly the Hilton honeymoon suite, but clearly this was where the magic was supposed to happen. My teammates entered right behind me, and Charlotte was arrested. She wasn't happy about that. She was handcuffed and seated on one of the folding chairs.

Guys from the team completed a sweep of the house, just to see if there was anyone else inside or any dangerous conditions to deal with. Inside one of the bedrooms they found the source of the weed smell. It was a drying room with dozens of large marijuana plants hanging upside down on racks. In addition to being a house of prostitution, this place was a grow operation.

While Charlotte was being interviewed to determine if she was a victim of human trafficking (she 'lawyered up' and refused to make any statement, which was totally her right to do), Frazier went outside to his vehicle to get some gear and call for a patrol car to transport Charlotte to the county jail. At this point it was just MCU detectives in plain clothes and, although each man except me was wearing a tactical vest and badge on a chain around their neck, there were no uniformed cops and no marked police cars on the scene.

While Frazier was in his car, he noticed some movement off in the distance about 100 feet away. A dark figure emerged from behind some bushes and headed for the trailer. The figure was wearing a hooded sweatshirt with his face covered as he picked up speed, walking purposely toward us.

There was no time for Frazier to warn us or stop the man, so the guy burst through the door into the living room where eight cops were standing with Charlotte sitting handcuffed in a chair. When he saw all the cops, this dude's eyes got as big as dinner plates. He looked like Jim Carrey's character in *The Mask* as he spun around and sprinted out the door.

Several of the MCU guys lit out after him. One of those cops was Brendt Smith, an Agent assigned to MCU from US Customs and Border Protection. Brendt was the youngest guy on MCU at that time, and he was in superior physical condition. In fact, he went on to become a member of the US Customs Special Response Team, a federal SWAT team that requires its members to complete a grueling entry process similar to military special operations qualification.

The man was no match for the cops chasing him and he was caught in short order. He had three different strains of weed packaged for sale in his pockets, and we figured out that Charlotte was his girlfriend. We had a laugh about what a dumbass this guy was, but what wasn't funny was the fact that he had been armed with a large knife when he came through the door. He'd thrown it on the ground outside as he ran away, but his plan had been to rob me while I was in a vulnerable position inside the trailer with Charlotte.

If some folks would work as hard at a real job as they do trying to sell drugs, pimp their girlfriends, and rob unsuspecting johns, the quality of their lives would be much improved.

Stereotypes

It's important to avoid having preconceived notions in police work, and that is true when investigating human trafficking. You never know who could be preying on victims and you're guaranteed to miss some of them if you don't keep an open mind.

During an MCU investigation involving a victim named Sofia, I answered an online advertisement by sending a text message to the number listed. I got a quick response and reached an agreement that the female shown in the ad would provide sexual services in exchange for $200. In this case, she would come to me. MCU had a room reserved for the operation at a local hotel. It was a franchise of a popular chain that typically isn't thought of as a place where bad things happen, further evidence that human trafficking happens all around us.

Between the time of my first message and Sofia's arrival, I exchanged numerous texts with her, or so I thought. At one point the person with whom I was texting asked me to voice call her. I did so and we talked about what time she would arrive, what she was wearing, whether I was law enforcement, and other details that are routine parts of an undercover operation.

It took an unusually long time for Sofia to arrive after she said she was on the way. We discovered later that she came from Flint, an hour west of us down Interstate 69. MCU had surveillance set up on the parking lot and watched as a small dark SUV pulled in from Gratiot Avenue. The SUV had three people inside and made two circles of the lot before stopping in front of room 119.

The front seat passenger opened the door and got out, and I could see right away that it was the girl featured in the advertisement. She was a 22 year old Latina with long dark hair and a red dress. She had a cell phone in her hand, and I watched her make a call. My phone immediately rang so I answered and spoke to her. She told me she had arrived and asked me to come outside to meet her. At that point probable cause existed to arrest Sofia and detain the other two people so I radioed for the MCU guys to move in, but something was bothering me.

When I was speaking with Sofia on the phone I immediately noticed that it was not the same voice I had heard earlier, when the investigation was beginning. The three suspects were separated and transported to the police department for interviews. I learned a lot about Sofia's circumstances during the long conversation that followed.

Sofia had been living in public housing in Flint, with her 5 year old son. She had never finished high school and was recently laid off from her minimum wage job. She had no money other than her government food subsidy and no prospects. If she didn't find something soon, she was going to be evicted from the housing project where she and the boy had lived for several years. One day she was crying as she described this situation to her neighbor. The neighbor's cousin was there and heard Sofia's story. The neighbor's cousin was about to become Sofia's trafficker.

The trafficker in this incident turned out to be the driver of the SUV in which Sofia had arrived. Her name was Tonya. She swooped in when she heard Sofia's desperation and offered a way for her to make quick money. Sofia was hesitant when she found out the sordid details about what she'd have to do but agreed to Tonya's plan because she had no other option to feed her son and keep a roof over their heads.

Tonya took explicit photos of Sofia and placed them in the online prostitution advertisement she created. It was Tonya with whom I'd been texting and speaking the entire time, until the last phone call. In the past 48 hours Tonya had transported Sofia from Flint to Kalamazoo, then Lansing and Port Huron for "dates" with prostitution customers. Each time, Tonya would take half of the $200 fee. The third person in the car had been Tonya's brother, who provided "protection" and would sometimes drive when Tonya got tired.

Sofia was not charged with any crime and was provided transportation to Ohio, where her family lived. Tonya was charged with several felonies including Pandering, Transporting a Person for Purposes of Prostitution, and Accepting the Earnings of a Prostitute. As the case was about to go to trial, we learned that Tonya and her family members had been threatening to kill Sofia if she testified in court. After being charged with Witness Tampering, Tonya later agreed to a plea bargain and was convicted.

This was the first time we had encountered a female human trafficker and it was an important lesson. We also learned how the desperation of extreme poverty can drive people to make bad decisions, ones they would ordinarily never make.

30 Hour Day

On a sunny Saturday in late August, I traveled to Alma, Michigan with my wife Cyndi and daughter Jenna, to watch our son Travis play his first game as a freshman quarterback with the Alma College Scots. We had a great day enjoying the beautiful campus and watching the game. The college's marching band included bagpipes and drums, which I particularly enjoyed, and the atmosphere was electric. I don't even remember who won, just how proud I was of Travis and that we were all together on a beautiful day. After the game we had dinner at the Olive Garden in town, wished Travis good luck for the coming week, and headed home.

Just as we were southbound on State Highway 127 approaching Lansing, my Major Crimes Unit phone rang and the caller ID told me it was the boss, Detective Sergeant Chris Frazier. I pressed the green circle and answered on the second ring.

"Good afternoon, Sarge" I said.

"Hey, Jim" he replied. "Hey, listen, I need you to come in right away. The detective bureau is out on Rawlins Street with a deceased woman and it's going to be a homicide. Also, her husband and 5-year-old son are nowhere to be found so we've got some work to do." Frazier told me to meet my teammates in the MCU office and that we'd have a briefing when everyone was present.

I informed Frazier of my current location and estimated time of arrival, then ended the call. Under normal circumstances we were almost two hours from home. I made it to the office in about 90 minutes.

We assembled in the portion of the MCU office that looks west through a wall of windows at downtown Port Huron, five stories below. As Frazier began to speak, he also handed around several printouts of information that had been gathered by patrol officers and the on-call detectives who'd initially responded to the call of a deceased person. They were still there, now accompanied by technicians from the Michigan State Police Crime Lab, who were meticulously processing the brutal scene.

We learned that a 30-year-old female named Lydia Ball had been found in the basement of her parents' home by her mother, a woman about 60 years of age named Roxanne Jackson. Lydia had been beaten severely about her head and face with a blunt object, her head enclosed in a plastic bag. Bleach had been poured over her clothing; a lazy attempt by the perpetrator to conceal his identity. Near the body had been found a homemade mallet, the size of a small sledgehammer. Following an autopsy, Medical Examiner Daniel Spitz would later testify that the mallet's strike face matched the 14 heavy blows which had crushed Lydia's skull.

Lydia was married to a 39-year-old drifter named Doug Ball, with whom she had a 5-year-old son named Douglas. The husband and son were nowhere to be found, and every moment that went by was critical. If Lydia had been killed by her husband, would he then also murder their son and perhaps take his own life? Such murder/suicide scenarios are not uncommon, and MCU had certainly seen its fair share of them.

Frazier assigned duties to each member of MCU, then made sure that a statewide AMBER Alert was issued. A description of young Douglas was sent out via local television news stations, newspapers and their social media platforms, radio, and wireless cell phone providers, along with a description of his father and the brown Chevrolet Malibu in which they were believed to be traveling.

Detective Grafton Sharp and I were assigned to complete a full workup of Doug, to determine where he may have fled with the child. This entailed gathering as much information as possible from interviews with family, friends, neighbors, or anyone who may have details about Doug, no matter how small. Then databases are explored for intelligence, such as the Law Enforcement Information Network and National Crime Information Center, which reveal a person's Computerized Criminal History. MCU investigators can access applications called Accurint and CLEAR, which reveal everything from address histories and utility bills to bankruptcies and social media accounts.

We started by interviewing Lydia's parents, Larry and Roxanne, and her brother Edwin Jackson, to learn more about Doug and what type of person he was. Lydia's family was emotionally distraught and in shock. They alternated between tears of sadness and quiet rage but remained focused to help us as best they could on the worst day of their lives.

From them we learned that Doug was a minimally educated man who rarely worked. Larry and Roxanne allowed Doug to live in their home so that their daughter and grandson would have a roof over their heads and food to eat. Doug spent most of his time watching movies and playing video games. He'd recently made a lame attempt to start a pit bull breeding business called Gorilla Kennels. He'd gone so far as to get the brand name tattooed on his arms but hadn't had any measurable success with it in real life.

Roxanne told me that she and Lydia had a checking account together. Doug was not on the account and had no debit card or other access to withdraw funds. Together we called the bank's 24-hour customer service and learned that Doug had recently used Lydia's debit card to make payments on a video gaming system he'd purchased at a local appliance store. Since Doug probably was in possession of Lydia's debit card, I arranged for the bank to notify us if the card was used for any future transactions, so that we could determine his general whereabouts.

Larry and Roxanne also told us that Doug had sent them on a wild goose chase over the last couple days. When Roxanne noticed that Lydia wasn't home on Friday, the day before she discovered Lydia's body, Doug told her that Lydia had walked to the unemployment office to look for a job. Later that afternoon Roxanne and Larry each received text messages from Lydia's phone number, stating that she needed a ride home from the unemployment office. They arrived separately only to find that Lydia wasn't there.

They returned home and soon received more texts from Lydia's phone, stating that she'd met up with a friend and would be staying the night at her house since they'd been drinking. Roxanne was immediately suspicious. Lydia rarely went out with friends and never spent the night away from her son.

Roxanne told us that when she sent text messages to Lydia Friday night, or received them, Doug would leave the room. Each time she received a text from Lydia, Doug was not present. She also said that the messages didn't seem like they'd been written by Lydia, who normally used lots of abbreviations and emojis.

When Lydia still hadn't returned late Saturday morning, Roxanne and Larry became very worried. Together they drove to an area 30 miles south of their home, near the riverside city of Algonac, to look for Lydia at the home of her friend. Doug had given them an address for the friend, claiming that Lydia had provided it to him. The couple quickly determined that the address which Doug had supplied them didn't exist.

Arriving home again on Rawlins Street, a dark anxiety came over Roxanne. She knew then that something was terribly wrong. As Larry smoked and paced outside the house, Roxanne went inside to find it empty. She called out to Doug but received no reply from him nor her grandson, Douglas. Roxanne wandered through her home, finding nothing and no one inside. Arriving at the stairwell near the kitchen, she decided to check the basement.

After moving carefully down the old wooden steps, Roxanne walked across the concrete floor of the musty cellar toward the washer and dryer. There, laying prone near a floor drain, was Lydia.

"I looked to the left and I saw her feet. When I touched her head, my hand went into her skull" Roxanne would later testify tearfully at Ball's preliminary exam. "And I yelled, 'Oh, my God, I found her! She's dead in the basement!'"

Hearing Roxanne's cries, Larry ran into the house. He made his way downstairs and witnessed the ghastly scene for himself. In shock and with understandable anger Larry climbed the stairs and burst outside to the yard, putting his fist through the glass portion of the door as he did so. The blood spilled from Larry at the crime scene would later be carefully explained at trial by MCU Detective Eric Krikorian, so that no inferences could be drawn by defense attorneys to confuse the jurors.

The interview of Lydia's family members was exhaustive and helpful to our investigation. It also gave us insight into their collective spirit and how much they loved her. Their sadness was palpable, but we had to rise above it because they were counting on us to do our jobs. Probable cause now existed to arrest their son-in-law, but first we had to find him and rescue their grandson.

Sharp and I believed, based on everything we could develop about Doug's personality, that he was soft and would likely run to a safe place and hide if possible. He didn't seem like a man prepared to strike out to parts unknown and survive on his own, much less care for a small child along the way. Though he could clearly be brutal to those physically weaker than himself, and that heightened our concern for his son, we believed that his laziness and lack of intelligence would assist us with his apprehension.

Sharp and I retreated to the MCU office and dived into all the data we could discover on our computers concerning Doug and his possible whereabouts. As I scrolled through arrest records, civil judgements, court dockets and property records searching for possible relatives and associates, a name kept appearing: Vickie Lynn Ball. Though she lived 60 miles to the southwest in Oakland County, she was the right age to be Doug's mother and seemed to have several relevant affiliations to him. I again contacted Lydia's brother, Edwin, who had been so helpful earlier in the day. He told me that he believed Vickie was indeed Doug's mother and that she had a sister who lived near her, an aunt to Doug.

I printed out the data on Vickie and showed it to Sharp. He had also discovered her name in his research, and we agreed that Vickie's home was a likely destination for a momma's boy like Doug. Together we walked into the office of our boss, Detective Sergeant Frazier, and made our case. Frazier listened carefully to our hypothesis and asked questions to clarify and challenge our position. When we'd finished, he agreed that Vickie's home was a high-priority target. Frazier directed us to gather our gear and head west immediately. After checking on the progress of our teammates' various assignments, Frazier would follow us to Vickie's house.

It was after midnight when Sharp and I pulled out of the underground garage beneath the police department, and raining heavily. We were in separate unmarked cars to double our mobility. We navigated south through downtown and then west on Griswold Avenue, a one-way thoroughfare that eventually became Interstate 69 west of the city limits.

Though our initial mission was surveillance, we were ready for a fight. MCU vehicles were undercover (UC) cars, just as our physical appearance was tailored to appropriately blend in wherever we operated. But secured in the trunks of those vehicles were rifles, spare magazines with ammunition, and "go-bags" with body armor, night vision scopes, and all manner of essential gear. MCU was a hybrid unit of great investigators who possessed tactical training and experience, and often included detectives with prior service in the military or on SWAT Teams.

Just over an hour later we arrived at the Orion Lakes trailer park, a humble collection of single- and double-wide units only a couple miles north of the Palace of Auburn Hills. As trailer parks go, it wasn't the worst one I'd ever seen; most of the small lots were landscaped and had a decent car in the driveway. The rain had eased in intensity, and it was plenty warm on that late summer night. The cloudy moonless sky made it super dark, but this worked to our advantage as we navigated toward the address of Vickie Lynn Ball. I found her trailer at the dead end of a cul-de-sac next to a large pond, in the shadow of a huge willow tree.

Since there was only one way in and out of her section of the park, I positioned my gold Chevy Impala in the middle of the block and began surveillance of Vickie's trailer. Sharp steered his UC ride through the park's narrow streets searching for Doug's brown 4-door Malibu without success. About 12 hours later, in the bright light of day, that car would be found by MCU Detective Eric Shumaker parked in a factory lot half a mile away. That was a significant piece of circumstantial evidence because it showed that Doug Ball tried to conceal his whereabouts after the murder.

Frazier was only 15 minutes behind us, and while in route he'd called the Oakland County Sheriff's Office to advise them we were in the area. Upon Frazier's arrival we approached Vickie's trailer on foot. Parked in the gravel space next to the unit was a white Dodge minivan. I quietly used my iPhone to call our central dispatch center, and the dispatcher confirmed that the registration plate on the van was registered to Vickie Lynn Ball at that address.

Frazier approached the main door of the trailer, while I positioned myself about 10 feet away underneath a window. Sharp had taken a spot on the backside of the home, where there was another door and more windows. Two portable air conditioning units hung from windows on opposite sides of Vickie's mobile home, both wet with condensation and humming loudly as they pumped cold air on that hot night.

"You guys good?" Frazier whispered in my direction. I silently used my Motorola radio to check with Sharp on the MCU encrypted frequency. Sharp confirmed he was in position, so I nodded and gave Frazier the 'OK' sign.

As Frazier knocked loudly on the flimsy door, a dog inside began to bark. He sounded large and pissed off.

"Goddamit!" I heard a woman inside the trailer exclaim. I didn't hear her voice again, nor any others, until hours later. We tried several more rounds of knocking and ringing the doorbell, alternating with pounding on the side of the trailer, but it was to no avail. No one came to the door and not a single light was visible inside.

Vickie's home was obviously a high-priority target, and we couldn't take our eyes off it even for a minute until we established contact with whomever was inside. We retreated on foot silently to where each of our UC vehicles were parked.

Frazier directed me to keep surveillance on Vickie's place while he and Sharp drove to the address we had developed for her sister, Doug's aunt. It was a few miles away, so I'd be alone for a good while as they tried to make contact. But between digital radios, smart phones, plenty of guns, and lots of experience I knew I would be just fine.

At 0330 hours I settled in behind the wheel of my car 50 yards up a slight incline from the trailer, with a perfect view of the main entry door and the minivan parked in the adjacent space. With the rain completely subsided, it was dark and quiet except for the faint rumble of distant traffic on Interstate 75. With the adrenaline worn away, it wasn't long before I had some heavy eyelids. I'd awakened at 0600 hours that Saturday to prepare for a day spent enjoying two of my favorite things, family and college football. Almost 24 hours later, I was whipped.

Sadly, surrendering to the sandman was not an option. I shook my head and sipped my cold coffee to stay awake until the predawn sky started to lighten. The clouds had cleared, and when the sun rose it was going to be a beautiful day. At 0635 hours I saw a blonde woman exit the trailer wearing pajamas and a bathrobe. I blinked hard a few times to make sure I wasn't hallucinating, as she stepped off the tiny porch and fired up a cigarette.

With binoculars I could see that the woman matched the driver's license photo of Vickie Lynn Ball. While she stood there smoking, I called Frazier on my cell. He and Sharp were headed back from their unsuccessful mission to locate Vickie's sister and were only a mile or two away. That was a very good thing because as I was speaking with Frazier, Vickie loaded up in the white minivan and began to back out of the short driveway.

Given the very serious and suspicious circumstances, following Vickie to her unknown destination would seem to be an obvious decision; perhaps she would lead us to our suspect. But it was just as likely that Doug Ball was inside the trailer with his 5-year-old son. Taking eyes off that residence was absolutely out of the question.

As the minivan slowly approached, I turned the key in my car's ignition. The motor came to life, and I yanked the transmission into drive. Just as the white van was about to pass, I pulled into the roadway and blocked Vickie's path. She hit the brakes hard, and I stepped out of my car to see her eyes wide in surprise; she had not expected that.

Walking slowly toward the driver door, I smiled and held my hands out palms up in a friendly "stop" motion. It was light enough for her to see the badge on a chain around my neck, and she rolled down the window as I approached.

"Good morning, ma'am. Are you Vickie Ball?"

"Yes" she replied. "What's going on?"

I identified myself to Vickie and handed her a business card. The words 'Port Huron Major Crimes Unit' surely gave her a good idea what was going on, since that was her son's current stomping grounds. She appeared extraordinarily nervous as we continued to talk.

"I'm trying to find Doug; I just need to speak with him about a matter we're working on." Pointing to her trailer I said, "Is he inside?".

"No" Vickie said. "He was here about three o'clock yesterday afternoon, but I haven't seen him since then." Vickie had a white-knuckle grip on the steering wheel as she spoke, and her voice trembled so much that I thought she was about to cry. She was clearly lying.

At that moment I heard cars approaching. I turned to see Frazier and Sharp park their UC rides on the side of the street just behind me.

"Ok, ma'am" I said to Vickie. "Stay here please, I'll just be a minute."

I walked quickly toward Frazier and met him in the street. With my back to Vickie, I said quietly "She's lying, Sarge. She says he's not inside, but I feel like he definitely is in there."

Frazier approached the van and spoke to Vickie, who's driver door was now open. After identifying himself, Frazier got straight to the point.

"Ma'am, it's OK. We know Doug is inside. Is your grandson with him?"

That was all it took. Vickie burst into tears as she nodded her head. She told us they were sleeping in a back bedroom. Doug had forced her to be quiet and not answer the door when we'd first arrived, and he'd made her grandson pee into a wastebasket to avoid turning on lights inside to use the bathroom. Doug had even told his mother that no one was going to take his son away from him. She'd thought it odd that Doug had showed up Saturday with her grandson and not his wife, but she hadn't known about the homicide until seeing it on the 11pm local newscast. She'd been mortified ever since.

As the sun began to rise, we had to move fast. Frazier took Vickie and her minivan around a corner about 50 yards away. The spot was out of sight from the trailer and would serve as a command post as deputies from the Oakland County Sheriff's Office began to arrive. To that end, and since we didn't have their frequencies programmed on our police radios, Frazier said to me "Call 911." He then directed Sharp and me to cover down on the trailer until the cavalry arrived.

I hopped in the Impala and moved it again to the side of the street. Using the key fob, I popped the trunk as I walked to the rear and keyed open a padlock on the black Pelican case inside. I removed the Colt AR-15 rifle inside, along with a MAGPUL magazine filled with 30 rounds of Federal Match Grade .223 caliber ammunition. Inserting the magazine and dropping the bolt to chamber a round, I looked quickly through the EOTECH Holographic Weapon Sight and saw the reticle light up red with a push of the side-mounted switch. The Kevlar vest in the trunk had two additional magazines attached to the carrier, so I threw it over my head and secured the Velcro straps.

Walking quickly across the street, I hugged the front side of several trailers as I moved down the cul-de-sac toward Vickie's property. Sharp was on the street's other side, moving behind trailers to the same destination. There was a low-rise hill west of the trailer, between it and the pond. I took a prone position behind the crest of that hill near some scrub brush, where I could cover the north and west sides of the structure. Sharp positioned himself between some vehicles and an adjoining trailer where he could lock down the south and east sides. In addition to his duties as a detective with MCU, Sharp was a highly trained, experienced sniper with the Port Huron Police Special Response Team. His fieldcraft expertise made him virtually invisible that morning.

With the situation as squared away as we could make it, at least temporarily, I pulled the iPhone out of my pocket and dialed 911.

"Oakland County 911. What is your emergency?"

"Good morning, ma'am" I said. "My name is James Disser and I'm a detective with the Port Huron Major Crimes Unit. I need to speak to the desk sergeant immediately."

"You got it" she replied. "Stand by."

Click. Dial tone. She hung up on me. Talk about Murphy's Law; that was it.

I punched the same three digits again and this time the dispatcher was able to put me through directly. I explained the situation as completely but efficiently as I could, since the sun was rising, and the clock was ticking. The sergeant was a pro. I don't know if his shift was beginning or ending at that hour, but after hearing about a suspected murderer hiding in a trailer with a child as a potential hostage, he didn't even blink.

"Well, detective" he said. "That sounds like a job for our SWAT Team."

"I couldn't agree more, sir" I replied.

Well over one million residents populate Oakland County, Michigan; along with robust industrial and technological sectors surrounding the automotive industry, they provide a massive tax base. As you might imagine, their Sheriff's Office is well-funded. That is as it should be, and it includes a SWAT Team that is trained up and experienced from many callouts over the years. The desk sergeant put out the call for the Team and sent uniformed deputies in patrol cars to secure the area surrounding us.

Prone on the wet grass and dirt, I shouldered my rifle and looked over the top of its sights at Vickie's trailer. Sharp and I just had to hold it down until the Team arrived or the suspect exited. Either way, the familiar rush of adrenalin meant I was no longer sleepy. The only distraction was the sound of mosquitoes buzzing around my head at their unique and annoying frequency. They descended on me in the warm wet morning light, almost like they knew I couldn't move and told all their friends. Since I'd left the can of Deep Woods OFF in my go-bag, I just had to endure the little bastards.

For the next 45 minutes, nothing moved. Since it was Sunday morning, there wasn't even the normal weekday bustle of people leaving home for their daily drive to work.

"Psst!" a voice whispered. "Coming up on your six, detective."

I turned my head to see an Oakland County SWAT sniper approaching in a low crawl. He'd made his way behind the mobile homes to our west, then silently along the pond's edge and up the small rise to my position. The dude was good; I hadn't heard a sound. As a former SWAT entry team operator, I knew that his Team's response time was impressive. It's not easy to get everyone spun up and deployed to an active scene that quickly.

I quietly briefed him up and then slid out of his way so that he could set up his Heckler & Koch precision rifle on its attached bipod. He invited me to stay right there with him since it would be tough to exfiltrate without possibly being seen, so I stayed hunkered down behind my own long gun.

Another sniper had approached from the opposite side and was setting up near Sharp's position. It wasn't long until we heard the low tone of a Bearcat's engine approaching. It was the Oakland County SWAT entry team rolling down the street toward Vickie's trailer, and they were not wasting time. They'd decided to enter the home and perform a hostage rescue maneuver to recover 5-year-old Douglas Ball and arrest his father. It was an aggressive move and I liked it.

MCU had established probable cause to arrest Doug Ball. Since the charge was murder and we could articulate the danger to his son, a search warrant wasn't required to enter the home; it was a classic example of 'exigent circumstances'. The suspect was likely still asleep, making the time to strike immediate. The Team could have surrounded the house and called out to the suspect with bullhorns, but that would possibly have created a hostage crisis where one didn't yet exist. Truly, in this instance, there was no time like the present.

The SWAT vehicle came to rest in the short gravel driveway and eight camouflage-clad operators quickly and quietly exited. They formed up in a line and smoothly moved to the door. The line of SWAT cops paused near the entrance as two of their members advanced; one pulled back the screen door as the other swung a black steel battering ram, crushing the thin trailer door with one hit. The two breachers fell into the back of the line as it passed by on the way into the home.

After no more than 30 seconds, one of the SWAT officers came back out the same door carrying Douglas Ball.

"Suspect's in custody" the sniper said quietly to me. "They're clearing the rest of the house now." His radio was equipped with an earpiece, and he'd been monitoring his teammates' communications silently.

Their plan had worked to perfection. Doug Ball and his son were asleep and taken by complete surprise when the Team entered the dingy small bedroom near the back of the trailer. After several minutes a large Black SWAT Team operator escorted Doug out of the home, handcuffed behind his back and bent over at the waist. He planted our murder suspect face down on the battered hood of a nearby Chevy Camaro. It was a great moment.

I exhaled a big sigh of relief and clapped the sniper on the shoulder.

"Thanks, brother." I said to him with sincerity. "You guys' kick ass."

"Aw no problem, man. Anytime. Thanks for the work!" he replied with a smile.

I walked back to my car while talking to Frazier on the phone. He'd received consent from Vickie Ball to search her trailer for any evidence related to our homicide investigation, so after downloading my rifle and stowing my gear I joined him and Sharp near the dead end of the cul-de-sac.

Lots of people started to arrive then; the rest of our MCU teammates, a Port Huron PD patrol car summoned by Frazier to transport our arrestee back to our station, serious-looking plainclothes cops who I took to be Oakland County bosses, even the Sheriff himself showed up. Near the makeshift command post, news reporters began to gather as a helicopter circled overhead.

During our search of the residence, Frazier and I found some valuable evidence including bleach-stained sweatpants and a pair of size 12 white Lugz sneakers, with treads on the bottom that matched marks left at the crime scene. We contacted an agent from the state Child Protective Services, who recommended that Douglas Ball be placed into the custody of his maternal grandparents in Port Huron. The only problem was that the boy was terrified of police officers and refused to get into a patrol car, crying and hugging Vickie's leg as he resisted her efforts to put him inside. Since she had been so cooperative with us after our initial contact, it was decided that Vickie would transport the boy in her minivan to the Port Huron Police Department, where he could be turned over to Larry and Roxanne.

I was assigned to escort Vickie and Douglas the 60 miles home, along with my MCU teammate Detective Ryan Mynsberge. He took the lead and I brought up the rear as Vickie followed him. I can say that I have never struggled to keep it between the lines quite like I did that day. But we arrived safely back at our office and the expressions of pure joy and relief from Larry and Roxanne made it all worthwhile.

Sometime after 1300 hours that Sunday I collapsed in my basement recliner with a glass of Woodford Reserve Kentucky straight bourbon whiskey and tried to watch some preseason NFL football. That didn't happen. After nodding off and on for a few hours I ended up in my bed, dead to the world until Monday morning.

Eight months later, Douglas Ball was convicted of Murder in the First Degree following a jury trial in the 31st Circuit Court courtroom of Judge Michael West. The jurors were out for less than 30 minutes before rendering their verdict. St. Clair County Assistant Prosecuting Attorney Jennifer Smith Deegan was masterful in her litigation against a defense lawyer who tried to blame anyone else for the crime, including Lydia's brother Edwin.

Tragically, Lydia's mother Roxanne Jackson passed away before the trial. Her testimony was played for the jury via video recordings of the preliminary exam. Roxanne had serious health problems, but her family believes it was a broken heart that took her life.

Doug Ball never admitted to the killing, later losing an appeal of his conviction. He was sentenced to life in prison without the possibility of parole and now lives as a permanent tenant of the Michigan Department of Corrections.

From the initial responding patrol officers to the Port Huron Detective Bureau, Major Crimes Unit, Oakland County Sheriff's Office and SWAT Team, this case was a model of good teamwork and cooperation. But it was also a very long day.

Father's Son

On a beautiful June morning I stepped out of the shower to my iPhone blaring Ozzy Osbourne's 'Over the Mountain', one of my favorite ringtones. The caller ID told me it was Officer Danielle Quain from the Marysville Police Department.

"What's up, Dani?" I asked.

From the tremor in her voice, I knew it was something serious. Quain told me she was at the scene of a homicide.

A man named Jonathan Stahl had called 911 and told the dispatchers that he'd just killed his father. When they arrived, Quain and her partner, Officer Dan Levey, approached the home and saw Stahl inside. While Quain covered him with her .45 caliber Glock, Levey ordered Stahl outside. Stahl was silent but offered no resistance, doing exactly as Levey directed.

As Stahl exited through the front door, Quain and Levey saw that he was splattered with blood. When Levey put him face down on the front lawn, he noticed chunks of flesh and brain matter on Stahl's clothing and shoes. Levey placed Stahl in handcuffs and stood by with Quain for the arrival of backup officers.

Chief Tom Konik and Deputy Chief Ron Buckmaster arrived within minutes and completed a sweep of the home's interior. They didn't find anyone else inside except a man later identified as Stahl's father. They knew immediately that he was far beyond any help they could provide. As Quain called me to request detectives from the Port Huron Major Crimes Unit, Konik and Buckmaster locked down the scene to preserve its integrity.

A quick phone call and a few messages on the MCU text string were all that was necessary to get the team on its way. We were lucky that day to also have Detective Sergeant Eric Shumaker from the Michigan State Police available to assist with our investigation. Shumaker had been assigned to MCU for several years prior to being promoted out of the unit, and I valued his expertise.

I parked my unmarked white Chrysler 300S outside the crime scene tape 15 minutes after hanging up with Quain, and within the hour my entire team had arrived.

The crime scene was part of a handsome modern condominium development, just a couple blocks from the St Clair River. Behind the white vinyl siding and black trim were 3-bedroom units with granite countertops, tile floors, and full basements. There was no need to rush inside so I lifted the tape and ducked underneath it, crossing the black asphalt of the circular drive to where the cops and bosses were gathered near the back of a police car.

I listened to the details described by Konik, including the horrific injuries suffered by the man inside. I learned that the suspect was currently in the back seat of another nearby car, so I asked if anyone had advised him of his Miranda rights; thankfully, no one had.

It looks cool in movies when cops growl *You have the right to remain silent* while slapping handcuffs on someone pressed against the wall of a bank they just robbed.

In reality, it's better not to ask an arrested person about their involvement in a crime until later. When restrained in the back seat of a patrol car, the suspect's blood is pumping, and his emotions are probably running high. There's no doubt some uniformed cops moving around, maybe a police dog barking; it's a natural time for him to answer with '*Fuck you, I want my lawyer!*' At that point, detectives are screwed. We can't ask him if he wants to change his mind an hour later. If he 'lawyers up', the conversation is over.

I asked Levey to transport Stahl to the Port Huron Police Department and told him I'd meet him there. The MCU office was on the 5th floor at PHPD, and we frequently used the interview rooms in the detective bureau downstairs. The rooms were wired for high definition video and sound, and preserved conversations as digital evidence using special software. Since Shumaker had just arrived, I asked him to accompany me and sit in during the interrogation. While I was proficient at extracting confessions by empathy and rapport, Shumaker's inquisitive mind and attention to detail were things I just didn't possess.

Before leaving, I was able to observe the inside of the residence. After placing a pair of blue disposable booties over my shoes, I entered through the front door. Progressing into the kitchen, I saw spatters of blood and brain matter in patterns on the ceiling and walls. On a leather reclining chair in the living room sat the remains of Stahl's father, the television in front of him still tuned to the Fox News Channel. A softball-sized hole above the man's left eye allowed for a view inside his skull; it was dark and void of any visible brain tissue. The two-pronged red Odyssey golf putter lying next to the recliner bore silent witness to the violence which ended the man's life.

Watching my step, I slowly walked back outdoors, careful not to disturb the scene or leave any trace of my presence inside. Due to the complexity and sheer volume of blood evidence, I called for a Crime Scene Response Team from the Michigan State Police Forensic Science Division. Their technicians and scientists were equipped to handle large amounts of evidence at major crimes scenes, and were qualified experts for courtroom testimony.

Since the evidence team wouldn't arrive for several hours, Shumaker and I left to interrogate Stahl while MCU detectives spread out through the complex. They would canvass Stahl's neighbors for any relevant information while uniformed officers continued to guard the scene. As I fired up my undercover car's engine and turned north onto the nearby highway, I saw a TV news helicopter start to circle overhead.

Once at PHPD I met with Levey, who was guarding the still-handcuffed Stahl in the booking room. Calls for service from the county dispatch center continued to roll in during the homicide investigation, so I knew Levey had to return to Marysville and handle some of the regular business that never ends for uniformed patrol officers. They are truly the backbone of any police department and the 'face of the franchise' that citizens expect to promptly see when they dial 911. I thanked Levey as he walked down the hallway toward the police garage and told him that I'd get his handcuffs back to him the next day.

Stahl was silent as I led him through the series of locked doors leading to the detective bureau, his calm demeanor betrayed by blue eyes glaring daggers as we walked. Rounding a corner into the area occupied by the PHPD Investigative Division, we drew a few sideways looks from secretaries and police cadets who'd heard about the man accused of killing his father. Waiting for us was Detective Eric Krikorian, who'd prepared a private area toward the back of the bureau with a blue plastic tarp spread out on the floor. Krikorian, himself an expert evidence technician, directed Stahl to disrobe as I removed the handcuffs from his wrists.

Stahl's clothes, heavily soiled with blood evidence and other tissue, were carefully placed in brown paper bags and preserved as crime scene evidence. While Stahl stood on the blue plastic tarp, Krikorian photographed his body with a Nikon digital single lens reflex camera, then carefully swabbed some of the blood and tissue from Stahl's skin. The collected evidence would be later sent to the crime lab for DNA analysis. When the process was finished I gave Stahl some hospital scrubs to wear and took him to a men's room down a nearby hall. I let him use the toilet and then scrub his face, hands and arms with soap and hot water.

Back in the bureau, I sat Stahl in a chair inside the interview room and placed a bottle of water on the table in front of him. I left him to chill for a bit while Shumaker and I discussed our strategy for the interrogation. As it turned out, we didn't need much of one.

As soon as we returned to the interview room and I finished reading Stahl his Miranda warning, he started talking.

Stahl had been a regional manager for a large hardware and tool supply firm, managing a network of stores from Kentucky to Idaho. For the past three years he'd lived at the condominium home of his father, following the death of his mother. During that time, he'd encountered trouble at work and his responsibilities had been reduced by the company, to the point he was responsible for just one store in a nearby city.

Stahl said the stress he felt from his mother's death, his workplace failures, and increasing debts had recently caused him to consider suicide. Stahl informed us that he told his dad that he was going for coffee and cigarettes early that morning. He drove down Interstate 94 and exited at Wadhams Road, where he considered jumping off the overpass into oncoming traffic. Stahl told us that he couldn't go through with it so, while driving back home, he looked for an 18-wheel tractor trailer rig on the freeway. Stahl said he wanted to drive into the big hauler and be killed by the collision but couldn't conjure the courage to complete that mission either.

Later, we'd find Stahl's laptop computer in the condo's basement, where he resided. The computer's browser was open to a website which provided specific instructions for various types of suicide; from hanging oneself to drug overdose and gunshots, it was all there for viewing. It ranked different forms of suicide according to how much pain one would endure before death and the amount of trauma to be suffered by family members who discovered the body. It even had forums for discussions and posting "farewell messages". The forum posts were often 'liked' by other readers who encouraged the authors to follow through with their fatal plans. It was very disturbing.

Back at home Stahl was using the large custom bathroom in his father's master suite, while his dad enjoyed some breakfast and watched the news on television in the next room. Stahl told us that as he walked out of the bathroom and into the master bedroom, he saw a collection of his dad's golf clubs leaning against a wall in the corner. Stahl said it was at that very moment he decided to murder his father.

Stahl's reasoning was that after killing his dad he would be imprisoned for life, thereby eliminating all the stressors which were making him feel so bad. He wouldn't have to go to work, where everyone made him angry; the management, his co-workers, even loyal customers. He wouldn't need to pay any of his mounting bills and could live debt free while having all his needs met by the Michigan Department of Corrections. Without any further consideration Stahl grabbed the Odyssey putter and marched into the living room, where his unsuspecting father relaxed in his chair.

Stahl described drawing back the golf club in his grasp as he rounded the chair in front of his elderly father, swinging it forward and striking him squarely in the head almost immediately. The man never saw the attack coming and didn't suffer for an extended time, as the first blow certainly rendered him unconscious and was likely fatal.

Stahl continued to strike his father's head with the club, each impact further destroying the man's skull. As he drew back the club each time, the blood, skull fragments, and tissue were launched into the patterns I had seen on the walls and ceiling.

"Twelve or fourteen times", was Stahl's answer when I asked how many times he had struck his poor dad with that club. "For the first time in my life, I wanted to do something right" he said, explaining that he wanted to make sure his dad was deceased, thereby ensuring his lifetime incarceration.

I'm not an expert in forensic psychology, but Stahl seemed like a man conscious of his own actions yet struggling mightily to retain his sanity.

There came a point during the interrogation when I was satisfied with the depth and breadth of Stahl's confession. Shumaker, though, kept digging to explore the reasons why Stahl felt the need to solve his problems in such a violent manner. Surely there must have been some abusive incident buried deep in their family history which triggered Stahl, but we were unable to discover it.

Stahl described his dad as his "best friend" and recalled their attendance at a recent Detroit Tigers game. When his dad wanted to leave in the seventh inning, Stahl reminded him that he never left early during Stahl's little league baseball games.

"That's because you were playing, son" was his father's response.

I felt a chill when Stahl described his father's devotion, and we ended the interrogation shortly afterward.

A few weeks later Stahl became the first, and only, arrestee to plead guilty to First Degree (Premeditated) Murder resulting from one of our investigations. The conviction carries a mandatory life sentence with no chance of parole, and offenders always go to trial in the hopes of being convicted of a lesser included offense. A conviction for Second Degree Murder allows for the hope of eventual parole, even if it comes many decades in the future. Stahl got his wish, though at an unfathomable cost.

Over a 31-year career I've been to the scene of brutal homicides and gruesome suicides. I have absorbed the suffering and pain of people experiencing shock and a mournful sense of loss when I inform them of their loved one's death. I've discovered sickening child pornography and had to describe it in reports and court testimony. I've even faked empathy during the interrogations of twisted individuals, just to get them to confess. Through it all, I've been able to compartmentalize my own feelings. When an investigation is over, I simply put the whole matter into a mental drawer and close it.

The Stahl murder made me wonder if all those drawers might one day fly open. I started to dream about it. Up north at my in-law's lake house over the Independence Day weekend, I woke up next to my wife and told her I needed to talk to someone. I just felt super stressed, sad and anxious, and I didn't understand why.

I made an appointment with a professional counselor a few weeks later and used that opportunity to describe in detail how I felt. I told him about recent events I thought might be affecting me; a battle with throat cancer the year before, the financial stress associated with paying college tuition for the two outstanding student-athletes Cyndi and I had raised, and the recent death of my own father. My dad was an accomplished and highly decorated 33-year veteran police officer and detective who succumbed to alcohol-induced dementia after a lifetime of not talking about his own feelings.

The counselor listened intently and patiently, occasionally asking questions to elicit more details. When I had let it all out, he assured me that things would be OK. He encouraged me to do some basic mental exercises to keep my mind clear and said that the Stahl homicide had probably 'plucked a string' inside my mind, due to the recent loss of my father. He said that string was vibrating in a way similar to a musical instrument but that it would probably soon stop, and it eventually did. I only met with the counselor that one time, and I should return someday, but I'm glad that I did. It was a relief to know that my feelings were normal.

Law enforcement culture often prevents cops from seeking help; toughness and stoicism have always been valued above anything that could be perceived as weakness. But I encourage any police officer who feels disturbed by the daily violence and mayhem to find a sympathetic, professional counselor to listen and advise them. It made me a happier and more effective person, able to continue in my chosen profession with less fear and anxiety.

Jump N Jam

Near the intersection of Gratiot Avenue and Interstate 94 in Marysville was a large L-shaped strip mall filled with many businesses and anchored by a grocery store called Wally's Supermarket. Near the center of the mall, between the Tractor Supply Company and an AT&T phone store, was a retail space once occupied by a business venture named Jump N Jam.

Owned by a woman named Cheryl Myny, Jump N Jam's rectangular footprint was about 10,000 square feet and it was an absolute oasis of insane fun, food, and exercise for kids. Underneath the high ceilings inside were a half dozen huge inflatable bounce houses in bright colors with names like 'Blast Zone', 'Roaring Rainforest Gauntlet', 'Crayon House' and 'The Mushroom'. They were designed in neon shades of blue and red, green and yellow, and had walls of mesh so that parents could supervise from a distance. There were slides, mazes, and even a bouncy boxing ring in which kids could harmlessly battle each other wearing giant inflatable gloves.

Toward the back of the establishment was an arcade with an air hockey table, video games, Skee-Ball lanes, Pop-a-Shot basketball hoops, and Foosball. Behind the arcade was a section with booths, tables and chairs dedicated to serving pizza, soda pop, and ice cream. Throughout the business were strategically placed couches to flop down on for a brief rest, wall-mounted flat screen TVs, and even a couple massage chairs for exhausted parents. Finally, behind a door near the back wall, was a room dedicated to private parties for parents who wanted to host a child's birthday at Jump N Jam.

Through her dedication to detail and tireless labor, Myny's vision had become a successful business which brought unbridled joy to hundreds of children. The first time I set foot in the place was the day she died.

As it was Veteran's Day, I'd begun that Saturday by playing bagpipes in the formal ceremony at the Allied Veteran's Cemetery, held each year at the eleventh hour on the eleventh day of the eleventh month. In the afternoon I traveled to an industrial area on the west side of Port Huron, parked my undercover Volvo S60 near some Little League ballfields, and walked through tall grass toward the rear of a small factory. I took digital photographs (from a distance) of the portable concrete barriers blocking its doors and the external cameras mounted high on its walls, providing 360 degree surveillance. Of particular interest was the enormous electrical hookup to nearby power poles, suitable for the type of heavy equipment the building formerly housed. A few days later the Major Crimes Unit would serve a search warrant there and we discovered, as suspected, a massive marijuana grow operation.

Back at home, I'd poured a cold pint of Bell's Amber Ale and crashed on the couch to watch the University of Michigan play football against Maryland. Just then, my work phone vibrated to life and began to play its newest ringtone, 'The Mob Rules' by Black Sabbath. The caller ID displayed the message 'Chief Konik'. Not good. Tom Konik was a fine leader and friend, but we didn't often socialize outside the police department. My Saturday plans were about to change.

Swiping the green circle to the right with my thumb, I answered.

"Hey, Chief," I said. "How are you today, sir?"

"Has anyone called you about Jump N Jam?" he asked, getting immediately to the point.

"No, sir," I replied. "They have not."

"I need you down here right away," Konik said. "Fire Department got called to the business about a woman being injured, but this is gonna be a homicide. There's a woman here with a gunshot to the head. We'll need a full MCU call out, too."

Heading for the sink to pour out my beer, I replied, "Roger that, Chief. I'm on the way and I'll get the team headed there now."

"Ok, see you in a few," Konik said before disconnecting.

As I turned and took my first step out of the kitchen to grab my boots and jacket, I had to pause for just a moment and think about exactly where Jump N Jam was located. I'd heard the buzz about it but had never been there; our kids were too old by the time it had opened. Too bad, they'd have loved it when they were little. Quickly I remembered and headed for the door. It was only a mile away.

Traffic was light as I exceeded all posted speed limits, the Volvo's leather-wrapped steering wheel in my left hand and iPhone in my right. Detective Sergeant Chris Frazier, boss of MCU at that time, listened intently as I relayed Konik's message and requested a full team response. As usual, Frazier didn't hesitate. He assured me that he and our entire team would be up on our dedicated radio frequency and on the way shortly, then directed me to call him back with any critical developments before his arrival. We hung up as I turned off Gratiot Avenue and into the expansive parking lot. The sun had set an hour before, the darkness now illuminated by blue and red flashing lights of police cars from multiple jurisdictions and a Marysville Fire Engine.

Slowing down as I approached the active crime scene, I observed Marysville PD Deputy Chief Ron Buckmaster out front securing yellow tape from a corner of the building to a light pole near the asphalt lot, then running the full width of the business along the sidewalk, around another light pole, and then back to the far corner. Buckmaster was a proud veteran of the United States Marine Corps and had experience bringing order to chaos. As I climbed out of my car, I could see inside the business through the 10 feet tall, tinted glass windows which ran its full breadth. I began to take in the scene as I walked toward the front door.

"Hey, Jim," Buckmaster said, lifting the tape and holding it as I stepped underneath.

"Hey, Ron," I replied.

A list of tasks started to form in my head, but I was always careful to not bark commands at people who severely outranked me. Fortunately, Buckmaster couldn't have been more down to earth or easier to work with. He was all about solving problems and getting the job done.

"Ron," I asked. "When you're able, would you post a patrolman at that door with a clipboard? Have him deny entry to anyone who doesn't need to be inside and keep a log of those who do, with their name and the exact time they enter or exit."

"You got it," Buckmaster replied.

I removed a pair of black latex gloves from my jacket pocket and put them on before pulling open the dark metal-framed glass door by the edge of its flat, rectangular handle. I hoped everyone else had done that too, but knew it was unlikely in the craziness. Stepping through the doorway I was greeted by music that was still playing from speakers in the ceiling. To my immediate left, adjacent to the main door in the building's southwest corner, was the service counter. A cash register stood unattended, along with racks of cubbyholes filled with the shoes and jackets of children.

Stepping behind the counter through an opening nearest the main door, I saw the source of the music; a low-profile JBL commercial amplifier was tucked under the counter on a top shelf. I clicked its black power button and the music stopped. The sudden hush caused Konik to turn toward the front and see me from 40 feet away. As he approached, I walked out from behind the counter to meet him.

The service counter had a 90-degree corner, which I passed while walking toward the center of the big room. Once clear of it I noticed floor space beneath the wall which I couldn't previously see, and another opening which provided access behind the counter. The area was between the counter and the first inflatable bounce house. I stopped to take it in visually. Soaking into the carpeted floor was a large pool of blood. It was the kind of blood which, in my experience, comes from severe head wounds. Particularly gunshots. It appears very dark and thick and its never a good sign. Scattered around the blood were the remnants of treatment that Marysville Fire Department paramedics rendered to the victim; the torn blue paper packages that had contained bandages, empty syringe packets, and a few sticky EKG electrodes. Konik's voice brought me back.

"They transported her," Konik said. "But it doesn't look good."

Konik had seen me examining the bloody scene and removed his smart phone from a jacket pocket. He brought up a digital image and handed me the phone. It was a photo of Cheryl Myny. Just before she was moved to a backboard and then onto the bright yellow and black ambulance stretcher, one of the Marysville Fire Fighter/Paramedics had the presence of mind to take a high-quality photo of her. He'd suspected that Myny was already gone and knew the image might help us solve the crime. He then sent the image to Konik via text message.

The photo showed Myny's body 'in situ', the original position where she fell. She lay partially on her left side, one knee slightly raised in the way that some people sleep. The very first thing I noticed was the folded cash money she still grasped with one hand. She had likely been at the nearby register, and this probably wasn't a robbery. Next, the wound to the back of her head. Her hair was soaked and matted from the massive blood loss. Her face was not completely visible to me, as it was turned toward the floor and partially covered by her dark blond hair. I asked Konik to send me the photo, and then continued moving toward the back of the business.

Marysville Police Officer TJ Williams was the next person I encountered. I asked him to grab some more yellow police line tape and cordon off the entire southwest portion of the building's interior, including the service counter and the area next to it where Myny's body had been. I was about to ask Williams where all the children and parents were and if he could get them into the back room, where the private parties were held, so that MCU could interview each of them separately and record their observations. He was two steps ahead of me.

Williams had been first to arrive. Stepping into the business that day one can only imagine the stress level Williams felt as he was directed to the spot where Myny lay, everyone expecting him to 'do something'. He did. Williams immediately assessed Myny's condition as extremely grave and used his police radio to have the ambulance 'step it up' and arrive as quickly as possible. The paramedics did arrive very swiftly, though their efforts were in vain.

Knowing that the dozens of children and adults could not be allowed to leave until they were identified and interviewed, while also aware that they could seriously compromise the fresh crime scene if allowed to wander, Williams gathered them all near the back room. He even screened them and identified two eyewitnesses, then had them remain separate from everyone else so their memories would remain fresh and unadulterated from speaking with others. These small actions made a big difference.

As Williams left me to secure the interior crime scene as I'd requested, I briefly contacted the two witnesses and had them wait in the food court area. I promised I would return to them soon and left to go out front and speak with Frazier, who'd advised me by radio that he had arrived. As I walked outside, a police cadet assigned to the door by Buckmaster recorded my name on her clipboard.

"How's it going in there, Jim?" Frazier asked.

I told him about the two witnesses I was about to interview, then showed him the photo and explained the crime scene in brief. While we spoke, our MCU teammates began to roll in. As they did, Frazier gave them assignments. Regardless of rank or jurisdiction, Frazier, as the supervisor of MCU, was now the on-scene commander.

MCU would be responsible for the documentation, collection, and preservation of all evidence. Two spent shell casings had been observed on the floor near Myny's body and a live round lay outside on the sidewalk; they would need to be collected along with other relevant items. A top priority was locating and downloading all available surveillance video. Prior to that, the scene needed to be properly photographed. A search warrant affidavit needed to be written and signed by a judge, just to ensure we had the legal right to be as thorough as necessary in our search and seizure of possible evidence. We had our work cut out for us and we all got busy doing it.

I returned inside and sat down with my first witness, a man of about 35 years who'd brought his son to the facility for a birthday party. As his boy romped in a bounce house, the man walked forward to exchange some cash for coins at the service counter. Just as he rounded the corner of the bounce house nearest the counter, he heard the heavy crack of a pistol shot. He looked up to see a white man standing over Myny. The suspect fired again, as this witness looked on. He then sprinted away to rescue his son.

My next interview was with the assistant manager of Jump N Jam. She was a close friend to Myny as well as being her employee. On the rare occasion when Myny wasn't there, she ran the whole show. I was amazed by her composure, having witnessed her friend die in such a violent fashion. It was this witness who informed me that the suspect was Myny's husband, a troubled man called Matthew Pilarowski.

As the investigation progressed we would learn that Myny, who'd kept her maiden name after marriage, had informed Pilarowski earlier that day she was leaving him. She had signed a lease for a house in Chesterfield Township, and perhaps it was this fact that made Pilarowski realize she was serious.

According to the assistant manager of Jump N Jam, Pilarowski had arrived and confronted Myny outside the business a few hours before the shooting. They'd argued visibly near the parking lot for several minutes before Myny returned inside to work and Pilarowski left in his pickup truck. When he returned, there was no argument. The assistant manager heard the shots and ran to the front of the business to find her friend unconscious and bleeding, as Pilarowski again left in his truck, this time at high speed through the parking lot.

I walked outside to confer with Frazier about what I'd learned. At my request, the St Clair County Central Dispatch queried Pilarowski's driver license information to determine the residential address of the couple; I learned that it was only a few miles away in Smiths Creek.

Just then I was approached by Port Huron Police Officer James Gilbert. He, along with numerous other uniformed cops from PHPD, St Clair County Sheriff's Department, and Michigan State Police, had arrived at the scene without being dispatched because they wanted to help Marysville PD in any way they could. Gilbert, who would later become my teammate on MCU and then its supervisor, was someone I'd always liked and respected. I called him 'The Mayor' because he had that type of personality; people were drawn to him for his ability to listen and make them feel included. I shared some of the details of the investigation to that point, including the newly discovered address.

"Diss, hold on," Gilbert exclaimed. "That's my neighborhood! They live right around the corner from me. Do you want me to head over there?"

I asked Gilbert if Frazier had given him any other assignment. He had not. I then sent Gilbert on his way with another cop for backup, but insisted they only perform reconnaissance; they were not to enter the house or even knock on the door. Ten minutes later, my phone rang. It was Gilbert.

"Hey, what kind of truck is Pilarowski supposed to drive?" Gilbert asked.

I described the half-ton, extended cab pickup to Gilbert and gave him the license plate number, as I had obtained that from Central Dispatch after he'd left on his mission.

"It's in the driveway, brother," Gilbert said. "It's still running, and the headlights are on, but there's no one inside the truck."

"Can you guys secure that scene until we get more people headed your way?" I asked.

"Already done, my man," Gilbert replied. "We'll keep it locked down."

Smiths Creek is an area that is policed by the St Clair County Sheriff's Department. Since we now had two scenes to deal with, one a homicide and the other a potential barricaded gunman, and the latter was in their jurisdiction, we called county detectives for help. Detectives Kelsey Wade and Haley Bonner were off duty for the holiday weekend, but both immediately agreed to come in from home and assist us.

Wade and Bonner were excellent cops. They both possessed many years of experience as patrol officers, particularly Bonner, who came to the Sheriff's Department after several years as a Detroit police officer. Wade had been a narcotics investigator assigned to the St. Clair County Drug Task Force prior to promoting to her present position. As detectives they were thorough and diligent. They followed police procedure dutifully, but neither was afraid to think outside the box to solve problems. Both have my respect and friendship still today. While uniformed deputies were sent to beef up the perimeter around the Pilarowski home, Wade and Bonner prepared a search warrant and had the St Clair County SWAT Team called out to serve it.

I continued to investigate the scene with my teammates and finished up a few more interviews. With the help of Williams, I got the names and addresses of everyone else who had been inside Jump N Jam when this terrible event took place, even if they saw nothing. I would follow up with them in the coming days, but it was right to release them then and allow them to take their children home. We had them leave through a rear exit, to avoid further crime scene contamination, and told them all the shoes and jackets belonging to their kids would be taken to Marysville PD. They could pick them up the next day.

I received a text message from my wife, Cyndi. By this time, she knew about the shooting and that I was called to the scene, though she'd been at work when I left. She sent me a link to a local group page on Facebook. Someone on the page was live-streaming video of the St Clair County Sheriff SWAT Team as it approached the Pilarowski home to execute the search warrant prepared by Wade and Bonner. This was not good. If Pilarowski was inside and aware of the live-stream video, he could prepare to attack the SWAT Team when they made entry. It was my first experience with social media interference in police operations.

Frazier and I decided to head out to Smiths Creek while the rest of our team continued working the homicide scene at Jump N Jam. They would remain there long into the night collecting evidence. Prior to leaving we made sure the SWAT Team commander knew about the Facebook live-stream. By the time we arrived at the nearby command post, SWAT had entered the Pilarowski home and completed their sweep of the residence. Only one person had been found inside. It was Pilarowski, and he was dead.

The house was a beautiful two-story contemporary colonial which sat at the circular end of a quiet cul-de-sac, surrounded by houses of equal elegance and value. It had a curved concrete driveway and brown brick facade, accented by tan vinyl siding. This was a nice neighborhood.

When the SWAT officers were all clear from the residence, Frazier and I climbed the four masonry steps to the arch-covered porch. We entered the home with Wade and Bonner through the heavy wooden main door, which had custom side panels and a half-moon glass transom overhead.

Ascending the grand half-turn staircase we headed for the master bedroom, where the SWAT Team commander told us they'd found Pilarowski's body. Careful not to disturb any items of potential evidence, we slowly entered the room. To our right, centered in the bedroom but with the headboard against the far wall, was a sturdily built dark spindle bed frame with a king mattress covered in quilts. In line with the bed, but against the near wall to our left, was a matching highboy dresser. The space on the floor between the two was where Pilarowski lay, his face distorted and bloody from a self-inflicted gunshot wound which had pierced the roof of his mouth. The gun, a .380 caliber semi-automatic pistol with pink grips (it had belonged to Myny), was beside him. It was later confirmed to be the same gun with which Pilarowski killed his wife.

We retreated to the kitchen and conferred with Wade and Bonner about how this scene would be processed, and by whom. I notified the St Clair County Medical Examiner's Office they would be needed at the home, and then I received a bizarre phone call. It was from an on-duty lieutenant at a police department in neighboring Macomb County. His call had been forwarded to my phone by the St Clair County Central Dispatch after he'd called there initially. He told me that his officers had just responded to a home in their city where a resident called 911 and asked the police to inspect the property outside his house. The resident told police that his "girlfriend" had just been murdered by her husband in Marysville and he was afraid the killer would next come for him. The lieutenant gave me the man's number and I called him. When he answered, the man was in his car driving as fast as he could to a relative's home out of state. He'd left as soon as the police told him it was safe to do so. The man spoke enough accurate details to me concerning Myny that I knew he was being truthful about their relationship. I told the man to slow down and head back home. He had nothing to fear.

Eventually, Frazier and I left Wade and Bonner to work the Smiths Creek scene along with investigators from the Medical Examiner's office, while we returned to Jump N Jam. Once there, we learned that MCU detectives had located the digital video recorder and recovered surveillance video showing the murder. It was difficult to watch.

From a ceiling-mounted camera above and just outside of the service counter area, Myny was seen at the register conducting her business as usual. Pilarowski entered the business, walked directly to Myny and brandished the gun. Myny turned and quickly walked away from him. Pilarowski followed and fired the gun, causing Myny to fall where I'd seen her. Then, in an act witnessed by the man I'd interviewed earlier, Pilarowski stood over Myny and shot her a second time. After firing the fatal shots, Pilarowski could be seen placing the gun in his own mouth and pulling the trigger. It was a misfire. The gun had somehow jammed after the second shot. The video captured Pilarowski leaving and attempting to shoot himself again outside the door, to no avail. He racked the slide of the gun, which ejected a live round and accounted for the bullet found on the concrete near the entrance. Pilarowski then entered his pickup truck and, according to eyewitnesses in the parking lot, sped away from the scene at dangerously high speed. I was grateful there had been no traffic cops in the area that day who might have stopped a speeding pickup truck on its way to Smiths Creek, because a deadly shootout would certainly have been a possibility.

It was after 0300 hours when my MCU teammates finished their work and closed the crime scene at Jump N Jam. It was later still when Frazier and I made our way to the southern end of St Clair County, approximately 20 miles away, to notify Pilarowski's parents of his death. It's just about the worst thing in the world to be awakened by cops in the middle of the night, only to be told a loved one has died. It's not fun for the cops, either. An official notification and identification requires the next of kin to view the remains. Often, as in this case, a black-and-white profile photo of the decedent's face is taken after some cleansing. It helps to soften the blow, though probably not very much. Pilarowski's parents were stunned but remained cordial and helpful. Frazier and I sat with them at their kitchen table for a good while, not leaving until the eastern sky started to lighten through the windows.

An unexpected blessing to me during this horrific episode was getting to meet Cheryl Myny's mother. I'll call her Grace because that is what she exhibited in spades throughout my experience with her. She was inspirational. Her sadness at the loss of her beloved daughter was clearly profound, but her concern remained with others; family members, friends, Myny's staff at Jump N Jam, even me. I went out of my way to help her in any way that I could, which wasn't saying much, in truth. With the assistance of Marysville PD Sergeant Curtis Babb, I retrieved Myny's car from the parking lot at Jump N Jam the next day and drove it to Grace's house instead of ordering a tow truck to impound it. It had become a makeshift shrine, with sympathizers tying inflatable balloons to the door handles and writing messages on the windows. I cleared the messages and disposed of the balloons beforehand. I called

Grace with any updates I developed and stopped by her house a couple times to check on her. A few weeks later I received a handwritten thank you card from Grace, and I still have it. I hope she is as happy and healthy as she can be today.

The investigation of Cheryl Myny's murder was closed by 'Exceptional Clearance', a legal term used when a crime is committed and an offender is positively identified, probable cause exists to arrest the offender, but the arrest is made impossible by reasons outside the control of law enforcement officers. In this instance, the offender was deceased. All investigative functions are still diligently executed by police; the scene is documented with photographs and video, evidence is gathered and preserved, interviews are conducted, and reports are written. Even autopsies are performed, and I attended both in this case. In the end, no justice is served when a case is closed in such a manner. Perhaps Pilarowski received justice when he crossed over. I hope so, for the sake of everyone involved.

Acknowledgements

One year into my career as a cop, a new dispatcher was hired at the Mount Clemens Police Department. She had bright blonde hair and grey eyes. She was athletic and funny and so pretty, just a stone cold knockout. The humble angel on one shoulder told me, *"Sorry, pal. She's out of your league."* The cocky devil on my other shoulder said, *"Well that just means we've got nothing to lose. Let's roll!"* I snuck her a handwritten note one evening toward the end of our shift, asking her (like a schoolboy) if she wanted to come with me to Metro Beach after work. She agreed. We hung out together under the stars until sunrise. Eventually we had to leave; we both had to work again at 1600 hours, and we needed to sleep. I didn't want to let her out of my sight. I was in love.

Thirty years have passed by in an instant, and I'm still in love. Cyndi Jarrett Disser became my wife just more than a year after our midnight first date at Metro Beach. Through every victory and defeat, all the crazy assignments and special operations, the line-of-duty deaths and police funerals, every promotion I ever received, the calls from hospital emergency rooms after I'd been banged up, through all the joy and heartbreak, happiness and stress, Cyndi has been with me. She's my partner in this life and she's done it all while raising two children (often in my absence) and having a career of her own. After her time as a police dispatcher, Cyndi excelled as a veterinary technician, an animal control officer, a retail asset protection manager, and especially as a mother. Our kids, Travis and Jenna, are successful young adults due, in large part, to their mom. Cyndi is the best thing that's ever happened to me. She's my winning lottery ticket.

There are many people not mentioned in the book who had a positive impact on my life and career as a policeman. That list certainly includes my mother, Joyce VanderBurgh Rowe, who married a cop and then unintentionally raised another one. I can imagine, but never truly understand, the stress and anxiety she endured as a cop's wife before her marriage to my dad ended when I was 15. And then to learn that her son would travel that road, too; it had to be tough. But she was always present for me when I needed her, as good moms are for their sons.

At Mount Clemens PD, the tally includes Bill Pringnitz, Tom Dedenbach, Charlie Peace, Larry Szczesniak, Jack Biehl, Robert Most, David Willis, Sr., Mike Patrick, Brian Krutell, Dennis Rickert, Robert Anderson, LaFrance Bearden, Terry Boraks, Greg Ameriguian, Mark Masters, Steve Andrews, Josh Lewis, Ray Langley, John Twomey, Jeff Bishop, Mike Kenel, Bob Jacquemain, Pete Jacquemain, Michelle Bratton, Jason Bone, Bob Hey, Dan Gerkey, Dan VanLacken, Richard Ziegler, Don Lewis, Ron Balow, Geoff Wegehaupt, Pete Andrzejewski, Michele Lubeckyj, Jennifer Morris, Dawn Jay, Patricia Marshall, and Ann Wyszczelski.

From Marysville PD, I'm thankful for Bradley Owen, Mark Thorner, Tom Cowhy, Tim Raker, Justin Reeves, Dan Stocker, Matt Golembiewski, Matt Scheffler, Tim Phipps, Bill Trout, Becky Vargo, Cathy Braden, Jenny Orr, Andrea Harmon, and especially Ed Gerrow. Gerrow and I spent years working the midnight shift together as patrol officers before he promoted to Sergeant and later Deputy Chief of Police. During my years assigned to the Major Crimes Unit, Gerrow ran interference for me with the bosses when needed and helped ensure I always had necessary resources such as undercover vehicles, radios, cell phones, firearms, body armor, and the best training.

The guys I served with in the Port Huron Major Crimes Unit included Jason Barna, Jeremy Young, Chris Bean, Matt Finnie, Ryan Sheedy, Travis Reed, Nate Tucker, Tyler Kolomyski, Steve Cavner, Mike Ball, Tom O'Rourke, Tony Clyne, Bob Philage, Jake Kierblewski, Ed Silver, and Devin Cleland.

I had the good fortune to work with many outstanding prosecutors, attorneys who were not afraid to stand in front of a jury and make an argument in the toughest cases. These litigators included Steven Kaplan, Jurij Fedorak, William Dailey, Jean Cloud, Dena Keller, Steve Guilliat, Melissa Keyes, Amy Goodrich, Dennis Rickert, Joshua Sparling, Paul Soderburg, Michelle Weeks, and the Honorable Mona Armstrong.

The many men and women from other police and sheriff's departments, federal agencies, and prosecutors' offices who've impacted my life and career positively would fill another page. I'm so grateful to all of them and proud that we served our communities together to the best of our abilities.

Finally, I'd like to thank John Borkovich, a retired Michigan Conservation Officer. I met John because Cyndi and John's wife Nancy are close friends, so the four of us started to hang out together a few years ago. John and Nancy are kind and generous people who share, among other things, our humor and sensibility. John wrote a successful book called *Wildlife 911* and encouraged me to do the same. He's given me countless nuggets of advice and acquired wisdom along the way, which I greatly appreciate.

Looking back on the stories in this book, I realize what a small fraction of my career they actually represent. The stories I didn't write would supply a few sequels, not to mention all the stuff I can't remember. I wish I'd kept a journal. Many of the names, places, and descriptions in this book were changed to protect certain identities. I hope you enjoyed these authentic adventures, and that the profanity wasn't too egregious. Believe it or not, I kept it to a minimum.

~ JD

Index